Banned Emotions

Banned Emotions

How Metaphors Can Shape
What People Feel

LAURA OTIS

Emory University

OXFORD
UNIVERSITY PRESS

Oxford University Press is a department of the University of Oxford. It furthers the University's objective of excellence in research, scholarship, and education by publishing worldwide. Oxford is a registered trade mark of Oxford University Press in the UK and certain other countries.

Published in the United States of America by Oxford University Press
198 Madison Avenue, New York, NY 10016, United States of America.

Library of Congress Cataloging-in-Publication Data
Names: Otis, Laura, 1961– author.
Title: Banned emotions : how metaphors can shape what people feel / by Laura Otis.
Description: New York, NY : Oxford University Press, [2019] |
Includes bibliographical references.
Identifiers: LCCN 2018044936 | ISBN 9780190698904 (hardcover : alk. paper)
Subjects: LCSH: Language and emotions. | Emotions in literature. |
Emotions in art. | Metaphor.
Classification: LCC BF582 .O85 2019 | DDC 152.4—dc23
LC record available at https://lccn.loc.gov/2018044936

9 8 7 6 5 4 3 2 1

Printed by Sheridan Books, Inc., United States of America

For Ute Frevert and the researchers and staff of the History of Emotions Group,
Max Planck Institute for Human Development, Berlin

CONTENTS

ACKNOWLEDGMENTS

I am grateful to all the people whose intellectual energy has helped to shape this book, especially to Ute Frevert and her team of researchers at the Max Planck Institute for Human Development, where I conducted the research and wrote the manuscript as a guest scholar in 2014–2018. I would particularly like to thank historians Benno Gammerl, Philipp Nielsen, and Daphne Rozenblatt and psychologists Edgar Cabanas Díaz and Mara Mather for their ideas about the project, and administrator Christina Becher and librarian Daniela Regel for their hard work and support. I am grateful to Hilmar Preuss and Frau Heinze at the University of Halle for helping me to understand Dostoevsky's use of some Russian words in *Notes from the Underground*, and to Catherine Dana for correcting my transcription of *Caché's* French dialogue.

I am grateful to Emory University for granting me a sabbatical leave in 2014–2015 so that I could conduct the research for this project and write the first draft. I am indebted to my colleagues and former colleagues at Emory who have encouraged me and steered me toward valuable sources, especially Larry Barsalou, Sander Gilman, and Elizabeth Wilson. I am also thankful to Carol Colatrella, Lorraine Daston, Ben Johnson, and Sianne Ngai, who helped and inspired me with this project. I am grateful to Robert McCauley, Laura Namy, Lynne Nygaard, and the administrators of Emory's Center for Mind, Brain, and Culture, who organized the superb Foundations of Emotions in Mind, Brain, and Culture conference in February 2016. I thank Pamela Scully and Donna Troka of Emory's Center for Faculty Development and Excellence for sponsoring my interdisciplinary course, Emotional Evidence, in the spring of 2016 and allowing me to bring the fine interdisciplinary scholar, Patrick Colm Hogan, to campus. I would like to thank the Emory English Department for letting me teach "Languages of Emotion"—three times! These teaching opportunities allowed me to learn from my wonderful undergraduate students, whose enthusiasm has been boosting mine since my interest in emotion metaphors began. I am also indebted to my graduate students, Amy Li and

Sumita Chakraborty, whose different approaches to human emotions have challenged me intellectually and kept me learning.

I am grateful to my editor at Oxford University Press, Abby Gross, whose wisdom and level-headedness have now guided me through two book projects, and to assistant editor Katharine Pratt. Finally, I would like to thank all of the anonymous readers who have devoted time to analyzing this book and its proposal and offering valuable ideas for its improvement.

Banned Emotions

CHAPTER 1 | Introduction

Discouraging Metaphors

It is hard to distinguish the physical from the cultural basis of a metaphor.

—GEORGE LAKOFF AND MARK JOHNSON

WHAT ARE THE POLITICS of telling someone what to feel? In the 1960s, activists proclaimed that the personal is political, and nowhere is this truer than in the emotion realm.[1] Emotions can't be represented neutrally, and the words and images used to convey them splatter them with cultural values. This book considers what is at stake in emotion metaphors, and who gains and who loses by depicting emotions in particular ways. The command to "move on," for instance, implies that life is a journey on which a person contemplating her pain is balking. Personal pains often have social causes, and orders to "move on" not only humiliate sufferers; they delegitimize protests; they drown accusations in shame. By examining literary characters who won't stifle their suffering, this book explores how a person might assert herself when a cultural description of what she feels belies her inner experience.

In metaphors for human emotions, physiology and culture meet.[2] Emotions emerge from human bodies, as the words for them often reveal (Lakoff and Johnson 14). The phrases "let go" and "move on" refer to common bodily experiences but use those experiences to convey cultural premises. The interaction between physiological urges and cultural demands becomes most revealing when the two clash, as in the case of socially discouraged emotions. This book analyzes metaphors for "banned" emotions to examine the ways that biological and cultural forces combine to shape emotional experiences.

How do authors and filmmakers represent emotions in which people are said to "indulge"? Only certain emotions get paired with this verb. One "indulges" in expensive, sensually pleasing items: furs, chocolates, or luxury cars that one shouldn't be buying and can't afford. One "indulges" in self-pity, resentment, and spite that feel good in the short-term but can lead to moral "bankruptcy." Supposedly, one can't "afford" these emotions that bring a rush of pleasure, because they drain one's psychological resources. *Banned Emotions* challenges this metaphoric linkage of emotions, economics, and theology.

The emotions of "indulgence" are an unsavory lot, but they are familiar and widespread. They include self-pity, prolonged crying, resentment, bitterness, grudge-bearing, and spite.[3] They exist not just as negative labels or exaggerations of more encouraged feelings, such as self-esteem; they constitute internal experiences in their own right. Often these emotions occur together, and they share a family affinity. Their common feature is anger, anger flattened by fear so that it arises in unpleasant forms. In a lifetime, most human beings may feel some of these emotions, but they often occur in people who lack opportunities to express their rage. As Martha C. Nussbaum points out, "it is people with an overweening sense of their own privilege who seem particularly prone to angry displays" (Nussbaum, *Anger and Forgiveness* 40). Many people suppress their anger not because they are cowards but because protesting loudly could mean losing their jobs or incurring a beating. Not everyone who lacks power experiences these unsavory emotions, and not everyone who experiences them has suffered injustice. Self-pity can surge when one gets drenched in the rain, or when one wrecks a favorite shirt. Emotions tend to occur for reasons, however, and the language used to represent socially undesirable emotions often deflects attention from external causes to the sufferer's failings (Ngai 128–30). *Banned Emotions* focuses on discouraged emotions because when visceral anger meets cultural prohibitions, their conflicts, compromises, and negotiations can be observed through creative language.

Although emotions emerge from human bodies, culture shapes them so greatly that even fundamental emotions like anger can't be presumed to be identical from one country or century to the next. Emotions have histories in the sense that they are defined, understood, even experienced differently in distinct times and places. By approaching emotions from a historical perspective, one can learn how current understandings of emotions have evolved, and how familiar assumptions about emotional experiences have emerged from traditions that seem distinct. Historian Ute Frevert analyzes the ways that emotions have changed with time and cultural context. She has found that in the West, rage was long viewed as a privilege of the powerful and was used to intimidate minions (Frevert 92). Twenty-first-century calls to crush negative emotions continue this cultural tradition, which regulates who may express anger, when, and how.

Cultural rules about how to feel and express emotions vary with gender, and these variations form a concern of this book. Frevert has noted that in modern European women, rage and the strength it can bring have been "increasingly judged inappropriate" and that "even when women do feel anger, they express it differently" (Frevert 95, 97). Whether or not women experience more "banned" emotions than men, male authors and filmmakers have used metaphors in unforgettable ways to shape cultural assumptions about women's emotions. Nussbaum describes a classical tradition in which "females are taken to be inferior creatures who indulge in the doomed and fruitless projects of retributive payback, with great harm to both self and others" (Nussbaum, *Anger and Forgiveness* 44). Charles Dickens's descriptions of Miss Havisham in

Great Expectations and Adrian Lyne's shots of Alex Forrest in *Fatal Attraction* show that this tradition lives on in verbal and visual emotion metaphors.

Great writers develop metaphors brilliantly, and this book analyzes a cultural pattern not just in its most direct iterations (as in self-help books) but in its richest, most elaborate variations. When it comes to emotion metaphors, *Banned Emotions* studies not just the chorale tunes, so to speak, but Bach's elaborations of them. The stories and films it examines come from Europe and the United States during two periods of rapid social change: 1864–1925 and 1995–2015. The analysis focuses on more than one historical period because it seeks origins and tracks changes over time. This book also reaches further back to trace the Biblical, classical, medieval, and early modern roots of emotion metaphors used in more recent works. By offering variations on traditional metaphors, creative stories and films depict the emotions of characters trying to assert their humanity through their emotions when poverty, racism, sexism, and violence restrict the ways they can act creatively in the world.

Artistic depictions of emotions aren't "typical," but they can reveal aspects of emotional experience that conventional representations don't. By taking readers into characters' minds, skilled authors can show not just the emotional behavior that a culture demands but complex individuals' resistance to it. Creative literary language invites readers to "simulate" characters' emotions: to recall and recombine their own past sensory experiences so that they can feel what the characters are feeling.[4] Literary critic Elaine Scarry has proposed that finely crafted fiction works like a musical score, providing "a set of instructions for mental composition" (Scarry 244). Interdisciplinary scholar Patrick Colm Hogan believes that "widely admired depictions of emotions tell us something important about the way people in a given society think about emotions" (Hogan, *The Mind and Its Stories* 1). This collective thinking draws both on common bodily experiences and on particular cultures' languages. Hogan combines the methods of cognitive science and literary studies by seeking cross-cultural patterns in the ways that literary works depict emotions. Literature, he argues, is "well designed to solve problems that plague emotion research" (Hogan, *What Literature Teaches Us* 2). Analyses of rich literary descriptions can complement scientific studies because they avoid "the simplification and artificiality that affect laboratory research" (Hogan, *What Literature Teaches Us* 38). Hogan could not be more right about cognitive science's relevance to literature or about literature's potential to inform scientific studies. Examining the metaphors crafted to describe emotions may reveal not just cultural understandings of emotions but aspects of human physiology that make emotions possible.

Even when emotion metaphors have a clear physiological grounding, they can serve political ends. Commands to "let go" of a grievance can nip criticism in the bud. Some metaphors for socially undesirable emotions represent them as so inimical that fear of social stigma may drive people to deny feeling them at all. In *Ugly Feelings*, literary critic Sianne Ngai has revealed how representations of envy, irritation, anxiety, and other emotions born of "withheld doing" are "saturated with socially stigmatizing meanings and values" (Ngai 34, 11).[5] But are such emotions—self-pity, for instance—really as harmful as metaphors like "wallow" suggest? Like any description of a system, a metaphor emerges from one of many possible perspectives. Who benefits, and who loses, when emotions are represented through particular metaphors?

In her analysis of emotion language, cultural critic Sara Ahmed has noticed a hierarchy in which "good" emotions are "defined against uncultivated or unruly emotions, which frustrate the formation of the competent self" (Ahmed 3). *Banned Emotions* draws on scientific studies as well as literary works to challenge this notion of an imperial self, in which a "you" separate from "your" emotions is charged with ruling them like colonial subjects.[6] If you don't think about how your feelings may be influencing you, warn psychologists Travis Bradberry and Jean Greaves in *Emotional Intelligence 2.0*, then "your emotions will control you" (Bradberry and Greaves 98). A metaphor representing emotions as the possessions of a "you" distinct from them does not fit everyone's reality or serve everyone's interest. Theoretically, anyone, rich or poor, can foster culturally desirable emotions and beat back those that block social success. Supposedly, negative feelings such as self-pity and prolonged crying do no one any good. But whose interest does it serve to quash these emotions? Who gains from an injunction against public expressions of pain?

People thriving in a system often attribute their success to themselves; those struggling look critically at the system. To thwart protests, those prevailing may try to convince those less successful that their failure is due to their own defects. This hegemonic strategy, which drives people to stifle their own voices, works terribly well in the emotion realm. By "hegemony," I mean cultural practices through which the most powerful members of a society instill their worldview by teaching people to oppress themselves.[7] The people who suffer most in an economic recession may silence each other with accusations of "whining" or "wallowing in self-pity." These metaphors are so shameful that people may sacrifice their chances to protest rather than risk being associated with them. Being perceived as worthy of respect often involves managing one's emotions in ways that suit social elites.[8] In her study of emotion rhetoric, Sara Ahmed has found that "emotions are bound up with the securing of social hierarchy . . . Emotionality as a claim *about* a subject . . . is clearly dependent on relations of power . . ." (Ahmed 4).[9] Sianne Ngai's study of American literature supports Ahmed's finding by showing how representations of "ugly feelings" divert attention from situations to psyches. Descriptions of envy, especially, squelch social criticism by making people who protest inequities seem deficient and "petty" (Ngai 21, 128). As soon as the word "envy" comes into play, a protest is "stripped of its potential critical agency . . ." (Ngai 129). What might be the expression of a valid grievance becomes the revelation of defective character.

Probably, few writers have ever crafted emotion metaphors with a sinister intent. Appeals to stop "holding on" and "let go"; calls to stop "wallowing" and "clean up," have obvious bodily sources and, probably, evolutionary roots.

Seeking light, movement, cleanliness, and useful work promotes physical and mental health. It makes sense that emotions, which emerge from human bodies, would be described in terms of the physiological sensations that make emotions possible. But religion, politics, and millennia of human cultures have also entered into emotion metaphors that seem natural. The command to "move on" after one has been jilted or fired is both a common-sense appeal to the body and a cultural call to resume a progressive journey of self-improvement. "Letting go" of a grievance frees the hands to do useful work and buy a lot of new things.

Even without reaching critical awareness, verbal descriptions of emotions can instill ideas about how to feel. Linguist Katarzyna Molek-Kozakowska has described "coercive metaphors" that forcefully promote ways of seeing the world, such as "Britain will be '*swamped*' by TB unless high-risk immigrants are routinely given blood tests . . ." (Molek-Kozakowska 161).[10] The metaphor "swamped" encourages readers to envision a natural disaster and to imagine immigrants as threatening (Molek-Kozakowska 161). Emotion metaphors such as "she broke down" can spread cultural assumptions in related ways. Few writers who craft and use metaphors consciously want to promote a worldview, but regardless of the writer's intent, emotion metaphors reinforce certain ways of perceiving emotions and can work to invalidate other views.

From one perspective, self-pity, prolonged crying, and spite are the emotions of losers—sore losers unwilling to concede defeat. A loser should shake her opponent's hand, acknowledge that her opponent has beaten her (this time) owing to superior skills, look ahead, and prepare harder for the next match. Such would be the case if life were a game, and if every player had an equal chance. But losing gracefully assumes a different meaning when the rules ensure that one loses each time. In such cases, people who violate cultural rules about emotions may be asserting their right to *be*. "We create a scene," writes novelist Charles Baxter, "when we forcibly illustrate our need to be visible to others . . ." (Baxter 129). People who express "banned" emotions call attention to cultural rules invisible to those who benefit from them but glaringly obvious to those who don't. *Banned Emotions* looks at fictional characters behaving badly not just to learn how bodily urges combine with cultural rules, but to think beyond these rules to possibilities more inclusive and more just.

People unable to find nurturing relationships, stimulating careers, or chances for creative fulfillment may cherish their emotions as the only evidence that they are thinking, feeling human beings. Even people with the good fortune to have all these things value their emotions as central to their identities. Whether wealthy or impoverished, people will love, desire, worry, suffer, and feel hurt. Denying people the chance to speak of their suffering means denying them their humanity. "Tears are unreliable witnesses, but they are the only witnesses," writes art historian James Elkins (Elkins 37). If people build emotional altars, burn candles, and treasure their feelings (even painful ones) for decades, it may be to assert their value as human beings. Memorializing one's suffering may not be the best way to build an identity, but for some people, at some times, it is the only way they have to remind themselves and others they are alive. In a culture that discourages expressions of personal pain, calling attention to one's suffering can do subversive work.[11] Publicly expressing one's suffering can alert people to systemic injustice. Metaphors associating "banned" emotions with stagnation, darkness, and dirt make people ashamed of voicing their pain and ensure that these alerts never go out.

A culture that trains disempowered people to stifle their emotions can be notoriously hard to resist. Under almost any conditions, however, people find ways to express their feelings and, in the process, to assert themselves. Despite demands to be quiet, many have-nots suffer conspicuously, determined to make their presence known. The organizing axis of *Banned Emotions* marks increasing degrees of resistance to cultural rules about which emotions should be expressed, when, and how. Simultaneously, this book analyzes ways in which bodily grounded, culturally reinforced emotion metaphors reassert themselves in literary and film representations of rebellious characters. This book does not explore "banned" emotions one by one, because self-pity, resentment, and spite so often occur together, and it makes more sense to study metaphors that show how these emotions combine. Cultures and bodies suggest metaphors for emotions, and each human mind serves as an interface in which they interact.

To analyze Western metaphors for unloved emotions, Chapter 2 of this book surveys scientists' principal theories of emotions over the past half-century: the basic emotions, appraisal, and constructed emotion theories. The analysis focuses more on laboratory research in neuroscience, cognitive science, and psychology than on psychoanalytic theory. The second chapter goes on to examine cognitive studies of metaphor, including the work of philosopher Max Black, linguist George Lakoff, philosopher Mark Johnson, and linguist Zoltán Kövecses. To place emotion metaphors in cultural as well as scientific contexts, Chapter 2 explores their religious roots in Catholic and Protestant allegories: Dante Alighieri's *Inferno* and *Purgatorio* (c. 1308–1320) and John Bunyan's *The Pilgrim's Progress* (1678). These religious texts helped to establish impeded motion, asphyxiation, and filth as metaphors for self-pity and long-term anger. The second chapter concludes by analyzing contemporary variations on these metaphors in self-help books such as Daniel Goleman's *Emotional Intelligence*, Travis Bradberry and Jean Greaves's *Emotional Intelligence 2.0*, and Spencer Johnson's *Who Moved My Cheese?* These guides urge readers to keep their emotions from "hijacking" their lives, as happened with the unfortunates in Bunyan's Slough of Despond and Dante's hell.

Chapter 3 of *Banned Emotions* focuses on metaphors for self-pity, perhaps the least loved emotion in the West. It starts with late twentieth- and early twenty-first-century representations of self-pity to show the cultural pressure brought to bear on anyone who publicly complains of pain. This third chapter examines psychologists' and humanities scholars' metaphors for self-pity and considers cultural critic Tom Lutz's, literary scholar Franco Moretti's, and art historian James Elkins's studies of crying. It analyzes two popular films with female protagonists, Ridley Scott's *G. I. Jane* (1997) and Paul Feig's *Bridesmaids* (2011), both of which use metaphors to depict self-pity in the worst light. *G. I. Jane*, a story of enabled movement, suggests that challenges such as breaking a gender barrier can be met only if self-pity is shunned. *Bridesmaids* associates self-pity not just with arrested motion but with moral and physical filth. These associations with dirt and paralysis reinforce a cultural fear of the "self-pity" label: no one to whom this label can be stuck will be respected or believed. Under these conditions, expressing pain takes not just courage, but skill— although some clever literary characters have managed to complain anyway.

Chapter 4 initiates this book's strategy of analyzing fictional characters behaving badly. Two complex female characters who subtly break cultural emotion rules are Charlotte Bartlett in E. M. Forster's *A Room with a View* (1908) and Doris Kilman in Virginia Woolf's *Mrs. Dalloway* (1925). Both characters play vital roles in their intricate novels' plots, and although they annoy the protagonists, they may win readers' sympathy. Dissatisfied with their lots in life, they assert themselves through suffering, and they make sure that the more privileged characters perceive their unhappiness. Forster and Woolf represent these suffering characters' emotions through metaphors of movement and stasis, light and darkness, stuffing and bursting—and body odor.

Chapter 5 of *Banned Emotions* builds on Chapter 4 by analyzing three male characters that manifest their pain more aggressively. Whereas Charlotte Bartlett and Doris Kilman convey their discontent through sounds and smells, the Underground Man in Fyodor Dostoevsky's *Notes from the Underground* (1864), Gregor Samsa in Franz Kafka's *The Metamorphosis* (1915), and Majid in Michael Haneke's film *Caché* (2005) show their suffering visually. All three male characters take extraordinary measures to ensure that the characters ignoring them will have to *see* their suffering. In their efforts to manifest their pain visually, these three characters hurt themselves as their demonstrations turn violent. Metaphors in these stories operate visually, and in a certain sense, all three works try to show what pain looks like.

In expressing culturally discouraged anger, women can turn as violent as men. The combination of self-pity, prolonged crying, and spite occurs with high frequency in rejected lovers, and people socialized to build their identities through relationships are more likely to be devastated when those relationships end. Chapter 6 examines metaphors associated with jilted women from classical times to the present day. It opens by analyzing psychologist John Bowlby's classic studies of attachment and critically examining attachment as a metaphor for human relationships. The characters studied include Dido in Virgil's *Aeneid* (29–19 BCE), Miss Havisham in Charles Dickens's *Great Expectations* (1861), Agnes Wessington in Rudyard Kipling's "The Phantom Rickshaw" (1885), Evelyn Draper in Clint Eastwood's *Play Misty for Me* (1971), Alex Forrest in Adrian Lyne's *Fatal Attraction* (1987), Mia Williams in Andrea Arnold's *Fish Tank* (2009), and Mia Fredricksen in Siri Hustvedt's *The Summer without Men* (2011). The metaphors associated with these fictional women's emotions vary considerably. Some build on the traditional patterns revealed in the earlier chapters, such as the rejection of daylight, the use of one's bodily scent, and paralysis or circular motion rather than linear progress. The emotion metaphors in the film and novel by female artists differ significantly from those developed in the works by male writers and directors. Hustvedt depicts Mia Fredricksen's devastation through shattering, and Arnold uses Mia Williams' body language to show how she gains control of her movements. The metaphors of arrested motion, asphyxiation, darkness, and filth may seem naturally appropriate for "unhealthy" emotions, but these metaphors convey a particular perspective and do not constitute the only way to represent unhappy people's emotions.

Chapter 7 concludes the book by analyzing recent scientific studies of emotion regulation. These psychological experiments indicate that reappraisal, or cognitive reinterpretation, works better than suppression to ease inner pain and promote mental health (Gross, "Emotion Regulation in Adulthood" 214). Modulation understood as occurring *within* a self shapes emotions more effectively than attempts to stifle alien forces threatening a self from the outside. Although neuroscientists and psychologists disagree about how emotions work, current research on emotion regulation does not support the popular notion of a self completely separate from emotions with unrestricted power to control them.

Emotion metaphors need to catch up with science and escape the rigid, implied model of "control or be controlled." More accurate metaphors would need to depict a system of "cooperative treaties," as psychologist Daniel Goleman has described (Goleman 30). Metaphors are integral to human thought (Lakoff and Johnson 3), but I ask readers to reconsider the traditional metaphors for "banned" emotions (paralysis, asphyxiation, darkness, and filth), since people do have some choice about the kinds of metaphors they use. I would like to discourage the spread of these metaphors, because they are so discouraging to the people at whom they are hurled. By exposing the roots and literary outgrowths of emotion metaphors, I hope to inspire new, creative metaphors that will be more accurate and empowering. I would like to free people to express emotions that may lead to a more just social order.

Notes

1. Both Sara Ahmed (in *The Cultural Politics of Emotion*) and Sianne Ngai (in *Ugly Feelings*) have begun examining the political consequences of the ways that cultures represent emotions, especially the emotions of marginalized people. I refer to their work throughout this book (Ahmed; Ngai). The phrase "the personal is political" cannot be traced to a particular writer.

2. In this book, I use the term "emotion" rather than "affect" because I am analyzing ways of representing biologically based, culturally and historically shaped internal experiences. I will explain my choice of terminology in Chapter 2.

3. I do not include racial, ethnic, religious, or any other form of group-hatred among these emotions, because mass-hatred is not acceptable in any form.

4. Psychologists Lisa Feldman Barrett, Christine Wilson-Mendenhall, and Lawrence Barsalou define simulation as an interpretive cognitive process in which one can "connect immediate sensory input with a vast body of sensory, motor, affective, and other, related information stored in memory" (Barrett et al., "A Psychological Construction Account" 449).

5. Ngai also examines representations of "animatedness," "stuplimity," paranoia, and disgust and argues that depictions of "ugly feelings" are rooted in "the politically charged problem of obstructed agency" (Ngai 32). She demonstrates that, aesthetically, these feelings are represented as offensive to the senses.

6. In *Postcolonial Biology: Psyche and Flesh after Empire*, Deepika Bahri analyzes the ways that colonialism has influenced understandings of human bodies and minds.

7. This working definition of hegemony relies on the theory of Antonio Gramsci as analyzed by Terry Eagleton. Gramsci proposed that political ideologies become instilled in practical, everyday life through "systems of representations" (Eagleton 136, my trans.). Emotion metaphors can certainly be included among these representations that shape people's understandings of how the world works.

8. Lauren Berlant has described how, in the United States, cultural pressures to develop unrealistic fantasies of success can hurt people who earn little money. Berlant criticizes "the cruelty of optimism revealed to people without control over the material conditions of their lives . . ." (Berlant 114).

9. "Why is social transformation so difficult to achieve? Why are relations of power so intractable and enduring, even in the face of collective forms of resistance?" asks Ahmed (11–12). I agree with Ahmed that emotions which shape and are shaped by language have reinforced inequitable power structures.

10. Molek-Kozakowska defines coercive metaphors as "ones that have a high *potential* of making recipients accept representations that are congenial to the interests of the media industry more than of any other institution or social group" (Molek-Kozakowska 152, original emphasis). She studied the metaphors of the 400 most-read online *Daily Mail* news headlines in 2012 and identified strategies such as simplification and (de)legitimization. The original source of the tuberculosis headline is www.dailymail.co.uk/health/article-2244512/Britain-swamped-TB-unless-tests-diagnose-brought-21st-century-experts-warn.html.

11. Sianne Ngai does not regard "ugly feelings" as mere symptoms of oppression and believes they have "*critical* productivity" (Ngai 3, original emphasis).

| The Bodily and Cultural Roots
of Emotion Metaphors

The appeal of some of our most widely accepted theories of emotion is
based . . . on their metaphorical associations rather than on their scientific
validity.

—ZOLTÁN KÖVECSES

TO WHAT EXTENT CAN emotion metaphors determine what a person feels?
Even researchers convinced that people worldwide share some basic emotions
believe that cultures influence the ways these emotions are expressed (Keltner
and Ekman 413). Some psychologists would go further to claim that language
shapes people's experiences of emotions (Barrett, "Solving the Emotion
Paradox" 34). Historians of emotions challenge the idea that human emotions
can be abstracted from languages and cultures at all. Depending on researchers'
fields and disciplinary training, those who study emotions may maintain
that emotions have their own physiological life independent of words; that
emotions are influenced by words; or that emotions come into being only
through the words that describe them. The ways that researchers investigate
emotions affect the kinds of knowledge that they build. In the many fields
that study human emotions, research techniques and research findings have
influenced each other in feedback loops. Methods and theoretical standpoints
mold one another, and in the realm of emotion research, clashes among fields
can provoke emotional responses.

To understand how emotion metaphors work today, it is vital to examine
their histories. This chapter reviews the most compelling scientific theories
of emotions, paying special attention to ideas about language's role in emotional experience. These experimentally backed theories include the basic
emotions theory, which posits some universally shared emotions; appraisal
theory, which regards emotions as cognitive interpretations of external stimuli;
and constructed emotion theory, which characterizes emotions as individually
variable and linguistically influenced. These theories resonate with recent evidence that colloquial metaphors are corporeally grounded and do cognitive
work. Emotion metaphors have a physiological basis, but Dante Alighieri's

Inferno and *Purgatorio* and John Bunyan's *The Pilgrim's Progress* reveal the religious roots of metaphors such as "getting bogged down." Dante's and Bunyan's treatments of emotions live on in contemporary self-help books such as Spencer Johnson's *Who Moved My Cheese?*, which depict "negative" emotions like anger and fear as hindrances in a goal-oriented quest. By bringing scientific and literary sources into conversation, this chapter examines the roles of physiology and language in creating emotional experience.

Fields of Emotion Research

"Emotion" derives from the Latin words, *movere*, "to move," and *ex*, "out" or "out of." ("Emotion"). In English, the terms "emotion," "feeling," and "affect" overlap as alternate ways to describe internal responses to a changing external world. Different fields of learning embrace some of these terms, avoid others, and define all three distinctly depending on the fields' aims and practices. In neuroscience, "emotion" means a "set of physiological responses that occur more or less unconsciously when the brain detects certain challenging situations" (Kandel et al. 1079). "Feeling," in contrast, denotes the conscious experience of bodily and cognitive reactions (Kandel et al. 1079; Frazzetto 11). Interdisciplinary scholar Giovanni Frazzetto expands on this definition: "Feelings are internal, subjective and private states, fruit of introspection and awareness . . ." (Frazzetto 125). For many laboratory scientists who study emotions, the subject of this book would be metaphors for *feelings*. Not all neuroscientists think alike, however, and Joseph LeDoux, who co-wrote the definition in Eric Kandel's textbook quoted earlier, now advocates restricting the use of words such as "fear" to "*conscious* feelings" in human beings so as not to confuse complex human emotions with animals' threat-detection strategies (LeDoux 23, original emphasis).

Communications scholar Eric Shouse shares the neuroscientific view that feelings are personal, but he adds new dimensions to the discussion. For those working in the communications field, "feelings are *personal* and *biographical*, emotions are *social*, and affects are *prepersonal*" (Shouse, original emphasis). Shouse calls attention to the possibility of physiological and cognitive responses without personhood, the focus of affect theory in the humanities. Scholars in this field distinguish affect from emotion by proposing that emotion calls for an illusory integral, defined person, whereas "affect does not" (Ngai 25). Like neuroscientists, affect theorists regard minds and bodies as "open to life" and are interested in the ways that they influence and are influenced by the surrounding world (Seigworth and Gregg 12). From the perspective of these scholars who study language, affect and cognition blend into one another, and there is no lasting, bounded self that thinks and feels (Seigworth and Gregg 2–3). Researchers in affect theory would investigate metaphors for affects without relying on the notion of individual experience.

In this book, I use the term "emotion" rather than "affect" or "feeling" because of the social aspect of emotions that Shouse invokes. Whether or not emotions involve more than physiology, and whether or not people experience them as enduring selves, emotions are social phenomena. This may be the reason that historians prefer the term "emotion" to "feeling" or "affect." Like many historians, I am interested in the ways that individual experiences and cultural understandings shape one another. Psychologist Michael F. Mascolo follows philosopher Ludwig Wittgenstein in thinking that attempts to separate public and private aspects of emotions are misguided (Mascolo 259). Wittgenstein argues that words maintain their meanings not through fixed definitions but through the ways they are used in social interactions (Mascolo 261). To learn how language works, it helps to listen to conversations rather than to reconstruct people's mysterious, inner states. Mascolo proposes that the same holds true for emotions, whose expression can't be separated from their experience. "What we call an emotional expression is part . . . of the emotional process itself," he proposes (Mascolo 262). If Mascolo is right, the expression of anger is integral to the feeling of anger, and metaphors that emerge from some people's emotional experiences shape the experiences of others.

The scholars who study emotions—neuroscientists, psychologists, historians, philosophers, literary critics—differ about the degree to which verbal language affects emotional experience. I join those who hold that emotion metaphors influence but never fully determine emotional experience. If they did, why would writers struggle so desperately to describe complex emotions? The research presented in this book indicates that widely shared physiological experiences inspire emotion metaphors, but once in circulation, these metaphors mold people's understandings of their experiences.

Few writers have described emotions as deftly as William James, whose use of metaphor surpasses that of many novelists and poets. James's wisdom and eloquence have led emotion scholars from diverse fields to claim him as an ancestor even when their theories collide. Joseph LeDoux and neurologist Antonio Damasio credit James with initiating "the modern attempt to understand emotions" (Kandel et al. 1081). Psychologists Maria Gendron and Lisa Feldman Barrett point out James's emphasis on the ways that emotions vary and the ways they emerge from other mental and physical phenomena (Gendron and Barrett 324). Aspects of most twenty-first-century theories of emotion glimmer in James's essay, "What Is an Emotion?" (1884), as they do in his masterpiece, *Principles of Psychology* (1890). James is a strikingly original writer, but his writing also reveals the work of cultural ideology. His cultural assumptions have been carried to current discussions of emotion along with his brilliant insights.

In the 1880s, James grew tired of studies that treated emotions as individual things. "I should as lief read verbal descriptions of the shapes of the rocks on a New Hampshire farm," he wrote (James 448). In James's eyes, psychologists were regarding emotions as something "like the old immutable species in natural history . . ." (James 449). Like biology, the emerging science of psychology needed a central theory that would explain the relationships among emotions and generate hypotheses that scientists could test. James proposed such a principle, now known as the peripheral feedback theory (Kandel et al. 1081). He called the human organism a "sounding-board" that resonates with each flux of its environment (James 450). According to popular notions at the time, external events caused mental (emotional) changes, which then expressed themselves in the body. James turned this idea around, arguing that "the bodily changes follow directly the perception of the exciting fact, and . . . our feeling of the same changes as they occur *is* the emotion" (James 449, original emphasis). Bodies caused emotions to arise in minds, not the other way around. If emotions emerged as components of simpler mental and physical phenomena, it was clear why they varied so greatly, both within and among individuals (James 454).

James supported his theory by describing familiar emotional experiences. He reported that "each fit of sobbing makes the sorrow more acute . . ." and noted that crying "is not without a certain pungent pleasure . . ." (James 462, 444). James hoped to show that enacting an emotion reinforced it, and that without a bodily basis, an emotion could have no life. Without flushing, a fast heartbeat, and clenched teeth, what would be left of rage? "The only thing that can possibly be supposed to take its place," speculated James, "is some cold-blooded and dispassionate judicial sentence . . ." (James 452). He noted that emotions could intensify with time if one remembered and dwelled on them. For instance, one might "get angrier in thinking over one's insult than at the moment of receiving it" (James 443). If emotions lived through the body, then, like the body, they could be controlled.

Rhetorically, James argued for his corporeal theory of emotion with culturally persuasive metaphors. His references to New Hampshire rocks and immutable species belittled descriptive approaches to emotions as obsolete, pre-Darwinian scientific attitudes. James asked readers to imagine the sound of one knife blade moving against another and to observe the ways their bodies reacted. He proposed that "the entire fund and capital of the emotion . . ." they would feel consisted of their bodily responses (James 458). Together, the body and mind formed a capitalist economy in which conscious perceptions of emotion might be regarded as the interest on capital. In his descriptive language, James combined economics with aesthetics to claim that without bodily effects, the "purely cognitive" perceptions of an environmental change would be "pale, colorless, destitute of emotional warmth" (James 450). He asked readers to exercise their imaginations and claimed that if they fancied a strong emotion and abstracted its "bodily symptoms," there would be nothing left (James 451). James himself spoke of an emotion as a thing when he asserted, "a purely disembodied human emotion is a nonentity" (James 452). James moved in a different direction than the scholars who had meticulously described types of love. He aimed to show that emotions had a bodily basis and could be regulated by governing the bodies that produced them.

James's *Principles of Psychology* is no self-help book, but it promotes the same ideology as some late twentieth-century guides to emotional health. Some emotions, James presumed, are undesirable and can be extinguished by keeping bodies from enacting them:

> Sit all day in a moping posture, sigh, and reply to everything with a dismal voice, and your melancholy lingers. There is no more valuable precept in moral education than this. . . . If we wish to conquer undesirable emotional tendencies in ourselves, we must assiduously, and in the first instance cold-bloodedly, go through the *outward movements* of those contrary dispositions which we prefer to cultivate. . . . Smooth the brow, brighten the eye, contract the dorsal rather than the ventral aspect of the frame, and speak in a major key . . . and your heart must be frigid indeed if it do [sic] not gradually thaw! (James 463, original emphasis)

James implies that emotions don't belong to individuals alone. Any emotion expressed will affect other people, and "morally educated" adults bear the responsibility of suppressing emotions that could cause communal harm. James acknowledges that in some cases, quashing emotions can cause ill effects, but he dismisses these as exceptions. "When we teach children to repress their emotional talk and display," he maintains, "it is not that they may *feel* more. . . . It is that they may *think* more" (James 466, original emphasis). For James, emotions are social as well as personal. They emerge from bodily phenomena, their "fund and capital," and these funds can be regulated to suit moral educators' interests.

Antonio Damasio and Joseph LeDoux identify James as a progenitor for good reason.[1] Like most researchers in their field, these experimentalists view minds and bodies as inseparable and emotions as corporeally grounded. Most neuroscientists conceive of emotions as evolutionarily conserved and rooted in homeostatic systems that evolved to regulate organisms relative to their changing environments (Kandel et al. 1079–80). These scientists define emotions as unconscious physiological responses for a practical reason as well as a philosophical one: reactive behaviors that humans share with other animals can be studied in laboratory experiments. Because neuroscientists focus on basic emotions such as fear and rage, many researchers in this field think that emotions—as they define them—are universal and characterized by distinct neural activity patterns. Few would make this claim about self-pity, a subjective feeling that does not exist in all cultures. Neuroimaging experiments offer some evidence that even more complex feelings such as sadness and happiness show distinct activity patterns in brain areas that monitor bodily states (Kandel et al. 1090). Emotions intrigue neuroscientists because they emerge from combinations of regulatory and cognitive processes (Kandel et al. 1092).

Fear has been a revealing emotion to study because it has let scientists integrate data from animal, anatomical, physiological, clinical, and neuroimaging research. In the early twentieth century, Ivan Pavlov's conditioning studies showed that animals can learn to fear a harmless signal if it is paired with a painful event. Animals (including humans) with damaged amygdalae (almond-shaped structures deep in each brain hemisphere) cannot make these associations (Kandel et al. 1084–85). People with impaired amygdalae who undergo fear conditioning can recall their training but don't respond emotionally to the harmless signal (Kandel et al. 1087). They even have trouble recognizing fear in images of human faces (Kandel et al. 1085). Together, behavioral, clinical, and imaging studies suggest that the amygdala does more than direct emotional responses. It creates and maintains the associations that form the essence of emotions (Kandel et al. 1084). It is necessary, though not sufficient, to produce fear and other emotional reactions.

In humans, the cortex—the wrinkled "bark" around the brain—works with the amygdala to shape behavior in which emotion plays a strong role. Both the cortex and the amygdala receive inputs from the thalamus, which processes incoming sensory information. Because the amygdala can respond faster, people may react to stimuli before they are aware of a situation's nuances (Kandel et al. 1084). The prefrontal cortex participates in complex cognitive functions such as making decisions and judgments (Kandel et al. 1089). The ventromedial prefrontal cortex is involved in shaping social behavior, and patients with lesions in this area have trouble making decisions in which emotions are an essential guide (Kandel et al. 1088–89). Other regions of the cortex also allow emotions to emerge. These include the insular cortex, which integrates information about the body's internal state; and the cingulate cortex, whose activity undergoes changes during depression (Kandel et al. 1090–92). These claims about brain structures' roles in producing emotions rest on clinical and experimental evidence and will continue to change as new evidence emerges.

The view that human beings share some "basic," discrete emotions extends far beyond neuroscience. The basic emotions theory predominates in psychology and also appeals to affect theory scholars in the humanities. Which emotions are basic remains controversial, but researchers who view some emotions as universal often include fear and anger and exclude complex feelings such as spite. The basic emotions theory represents emotions as externally activated, recognizable across cultures, and characterized by distinct patterns of neural and bodily activity. According to this view, emotions are unconscious and work as "complex reflexes that are automatically triggered . . ." (Barrett et al., "Of Mice and Men" 298). Once emotions emerge into consciousness, they become feelings.

Scholars interested in the dynamics of affect, language, and culture find psychologist Silvan Tomkins's description of basic emotions useful. In *Affect, Imagery, Consciousness* (1962–1992), Tomkins avoids the term "emotion" because he believes that "affect" better conveys the slipperiness of human responses. Tomkins notes that affects always have causes, but he points out the loose connections between affective responses and those mediated by homeostatic feedback systems (Tomkins 37). Humans try to maximize positive affect and minimize negative affect, and a human automaton would need an affect system in order to act in its own interest (Tomkins 48, 41). According to Tomkins, psychologists have been overlooking the most interesting feature of the affect system: its flexibility. People can "invest" affect in anything conceivable (Tomkins 49). A person can love a man, a woman, or a child; a garden, a book, or a pair of shoes. Like William James, Tomkins sometimes expresses himself in the language of economics. "If the cost of affect investment becomes excessive it is always possible to liquidate such investment," he writes (Tomkins 66). Tomkins's metaphor implies more conscious control over affect than his arguments might grant. Eight "primary affects" constitute Tomkins's economy: (1) "Interest-Excitement," (2) "Enjoyment-Joy," (3) "Surprise-Startle," (4) "Distress-Anguish," (5) "Fear-Terror," (6) "Shame-Humiliation," (7) "Contempt-Disgust," and (8) "Anger-Rage" (Tomkins 73–74). Tomkins believes that most human beings share these affects, and he specifies the facial expressions associated with each one.

Since Tomkins proposed this version of the basic emotions theory, a range of evidence for it has accumulated. Psychologist Paul Ekman's and his colleagues' studies of facial expressions have proved to be compelling and controversial. Decades of research have convinced Ekman and psychologist Dacher Keltner that "select emotions have distinct facial expressions" and that "there is agreement across cultures in judgments of the expression of emotion in the face . . ." (Keltner and Ekman 412). Keltner and Ekman believe, however, that "culture clearly shapes how emotion is expressed," and they are eager to move past debates about whether facial expressions associated with emotions are universal or culturally relative (Keltner and Ekman 413). More fruitful research topics would be how cultures influence emotional expressions and how individual manifestations of an emotion can vary. Some functional magnetic resonance imaging (fMRI) studies suggest that basic emotions such as anger and disgust are characterized by distinct activity patterns (Kandel et al. 1089–91). These studies need to be interpreted with caution, however, since they often focus on specific, preselected brain regions, and many brain areas are involved in producing emotions.

Even before the 1960s, appraisal approaches to the emotions offered an alternative to the basic emotions theory. Psychologists who view emotions from this perspective conceive of them as permeated by cognition. Advocates of appraisal theory believe that rather than discrete, automatic sets of physiological responses, emotions are "intentional states directed toward objects and dependent on our beliefs and desires" (Leys 438). In *Emotion and Personality* (1960), psychologist Magda Arnold emphasizes the ways that human nervous systems evaluate sensory information as soon as it arrives. Convinced that "appraisal and emotion complete sense perception," she studies the ways that brains register sensations they like or do not like (Arnold 2: 34). For Arnold and the psychologists inspired by her work, emotions "arise from a meaningful interpretation of an object by an individual" (Gendron and Barrett 317). They emerge as a person senses physiological changes and considers how an external situation might have caused them.

Evidence for emotion as appraisal came from the 1962 experiments of psychologists Stanley Schachter and Jerome Singer. These researchers injected participants with adrenaline and observed that people who were "uninformed" or "misinformed" about how the shot would affect them more often attributed their increased heart rates to the angry or euphoric mood of a confederate (Lutz 143–45). These results suggest that emotions involve not just physiological arousal but "cognitive interpretation" (Gendron and Barrett 319). The interpretation might be instantaneous rather than deliberate, but it seemed indispensable for emotion. "Is the state of physiological arousal alone sufficient to induce an emotion?" asked Schachter and Singer. "Best evidence indicates that it is not" (Schachter and Singer 380).

In the past fifteen years, psychologist Lisa Feldman Barrett has developed the concept of cognitively permeated emotion into a theory that fits recent experimental evidence. Like appraisal theorists, Barrett believes that "core affect" means nothing in itself; it simply represents a human being's responses to an ever-changing flow of external events (Barrett, "Solving the Emotion Paradox" 30). Emotional experience begins when a person realizes that affect is "about something" (Barrett, "Solving the Emotion Paradox" 36). Emotion involves cognitive evaluation, but Barrett disagrees with appraisal theorists about what is being evaluated. In her view, emotional experience requires appraisal not of an external situation but of one's own mind-body complex (Gendron and Barrett 318). Barrett originally called her understanding of emotions "conceptual act theory" because her experimental findings indicate that an emotion is a categorization of an internal state (Barrett, "Solving the Emotion Paradox" 21, 35). Placing something in a category gives it meaning, and categorization is a fundamental aspect of human cognition (Barrett et al., "Of Mice and Men" 304). Like memories, emotions emerge from combinations of more essential activities that brains have evolved to perform (Barrett, "Solving the Emotion Paradox" 21). Because her evidence indicates that brains create emotions from a range of functions, she now calls her idea the "theory of constructed emotion" (Barrett, *How Emotions Are Made* xiii).

Barrett describes an "emotion paradox": popular culture characterizes emotions as discrete, identifiable things, and that is how most people experience them (Barrett, "Solving the Emotion Paradox" 20). Many of the novels and films discussed in this book represent emotions according to this "classical view": as recognizable entities that should be controlled by a separate self (Barrett, *How Emotions Are Made* x). But laboratory experiments suggest that emotions can't be so easily distinguished. Barrett has carefully reviewed studies of peripheral nerve activity, facial expression, situational behavior, and brain imaging patterns and found no "consistent evidence for particular neural correlates" of basic emotions such as anger (Barrett, "Solving the Emotion Paradox" 23). Even combined, these investigative methods offer insufficient evidence to prove that there are "neural signatures for distinct emotions" (Barrett, "Solving the Emotion Paradox" 23). Claims that fear, anger, joy, and disgust are neurologically distinct rest on shaky experimental ground. Why would different emotions have their own, dedicated circuits in brains so highly interconnected? (Barrett et al., "Of Mice and Men" 299). The basic emotions theory has trouble accounting for variations between individuals, within individuals in different contexts, and between distinctive cultures (Barrett et al., "Of Mice and Men" 298).

In her own neuroimaging experiments, Barrett and her colleagues have observed that an emotion such as fear can elicit distinct neural activity patterns in different simulated (imagined, or sensorily recreated) contexts, such as "physical danger brought on by one's own carelessness" or "social evaluation" (Wilson-Mendenhall et al. 1110). Her group's data indicate that "the situation in which an emotion concept was experienced shaped how the emotion was instantiated in the brain" (Wilson-Mendenhall et al. 1120). Barrett's theory of constructed emotion takes this variability as a point of departure. If emotions arise when momentary affects are compared with simulated past experiences, then each person's emotions will be unique, and they will vary with context. This understanding of emotions follows the logic of mammalian nervous systems, in which prior knowledge influences sensory perception (Barrett, "Solving the Emotion Paradox" 29). The theory of constructed emotion explains why emotions vary with context, since affect will activate a different range of memories in an individual depending on her situation (Barrett, "Solving the Emotion Paradox" 33). Neither the memories nor the environmental interaction needs to reach conscious awareness, and emotions can arise from their blending without anyone realizing why these emotions have emerged. Barrett notes that memory was once known as a "unitary facult[y] of the mind," with dedicated circuits and storage areas. Today, memory is understood as an "emergent phenomen[on]" that relies on the recreation of sensory and motor experiences (Barrett, "Solving the Emotion Paradox" 21). Barrett predicts that understandings of the emotions will undergo a similar transformation.

If emotions emerge when present affects meet past experiences, then individual instances of emotions can yield worthwhile knowledge. Barrett's theory of constructed emotion differs from the basic emotions theory in valuing individual experiences as a source of information (Barrett, "Solving the Emotion Paradox" 37). If researchers are seeking aspects of emotion common to most humans, they are likely to downplay the nuances of particular minds. For most of the twentieth century, many experimental psychologists rejected self-reports in favor of quantifiable data, but Barrett and her colleagues aim "to understand the richness and diversity of emotional life in humans" (Barrett, "Solving the Emotion Paradox" 37). She points out that "conceptualizing core affect . . . is a skill," and that people vary greatly in their "emotional granularity"—their ability to describe their emotional experiences with specific words (Barrett, "Solving the Emotion Paradox" 36, 25). Self-reports can't reveal the mechanisms by which experiences are produced, but when it comes to emotions, people are worth listening to.

Because the theory of constructed emotion views emotions as variable and dynamic, its proponents pay close attention to words. Barrett believes that "emotion concepts are directed by language" (Barrett, "Solving the Emotion Paradox" 34). Her behavioral experiments have convinced her that words influence emotional experiences, and she suspects that language stimulates people to combine affects and memories in ways that they have never before encountered (Barrett, "Solving the Emotion Paradox" 35). Barrett does not claim that emotions are created *entirely* by language and culture. Like basic emotions and appraisal theorists, she maintains that "every human thought, feeling, and behavior must be causally reduced to the firing of neurons in the human brain" (Barrett et al., "Of Mice and Men" 306). Currently, she represents the interaction of biology and culture in this way:

> Emotions are not built-in but made from more basic parts. They are not universal but vary from culture to culture. They are not triggered; you create them. They emerge as a combination of the physical properties of your body, a flexible brain that wires itself to whatever environment it develops in, and your culture and upbringing, which provide that environment. (Barrett, *How Emotions Are Made* xii)

Within the mind-body complex of each individual, words can shape experiences by activating simulations that will coalesce into emotions. Barrett doesn't think that language fully determines emotions, but because people use their experiences to define their emotions, the languages they speak and the words they use will affect their understandings of what they feel.

A Crop of Metaphors

In the late twentieth century, understandings of human language evolved as quickly as those of emotions. These new studies of metaphors challenged traditional notions of what metaphors do, why writers create them, and how they work. Philosopher Max Black doubted that authors were planting metaphors just to decorate their works and give readers pleasure (Black, "Metaphor" 282). Black found metaphors to be a useful tool for communication and argument, and he analyzed the ways that metaphors can transform thinking. Supposedly a metaphor stands for a literal expression, but it rarely works as a mere substitute (Black, "Metaphor" 279–80). "Memories of Paris" does not adequately translate Ernest Hemingway's title, *A Moveable Feast*. A metaphor might also be seen as a comparison that calls attention to similarities. But compelling metaphors are active, not passive, and rather than reporting preexisting similarities, metaphors often create them (Black, "Metaphor" 284–85). Crafting and interpreting innovative metaphors involve intense mental work because metaphors "stretch, twist, press and expand" concepts whose meaning one thought was clear (Black, "More about Metaphor" 448).

To replace the substitution and comparison views, Black proposed the interaction theory of metaphor. In his experience, the two terms in a metaphor become "active together" as the person encountering them considers cultural ideas associated with each one (Black, "Metaphor" 286). Literary scholars call the paired terms the "tenor" (the lesser-known concept that one is trying to characterize) and the "vehicle" (the better-known concept to which one compares the tenor).[2] Neuroscientists, cognitive scientists, and psychologists dissect metaphors with different terms, which are likewise metaphorical. In these scientific fields, a metaphor "shoots" meaning, so to speak, from the "source" or "base" (the more familiar term, the literary "vehicle") to the "target" (the less familiar term, the literary "tenor"). Consider the metaphor from the 1980s song, "Love Is a Battlefield."[3] In the implied metaphor of cognitive scientists, the source (a battlefield) shoots an arrow of meaning at the target (love). In the implied metaphor of literary scholars, meaning is carried in a vehicle (a battlefield) to the tenor (love), which then "holds" this meaning. Because of the interdisciplinary nature of this book, I will use the scientific terms but will remind readers of the corresponding literary terminology. According to Black's interaction theory, metaphors selectively call attention to certain aspects of the source and target.

Black has found that in thought-provoking metaphors, the source "organizes" one's view of the target (Black, "Metaphor" 288). It is as if the source were a screen of smoked glass with only a few lines scratched clear, and one were peering through it at the target (Black, "Metaphor" 288). By allowing meaning to emerge, the source or vehicle functions more as a system than a thing (Black, "More about Metaphor" 441). The metaphor "selects, emphasizes, suppresses and organizes" aspects of the target by attributing ideas culturally linked to the source (Black, "More about Metaphor" 442). If the source is well chosen, the paired concepts produce overtones like a musical chord in a resonant space (Black, "Metaphor" 290). Black was most intrigued by the transformative possibilities of resonant metaphors. He emphasized that metaphors create meaning, so that "literal translations" of them lose "*cognitive* content" (Black, "Metaphor" 293, original emphasis). In the search to understand the world that fields of knowledge share, metaphors can serve as "cognitive instruments" (Black, "More about Metaphor" 454).

To show how new thinking tools can transform knowledge, Black asks his readers a series of questions: "Did genes exist before their existence was recognized by biologists? . . . Did the slow motion appearance of a galloping horse exist before the invention of cinematography?" (Black, "More about Metaphor" 453–54). He argues that by stimulating the imagination, metaphors can offer new ways of seeing, and by implication, new ways of knowing. Black compares metaphors to maps and graphs, "cognitive devices" that structure experience and make it possible to see patterns in data (Black, "More about Metaphor" 456). He specifies that metaphors are culturally relative: for metaphors to work, the notions that link sources and targets need not be true, only accepted as true in a given culture (Black, "Metaphor" 287). One needs to consider this relativity when assessing the implications of Black's interaction theory. As cognitive instruments, metaphors don't just describe reality. By offering tools to structure perception, they build the realities that people know.

Linguist George Lakoff and philosopher Mark Johnson have offered an array of evidence that metaphors work as cognitive tools. Using expressions from everyday English, they have supported Black's claim that metaphors aren't just literary devices—they are integral to thought, and they shape the concepts that structure people's realities (Lakoff and Johnson 3). Lakoff and Johnson point out metaphors in colloquial language, quoting expressions so common, they don't seem metaphorical. The linguist and philosopher acknowledge cultural specificity throughout their argument, but they also show how often metaphors such as "I'm feeling down" describe abstract concepts through references to human bodies (Lakoff and Johnson 14–15). One can't make claims about human thought based on colloquial English, but Lakoff and Johnson's *Metaphors We Live By* has translated well.[4] Each translation of their book—including German, French, Spanish, and Italian—has examined popular expressions in its own language, and although none of them correspond perfectly to those in English, the families of structured concepts they form reveal the ways that metaphors can direct thought.

As cognitive tools, metaphors emerge from bodily and cultural experiences, but once established, they can shape future experiences in a feedback loop. "*Every* experience takes place within a vast background of cultural presuppositions," write Lakoff and Johnson. "All experience is cultural through and through . . . We experience our 'world' in such a way that our culture is already present in the very experience itself" (Lakoff and Johnson 57, original emphasis). Lakoff and Johnson agree with Black that rather than passively recording preexisting similarities between concepts, metaphors "*create* similarities" by offering new ways to structure people's experiences (Lakoff and Johnson 151, original emphasis). Inevitably, structuring one "concept in terms of another . . . will necessarily hide other aspects of the concept" (Lakoff and Johnson 10). An emotion metaphor such as "move on" highlights the importance of opening oneself to new experiences, but it erases the benefits a person may gain from dwelling on a feeling or thought. Even when emotion metaphors seem to have a common-sense, bodily basis, they are culturally molded and do not represent everyone's experiences, in all contexts.

Linguist Zoltán Kövecses worked with George Lakoff to study the conceptualization of emotions. The two scientists followed Black's lead in defining a conceptual metaphor as "a set of correspondences between a source domain and a target domain" (Lakoff and Kövecses 201). Lakoff and Kövecses noted that in English, many expressions for emotions emerge from a central, conceptual metaphor: "the body is a container for the emotions" (Lakoff and Kövecses 198). In the case of anger, on which they initially focused, rage is often represented as a hot fluid in a container. In expressions such as "she had reached the boiling point," anger is the target, and the heat of a contained fluid is the source (Lakoff and Kövecses 199). It is not hard to see how such expressions relate to the physiological aspects of anger that William James described. Of course, not all anger metaphors involve simmering, boiling, or exploding. Lakoff and Kövecses noticed some that depict anger as a "dangerous animal" whose owner needs to restrain it (Lakoff and Kövecses 207). Although many of these metaphors appear to have physiological roots, they share a cultural assumption. In English, most anger metaphors represent rage as a dangerous force that needs to be controlled (Lakoff and Kövecses 205).

Once Lakoff and Kövecses had gathered as many emotion metaphors as they could, they analyzed them for patterns. In the case of anger, everyday metaphors implied a common scenario, or prototype. This "script" for anger was cultural and did not necessarily correspond to the neural and physiological events underlying rage. One might think of it as a common theme that Lakoff and Kövecses inferred from the variations it produces:

> [Anger involves] an offender and a victim. The offender is at fault. The victim, who is innocent, is the one who gets angry. . . . The offense seems to constitute some sort of injustice. . . . Getting even is equivalent to balancing the scales of justice. . . . What anger "demands" and has an "appetite" for is revenge. (Lakoff and Kövecses 209)

Based on this narrative, Lakoff and Kövecses suggested a five-stage sequence summarizing the English-language prototype for anger: (1) "Offending event," (2) "Anger," (3) "Attempt to control anger," (4) "Loss of control," and (5) "Retribution" (Lakoff and Kövecses 213–14). No anger metaphor conveys all five steps in this sequence, but most elaborate some part of it. What makes this anger prototype so hardy is its ability to send off new shoots.

The anger prototype and the container metaphor associated with it invite creative improvisations. Lakoff and Kövecses observed that the fluid-in-a-container metaphor has a "rich system of metaphorical entailments" (Lakoff and Kövecses 199). These elaborations zoom in to reveal details of key moments in the implied narrative. Some metaphors depict the causes of anger as physical irritants, such as "a pain in the ass" (Lakoff and Kövecses 208).[5] One variation on the prototype ("Anger is an opponent") implies that "winning" means controlling one's anger, and "losing" means letting anger prevail (Lakoff and Kövecses 206). This variant emphasizes the social danger of releasing anger, even if one is ready to "explode."

Metaphors for "banned emotions," many of which involve suppressed anger, branch off from this prototype and the conceptual metaphors related to it. Lakoff and Kövecses regard "frustrated anger" as nonprototypical, since it occurs when retribution is impossible (Lakoff and Kövecses 214). The language of suppressed rage, however, often involves offenses and retribution. It has its own metaphors, although it may be represented in terms of pressure. Lakoff and Kövecses list "nursing a grudge" as another deviation from the prototype, a metaphor in which the source-target pairing suggests long nurturing (Lakoff and Kövecses 215). Other exceptions to the prototype include "redirected anger," "controlled response," "constructive use," "successful suppression," "controlled reduction," and "slow burn" (Lakoff and Kövecses 215). Together, these exceptions to the prototype strike one as strategies of people who cannot act on their anger. Colloquial English may support an anger scenario of pressure and release, but the language of emotion doesn't apply equally well to everyone in the culture that produced it.

In metaphors for anger, Lakoff and Kövecses have observed the combined forces of culture and physiology. Based on their linguistic study, they propose that emotion metaphors are grounded in physiological experience but that language influences people's understandings of that experience. They note that "our cultural theory of the physiology of anger corresponds remarkably well with the actual physiology" (Lakoff and Kövecses 219). But like Barrett, Lakoff and Kövecses maintain that anger doesn't exist as an independent thing. As a metaphor, "anger is an opponent" brings to life what it is trying to describe (Lakoff and Kövecses 206). The creation of metaphors plays a role in producing knowledge, but as Barrett's work shows, thinking of emotions as active things may block efforts to understand how they work.

In his more recent studies, Kövecses has continued to investigate the ways that physiology and culture interact to create emotion metaphors. To build useful knowledge of emotion language, he argues, researchers need to move beyond claims that emotions are purely corporeal or socially constructed (Kövecses, *Metaphor and Emotion* 14). As a cognitive linguist, Kövecses remains convinced that "all psychological phenomena ultimately depend on physiological processes" (Kövecses, *Emotion Concepts* 172). Cross-cultural studies of emotion metaphors have shown that people worldwide interpret their emotions differently, but some conceptual metaphors are "near-universals" (Kövecses, *Metaphor and Emotion* 139). Comparisons of anger metaphors in Chinese, Japanese, Hungarian, English, and other languages have convinced him that their common features reflect "certain universal properties of the human body" (Kövecses, *Metaphor and Emotion* 146). Embodiment limits the range of anger metaphors, which vary significantly among the cultures he has studied (Kövecses, *Metaphor and Emotion* 160). With some reservations, Kövecses supports the basic emotions model backed by many neuroscientists.[6]

To scholars who understand emotions as socially constructed, Kövecses would reply that people of different cultures "conceptualize their emotions in many different ways *within the constraints* imposed on them by universal physiology" (Kövecses, *Metaphor and Emotion* 165, original emphasis). Kövecses believes that in any given culture, the language used to describe emotions shapes and is shaped by conscious feelings. Close analysis of emotion metaphors promises to reveal how cultures influence emotional experiences (Kövecses, *Metaphor and Emotion* xi–xii). Often these cultural models affirm physiological ones, as in metaphors representing anger as a contained liquid. But sometimes the cultural patterns defy biology—as in the striking Western tendency to depict emotions as separate from the self.

When Kövecses sought an anger prototype in a squirming mass of metaphors, he noticed depictions of emotions as dangerous natural forces or opponents (Kövecses, *Emotion Concepts* 162–64). Like these metaphors, the fluid-in-a-container model implies that emotion "is capable of independent existence from a person" and "has to be controlled" (Kövecses, *Emotion Concepts* 151). Together, these metaphors serve the "folk" assumption that "an emotion is an entity separate from the self" (Kövecses, *Emotion Concepts* 165). This way of thinking about emotions seems rooted in an older folk model: the separation of the body from the mind (Kövecses, *Emotion Concepts* 206). Current research in neuroscience, cognitive science, and psychology does not support this mind-body separation. If psychological events are grounded in physiological ones, there can be no mind without a body. Kövecses suspects that behind metaphors depicting emotions and selves as separate things lies a notion of self based on control (Kövecses, *Metaphor and Emotion* 199). He points out that scientific understandings of emotion have drawn on the folk model—how could they not, when they are forced to rely on culturally saturated language? (Kövecses, *Emotion Concepts* 144). People who hear and propagate emotion metaphors may well experience emotions as alien forces. But the source of their experience lies in cultural teachings, not in their hearts or in their blood.

Religious Roots

In the Christian tradition, emotional responses to frustration figure among the seven deadly sins. Early Catholic theologians defined these transgressions: pride, greed, lust, envy, gluttony, anger, and sloth ("Seven Deadly Sins"). According to one contemporary religious website, these seven sins are "fatal to spiritual progress" ("Sins, Virtues, and Tales"). The "banned" emotions of self-pity, suppressed rage, grudge-bearing, and spite bear a family resemblance to pride, anger, envy, and sloth. Except in the case of anger, there is no one-to-one correspondence, but even in the twenty-first century, these unloved emotions smell like a reeking stew of sin. Understandings of these feelings are enmeshed with those of sins because they are described with the same metaphors. With time, cultural authorities change, as do rules for emotional expression and behavior. The metaphors that structure emotion concepts, however, have persisted and adapted themselves as cultures have evolved.

Vivid narratives in the Catholic and Protestant traditions associate banned emotions with unpleasant physical sensations. In evocative ways, Dante Alighieri's *Inferno* and *Purgatorio* (1308–1321) and John Bunyan's *The Pilgrim's Progress* (1678) represent metaphorical transgressions through bodily suffering, so that readers can *feel* the nature and consequences of sins. All three works depict exploratory journeys undertaken for spiritual growth. In these narratives, the emotions of anger and despondence (despair, or lack of hope) literally stop progressive movement. Those who feel prolonged rage sink into the mire, serving as a warning to all those who are emotionally stuck.

In the fifth circle of Dante's hell, sinners punished for anger suffer in the River Styx. As a reconstruction of divine justice, the inverted cone of the *Inferno* reconstructs moral offenses as physical punishments. Dante's sinners keep doing what they have done in life, but in the afterlife, they do it literally. Organized as a descending series of shrinking, concentric circles, Dante's hell houses sinners according to the gravity of their crimes. Those who have committed the most heinous sins against God lie deepest (Sinclair, Introduction

17). In this hierarchy, angry sinners fume between the heretics below them in the sixth circle, and the avaricious and prodigal above them in the fourth. In Dante's system, their anger is a sin of incontinence, worse than financial greed but not as bad as heresy (Sinclair, Note 108).

Guided by the Roman poet Virgil, Dante's shocked protagonist describes what he sees:

> I, who had stopped to gaze intently, saw muddy people in that bog, all naked and with looks of rage. They were smiting each other not only with the hand but with head and breast and feet and tearing each other piecemeal with their teeth. The good Master said: "Son, thou seest now the souls of those whom anger overcame; and I would have thee know for sure also that there are people under the water who sigh and make the water bubble on the surface, as thine eye tells thee wherever it turns. Fixed in the slime they say: 'We were sullen in the sweet air that is gladdened by the sun, bearing in our hearts a sluggish smoke; now we are sullen in the black mire.'" (Alighieri, *Inferno* 105)

This scene of people biting each other in purplish-black water might scare any angry person straight (Figure 2.1). But in its forward momentum, the passage draws the reader's attention to the angry souls bubbling alone in the mud. These sinners can only "gurgle in their throat, for they cannot get the words out plainly" (Alighieri, *Inferno* 105). In the "filthy pond between the dry bank and the swamp," they "gorge themselves with the mire" (Alighieri, *Inferno* 105). The protagonist is horrified, as many readers might be. Dante spurs them to imagine how these sinners' behavior in life corresponds to isolation and immersion in filth.

Dante's translator, John D. Sinclair, argues that in the structural logic of the *Inferno* (deeper = more sinful), those who bubble alone in the mud have committed a greater offense than those brawling:

> Incontinencies of the flesh do not sink the souls so deep in Hell as those of the spirit, and . . . the worst of all that class of sins is the sluggish, persistent bitterness of the souls which are so mastered by their resentments that they refuse the light of the sun, the goodness of God. (Sinclair, Note 108)

Wrathful people commit sins by refusing to relinquish their claims: they won't pardon those who have hurt them, in their perspective. Rather than seeing their pain as part of a divine order and trusting God to make amends, they arrogate vengeance to themselves. Their sin lies in preferring the immediacy of their own emotions to faith that God will set things right. Lacking the power to find justice—as they see it—they rage inwardly and reject social bonds that might broaden their perspectives. Dante represents their sin as one of willful misperception.

In Dante's *Purgatorio*, the fourteenth-century poet brings to life the faulty vision he associates with rage. Cantos XV to XVII depict his protagonist's journey through the occluded mountain regions of those atoning for wrath. Still led by Virgil, the protagonist notes that:

FIGURE 2.1 An illustration of Dante's *Inferno*, Canto 8 by Stradanus (1523–1605). Public domain.

A smoke was
Coming toward us that was as dark as night,
Nor was there anywhere to escape from it;
This took from us our sight and the pure air. (Alighieri, *Purgatorio* 151)

In Dante's description, the smoke of anger affects other senses besides vision; it becomes an entrapping, asphyxiating cloud. Canto XVI opens with a horrifying description of the protagonist's immersion in these fumes:

The murk of Hell and of a night empty
Of every planet, under a bare sky
Which clouds had made as dark as it could be,
Never drew over my sight as heavy
A veil as that smoke which there covered us,
Nor so rasping to the other senses,
For it would not let my eyes stay open . . .
As a blind man goes along behind his guide . . .
So I walked through the bitter and foul air . . . (Alighieri, *Purgatorio* 153)

Besides robbing people of sight, the smoke of wrath smothers them and immerses them in "foul" smells and "bitter" tastes. It exerts a "rasping" force, irritating their skin. Virgil explains that sinners in this realm of Mount Purgatory are "untying the knot of anger" (Alighieri, *Purgatorio* 153). Dante dramatizes the bodily roots of anger by combining sight with smell, taste, and touch. His poetry encourages readers physically to feel the suffering of people atoning for their wrath. At the same time, his description of oppressive smoke makes his cultural metaphors literal. Anger can be described as blinding, suffocating, or oppressive, and on Mount Purgatory, it *is*. In an enduring, metaphoric way, Dante associates angry refusal to relinquish one's grievances with darkness, suffocation, immobility, and filth.

In the Puritan tradition, which advocates personal religious experiences, the protagonist falls into the mud. John Bunyan's *The Pilgrim's Progress* depicts Christian's allegorical journey toward salvation, symbolized by a distant "Wicket Gate" and "shining light" (Bunyan 12). Accompanied by Pliable, Christian leaves his wife and children to struggle toward his far-off goal. The narrator, who describes a dream vision of Christian's quest, tells readers:

> They drew near to a very miry Slough that was in the midst of the plain, and they, being heedless, did both fall suddenly into the bog. The name of the Slough was Despond. Here therefore they *wallowed* for a time, being grievously bedaubed with the dirt; and Christian, because of the burden that was on his back, began to sink into the mire. (Bunyan 16, emphasis added)

The weight of Christian's pack, which symbolizes original sin, constitutes the greatest threat to him in this scene. Pliable abandons him, so that Christian is "left to tumble in the Slough of Despond alone" (Bunyan 16). He thrashes his way to the shore nearest the Wicket Gate, but his burden keeps him from climbing out (Figure 2.2). He can do so only when Help extends a hand and asks, "But why did you not look for the steps?" (Bunyan 16). Christian answers, "Fear followed me so hard, that I fled the next way, and fell in" (Bunyan 16). His explanation differs from the narrator's, which mentions only Christian's "heedlessness," or inattention. Christian reveals that he overlooked the bog and the steps across it because he was afraid.

Like Dante's tale, Bunyan's involves multiple voices and layers of narrative mediation. The curious narrator intervenes in Christian's story to ask Help

"Christian still endeavored to struggle to that side of the slough that was farthest from his own house."
33

FIGURE 2.2 Christian struggles to escape from the Slough of Despond in John Bunyan's *The Pilgrim's Progress*, Henry Altemus, 1890, illustrations by Frederick Barnard, J. D. Linton, W. Small, et al., engraved by the Dalziel Brothers. Public domain.

why the path to salvation isn't better maintained. Assuming the role of Dante's poet-guide, Help explains:

> This miry Slough is such a place as cannot be mended; it is the descent whither the scum and filth that attends conviction for sin doth continually run, and

therefore is it called the Slough of Despond: for still as the sinner is awakened about his lost condition, there ariseth in his soul many fears, and doubts, and discouraging apprehensions, which all of them get together, and settle in this place; and this is the reason of the badness of this ground. (Bunyan 17)

The Catholic and Protestant allegories have more in common than filthy water. "Despond" derives from the Latin *de* and *spondere*, implying abandonment of a promise: to "lose heart or hope, be dejected" or to "give up" ("Despond"). Falling into a bog from which one can't escape works as a vivid, suggestive metaphor for the bodily work of fear. Whereas anger immerses Dante's sinners in mud redolent of their own failings, Bunyan's protagonist falls into the Slough because of doubt. Unwary travelers sink in when they can't believe that God will rectify the world's pains and injustices. Bunyan stresses the burden of original sin, which ensures that no one will escape the bog without aid. The two scenarios have a strong resemblance: one sinks into slime if one fails to trust God. Without faith, there is no solid ground.

When one aligns Dante's narrative with Bunyan's, the lineage of self-pity metaphors starts to emerge. The fourteenth- and seventeenth-century writers both used immersion in dark water and formless muck (the sources) to describe chronic anger and doubt (the targets). Their metaphors denigrate a certain emotional attitude toward human pains: doubt that these aches form a part of God's order, and that God will make things right. Dante's representation of hell and Bunyan's image of despond suggest the immobility and isolation caused by rage and fear. Many unsavory emotions involve combinations of anger and *Angst*: rage that offenses against one have gone unavenged; and fear of the consequences of redressing them. In figuring "banned" emotions through darkness, immobility, and dirt, Dante's and Bunyan's works have reinforced a pattern that still shapes understandings of these emotions.

Metaphoric Messages

Cultures vary in the ways that they define emotions, but most have rules about which emotions can be expressed, when, and how. In many cases, individuals are held responsible for controlling their emotions for the sake of others in their societies (Frevert 16). For at least three centuries in the West, guidebooks have advised readers how to manage their emotions so that they can achieve success within systems of social constraints. As science has gained social prestige, these advice books have increasingly cited laboratory findings, but the metaphoric arguments of these self-help books draw on older sources.

In the mid-1990s, psychologist Daniel Goleman wrote *Emotional Intelligence* because of his concern about social violence. Aggression was on the rise, he believed, partly because people couldn't understand their emotions (Goleman xi). Goleman regarded an inability to control one's emotions as a "moral deficiency" and pointed out that many codes of ethics command people to "harness, subdue, and domesticate emotional life" (Goleman xiii, 5). He argued that people have an emotional intelligence independent of their psychologically quantifiable IQ. This intelligence of the emotions involves abilities to control and motivate oneself, and it can play a greater role than IQ in determining social success (Goleman xii).

When Goleman describes the neural mechanisms of human emotions, he emphasizes threats, conflicts, and control. In a series of similes, he compares the amygdala to a "psychological sentinel," a "neural tripwire," and an "alarm company" that threaten to "capture and drive much of the rest of the brain" (Goleman 19). He credits Joseph LeDoux with discovering a "neural back alley" from the sensory thalamus to the amygdala (Goleman 20). Metaphorically, Goleman terms the left prefrontal lobe of the cortex an " 'off' switch" or "neural thermostat" for the amygdala's urgent signals (Goleman 29). His comparisons suggest a mechanized brain built by someone concerned about security. In this system, the neural connections between the cortex and amygdala are the "hub of battles"—although they might also be a place for "cooperative treaties" (Goleman 30). The question is how to understand these connections, and Goleman varies in the ways he presents them. His simplistic claim, "We have two minds, one that thinks and one that feels," doesn't do justice to his argument (Goleman 9). He depicts a dynamic relationship and leaves the way open for cooperation, but he emphasizes battles for power. He calls his chapter on the amygdala and the cortex "Anatomy of an Emotional Hijacking."

Goleman's hijacking metaphor has spread so widely that it is worth analyzing. As Max Black argues, creating a resonant metaphor involves a complex, selective mapping of source features onto a target (Black, "Metaphor" 288). The first question Goleman's hijacking figure raises is what exactly the target is. Probably, it is an emotional episode in which a person runs amok. Goleman refers to "neural hijackings," an "amygdala hijacking," and "a neural takeover which . . . originates in the amygdala" (Goleman 16, 232). At first glance, one might think that the amygdala is the hijacker, but "originates" suggests that the amygdala is more like the hijacker's troubled home country. Goleman's claim that "people with greater certainty about their feelings are better pilots of their lives" provides context for understanding the hijacking metaphor (Goleman 46–47). Who is the hijacker, and what does she want? Unlike emotions, hijackers are sentient beings, and they have intentions. Goleman's metaphor suggests the displacement of a well-meaning pilot (probably associated with the prefrontal cortex) by an invasive alien with distinct aims. Goleman notes that "the neocortical response is slower in brain time than the hijack mechanism because it involves more circuitry" (Goleman 28). Possibly, Goleman's hijacking metaphor has its source not in neuroscience but in Plato's *Phaedrus* (370 BCE), which depicts the soul as a charioteer driving one rational and one unruly horse (Plato 50–52, 61–63). Goleman has taken a cultural story and modernized it to create a narrative with jet-age technology. He makes a much-needed call for a better understanding of emotions, but his hijacking metaphor has detrimental effects. Emotions are not alien, hostile, or threatening; they are not sentient beings trying to take over a brain. Hijackers take command of vehicles to win attention when they feel that their cause has been ignored. Possibly, Goleman was warning readers what could happen if emotions continued to be suppressed on a cultural level. If this is the case, his hijacking metaphor works against him because it represents emotions as foreign, dangerous people who need to be monitored and controlled.

Goleman's *Emotional Intelligence* offers other metaphors that give different perspectives on emotional life. His references to "swamping" and "flooding" draw on Bunyan's Slough of Despond, and they do not personify emotions (Goleman 10, 158). Still, this water-based family of metaphors depicts emotion as a force opposed to thought. Part of emotional intelligence, Goleman tells readers, is learning to "keep distress from swamping the ability to think" (Goleman 36). Goleman deserves credit for convincing a generation of people that emotions deserve cultural attention. He urges readers not to "do away with emotion and put reason in its place" but to "find the intelligent balance of the two" (Goleman 32). Perhaps because he draws on long-standing cultural metaphors, some of his figures of speech oppose his aims. Rather than emerging as equals who might cooperate to run a shared land, reason and emotion become opposing forces, only one of which can rule.

Travis Bradberry's and Jean Greaves's *Emotional Intelligence 2.0* (2009) builds on Goleman's work and recharges his emotion metaphors. These industrial psychologists offer strategies for developing self-awareness, self-management, social awareness, and relationship management, which they see as the components of emotional intelligence. They adopt Goleman's hijacking metaphor and tell the story of a real pilot, Chelsea Sullenberger, who saved the lives of everyone on his plane because he "kept his emotions from taking the controls . . ." (Bradberry and Greaves 126). Bradberry and Greaves warn readers that "when you don't stop to think about your feelings . . . you set yourself up to be a frequent victim of emotional hijackings" (Bradberry and Greaves 98). Rather than responding to emotional impulses, people should ask themselves, "What response should I choose?" (Bradberry and Greaves 189). In a less nuanced way than Goleman, they present a model of emotions that asserts: "Control, or be controlled!"

Many of Bradberry and Greaves's metaphors depict struggles for power. The psychologists note that "unmanaged stress . . . reduces our minds to something like a state of martial law in which emotions single-handedly dictate behavior" (Bradberry and Greaves 230). If mental life is the target, their sources involve scenes in which an incompetent ruler threatens to displace a competent one. They offer advice that will "keep your emotions from running the show" (Bradberry and Greaves 85, 110).

Often their metaphors refer to hand movements, classic metaphoric sources for representing the human will. They tell readers, "Catch yourself when your emotions get the best of you," a challenging maneuver given that "brains are hard-wired to give emotions the upper hand" (Bradberry and Greaves 55, 6). As in Plato's allegory, their sources for emotion metaphors often combine movement with directed hand-use. By implication, emotions are unruly animals, as in some of the metaphors Lakoff and Kövecses observed (Lakoff and Kövecses 207). "Your emotions will create trouble if you let them lead you around," write Bradberry and Greaves. "Grab the reins before you head in the wrong direction" (Bradberry and Greaves 104, 98). In a more modern version of the same figure, they tell readers to "take the wheel and drive" (Bradberry and Greaves 99). If the mind-body complex is a moving vehicle, emotions should not be choosing its path.

Implicit in these psychologists' metaphors is the idea that emotions disrupt movement. They exhort their readers, "Keep your emotions from holding you back" (Bradberry and Greaves 26). Motion—especially linear, progressive motion—comes across as the desired aim. Certain emotions, in contrast, hinder progress. When emotions are ungoverned, "you spend your day bouncing around from feeling to feeling" (Bradberry and Greaves 116). People driven by emotion move in random leaps, not in a line from Point A to Point B. Bradberry and Greaves draw on Bunyan when they advise the reader, "prevent yourself from getting bogged down by strong emotions . . ." (Bradberry and Greaves 134). Just as the Slough of Despond enmired unwary travelers on the road to salvation, emotions can entrap people on the path to success. Bunyan's allegory suggests how to avoid the Slough, but Bradberry and Greaves advise readers to "move toward the emotion, into it, and eventually through it" (Bradberry and Greaves 68). The goal is to keep moving forward, and some emotions can thwart that aim. Bradberry and Greaves represent fear as the most inimical because it can take hold of people and paralyze them (Bradberry and Greaves 4). The stories they tell focus on moments when quick, decisive actions saved lives and immobility would have been disastrous. Some of their metaphors involve violence, such as the "one-two punch of reading emotions effectively and then reacting to them . . ." (Bradberry and Greaves 98). Their self-help book uses images of predators, including the hawk whose perspective they advise readers to take (Bradberry and Greaves 75). Together, their metaphors imply that readers should pull themselves free of emotions; beat them back, if necessary; and work toward a state in which emotions can't inhibit their forward progress.

Like Goleman, Bradberry and Greaves argue that one shouldn't just control emotions for one's own sake. All three psychologists use disease metaphors to convey how "infectious" emotions can be. Goleman describes a "spreading virus of good feeling," and Bradberry and Greaves claim that "emotions are contagious" (Goleman x; Bradberry and Greaves 173). Goleman focuses more on the social benefits of emotional intelligence; and Bradberry and Greaves, on the personal career benefits, but these can be hard to separate. "It's as if the people who intentionally practice emotionally intelligent behaviors are infecting others," note Bradberry and Greaves, and they see this "infection" as positive (Bradberry and Greaves 228). It would appear that if people control their emotions—especially certain kinds of emotions—everyone will benefit.

Spencer Johnson's self-help allegory, *Who Moved My Cheese?*, teaches the management of "negative" emotions believed to harm individuals and societies. Written for workers in the age of the Internet, it addresses readers who need to reinvent themselves when social change has washed away their jobs. Unabashedly didactic, this parable for the new Millennium uses metaphor as a persuasive strategy. It works like *The Pilgrim's Progress* in its depiction of a journey to salvation and the need to overcome emotional drag.

Johnson, a medical doctor, offers readers a frame tale in which a group of friends at a reunion compare their lives. They express concern about how social shifts have affected them, until one of them tells an inspiring story about how he altered his attitude toward change. In his tale, four creatures live in a maze: the mice Sniff and Scurry, and the Littlepeople Hem and Haw. These characters represent four tendencies in any person's mind, and the Cheese, which they have always found in the same place, represents whatever makes that person happy. One day, the Cheese is no longer there, and the mice set out in search of more. Hem and Haw hesitate, and Johnson's allegory describes their emotions as they argue about what to do.

Human emotions—at least certain emotions—do not come across well in *Who Moved My Cheese?* In the past, Hem and Haw sometimes had trouble finding Cheese because, as in Dante's *Purgatorio*, "their powerful human beliefs and emotions took over and clouded the way they looked at things" (Johnson 27). Fear serves as the target in most of Johnson's metaphors, since he wants to free readers from its grip. Like Bradberry and Greaves, he uses metaphors that depict fear as a hindrance to motion. When Haw suspects that he may never find Cheese again, the narrator comments, "Such fearful beliefs were immobilizing and killing him" (Johnson 47). One is reminded of the Evangelist's words in *The Pilgrim's Progress*: "If this be thy condition, why standest thou still?" (Bunyan 12). In Johnson's text, visual illustrations of Cheese take the Evangelist's role, since each wedge bears an underlined message. "What would you do if you weren't afraid?" asks one (Johnson 48). Like Christian, the Littlepeople must move to survive, but Haw is "weighed down by fearful beliefs," and Hem is "paralyzed by his own fears" (Johnson 53). Haw, who emerges as the protagonist, begins to realize that he has been "held captive by his own fear" (Johnson 57). He has let his fear control him when he should have been controlling it, and he reflects, "The fear *you let* build up in your mind is worse than the situation that actually exists" (Johnson 63, original emphasis). Inspired, Haw ventures alone into the maze and feels better because "he was not letting his fear stop him" (Johnson 61). In Johnson's allegory, each individual is responsible for subduing the fear that hinders his soul-saving motion.

To describe the struggle with fear, Johnson combines metaphoric sources. Like Bradberry and Greaves—who may have followed his lead—he unites metaphors of motion with those of hand movements. Probably Johnson hoped that his metaphors would make readers imagine bodily acts of will. The most repeated phrases in his tale often occur together: "let go" and "move on." To motivate the "paralyzed" Hem, Haw tells him, "Life moves on. And so should we" (Johnson 45). As a metaphoric source for a desirable response to change, movement suggests the force of life—and of the free market. "Holding on," in contrast, implies a fear-induced grip on a crumbling structure that may take one down with it. Haw learns that "the fastest way to change is to laugh at your own folly—then you can let go and quickly move on" (Johnson 70). Johnson's heroic Littleperson survives because he "let go of the past . . ." in a metaphor that suggests a relinquishing of claims (Johnson 69).

Who Moved My Cheese? urges readers to subdue their fears, but it also pushes them to forget their anger. Johnson's treatment of rage is less obvious than his depiction of fear, but it forms an integral part of his message. Johnson represents anger, like fear, as the wrong response to change. He illustrates this reaction through the Littleperson Hem, the worst-behaved creature in the maze. When Hem discovers that the Cheese is gone, he throws a tantrum: "He put his hands on his hips, his face turned red, and he screamed at the top of his voice, 'It's not fair!'" (Johnson 33). One can almost hear a parent's voice responding, "Life isn't fair"—the statement of someone in a position of greater power. By depicting anger as childish, Johnson tries to dismiss rage as a response. Within the context of his allegory, Hem's anger serves no purpose because the Cheese has disappeared for no known reason. Hem and Haw, who "ranted and raved at the injustice of it all," are simply wasting their time (Johnson 35). Outside of Johnson's tale, however, injustice may be caused by powerful humans as well as natural forces. By creating a scenario in which no one is to blame, Johnson makes those who cast blame seem petulant. "Why did they do this to me?" Hem demands. "We're entitled. . . . Somebody else did this and we should get something out of it" (Johnson 37–38). These thoughts don't motivate him to budge from his spot, and as far as readers know, he never does. Hem and Haw's talk of injustice leads to depression, and for a while they stand, "immobilized like two statues" (Johnson 37). Within the artificial system Johnson has set up, fear and anger inhibit life-preserving motion.

Johnson's attitude toward anger emerges more clearly when his frame tale resumes. Cory, a doctor, agrees with the story's message: "Some people never change and they pay a price for it. I see people like Hem in my medical practice. They feel entitled to their 'Cheese.' They feel like victims when it's taken away and blame others. They get sicker than people who let go and move on" (Johnson 83). His recapitulation of the argument reflects Lakoff's and Kövecses's anger scenario, but here a person who feels he has been the victim of injustice and points to an offender makes himself sick. In Johnson's frame tale, the character Richard adds, "My children seem to think that nothing in their lives should ever change . . . they're angry," and Becky recalls her son's rage when her husband's change of job forced the teen athlete to leave his friends and enter a high school with no swim team (Johnson 88–89). These references to patients' and children's anger are no accident because *Who Moved My Cheese?* is written by the more powerful for the less powerful.

Within the context of Johnson's story, fear and anger block productive action, but in other circumstances they may not. By creating an artificial situation in which no one has caused a key change, *Who Moved My Cheese?* teaches people to govern their emotions in ways that serve the elite. A ban on blaming blames the blamer, so that vulnerable people will hesitate to point fingers. Johnson's metaphoric commands to "let go" and "move on" work to make potential critics feel obstructive and retrograde. If people can be convinced that anger inhibits progress, they may learn to stifle their rage. Some culturally sanctioned emotion metaphors work to make marginalized people ashamed of what they feel.

Thinking through Metaphors

Diverse families of metaphors represent unsavory emotions, and many sources for these figures involve bodily experiences. An emotion may be depicted as a hot fluid in a container, as George Lakoff and Zoltán Kövecses have found in their linguistic analyses. Dante Alighieri's *Inferno* and *Purgatorio* speak eloquently for a culture that links anger, spite, and resentment to darkness, isolation, filth, and blinding smoke. John Bunyan's *The Pilgrim's Progress* depicts despondency as a swamp, inspiring "wallowing" metaphors still used for self-pity and self-doubt. William James and Silvan Tomkins describe affects in economic terms, and Daniel Goleman, Travis Bradberry, and Jean Greaves claim that emotions can spread like viruses. No single feature links all these metaphors for self-pity, prolonged crying, suppressed anger, grudge-bearing, and spite. Figures for socially undesirable emotions may involve darkness, dirt, disease, paralysis, mire, and foul smells. A great number, however, have their sources in movement, especially in movements of the hand.

In Western cultures, metaphors often represent "banned" emotions as hindering forward motion, or locking the hands in a desperate grip when they should be free to perform new tasks. Emotions are all about motion, but certain emotions are depicted as blocking movement. Most human bodies can move in some ways, but the metaphoric linkage of emotion to movement is cultural as well as natural. In the West, linear, forward motion is often viewed as good for its own sake, regardless of its direction. Spiritually, many Westerners—especially Americans—believe that one should keep working one's way toward salvation. Economically, one should be progressing along a career path. Companies should be "growing"; countries should be "developing"; careers should be "advancing." When failures occur, there is no time for disappointment. One has to "move on"—change one's hairstyle, buy new clothes, relocate and buy a new home full of goods.

This cultural emphasis on linear, forward motion comes through in many emotion metaphors. As Max Black has observed, metaphors organize what they describe (Black, "Metaphor" 288)—and metaphors such as "let it go" depict emotions as things separate from the self that must be dropped because they hinder progress. Despite the differences among the basic emotions, appraisal, and conceptual act theories, these scientific models share an important feature. None of them posits a human self completely separate from the emotions. For neuroscientists, the self includes the prefrontal cortex *and* the amygdala, and an individual person emerges from information flowing among every part of her body and brain. For appraisal theorists, a person relies on internal affect and cognition about the world to create emotions. For constructed emotion theorists, emotions arise through interactions that involve perceptions, sensory memories, and their comparison. William James challenged readers to imagine an emotion, then to remove every physiological component. One might try the same thought experiment for a human brain experiencing an emotion. What brain regions not involved in the emotion would remain unimplicated to control it? In both cases, the answer would be the same: there is not much left. As will be shown in Chapter 7, many brain areas participate in generating and regulating emotions, and current research on emotion regulation points toward the modulation of emotion *within* a self rather than *by* a self (Gross, "Emotion Regulation" 6). If the human self includes what it is told to expunge, then crushing an emotion undesirable to someone else may mean suppressing a valuable part of one's being.

Notes

1. Together, Damasio and LeDoux wrote the chapter, "Emotions and Feelings" in Eric Kandel et al.'s respected textbook, *Principles of Neural Science* (2013). I rely on their summary throughout the following discussion of neuroscientific studies of emotions. Damasio is known for his clinical studies and his philosophical analyses of mind, body, and selfhood. LeDoux is respected for his experimental investigations of the amygdala's role in producing emotions. In his recent work, LeDoux has argued that the results of threat-detection studies in rodents should not automatically be applied to anxiety disorders in humans, which involve other kinds of neural activity and are more complex. Calling a mouse's threat-detection "fear" creates problems because it imposes human qualities on an animal that does not necessarily feel what a human feels. Animal studies of threat-detection remain relevant to human fear but cannot reveal everything about the way that human fear works (LeDoux 23–51).

2. Literary critic I. A. Richards coined these terms in *The Philosophy of Rhetoric*.

3. "Love Is a Battlefield" was written by Holly Knight and Mike Chapman and performed by Pat Benatar. It was released in 1983 by Chrysalis Records as part of Benatar's album, *Live from Earth*.

4. Psychologist Edgar Cabanas Díaz has told me that the Spanish language edition of *Metaphors We Live By* uses everyday expressions to support Lakoff and Johnson's argument in a fully convincing way (Edgar Cabanas Díaz, personal communication).

5. Sianne Ngai has noticed that emotional irritation is often represented in the language of physical irritation, such as a mild pain or an itch (Ngai 184).

6. Kövecses disagrees with scientists who claim that conscious experiences of emotion, which can be shaped by language, do not offer any information about the neural mechanisms underlying emotions. Kövecses believes that individual, conscious experiences of emotion can be informative and that studying emotion metaphors can indicate the ways that human brains organize information (Kövecses, *Metaphor and Emotion* xi).

CHAPTER 3 | Wallowing in Self-Pity

I had fallen into the ugly depths of self-pity, a terrain just above the even
more hideous lowlands of despair.

—SIRI HUSTVEDT, *The Summer without Men*

"DON'T WHINE WHEN IT hurts. It's like the first grade, Jerry. Nobody likes a
crybaby." So says the fictional magnate Gordon Gekko to his future son-in-law
in Oliver Stone's *Wall Street: Money Never Sleeps*. If one can believe the fallen
financier (and who wouldn't?), Gekko survived eight years in prison because
he didn't whine.

In the United States, contempt for people who cry from pain extends well
beyond the first grade. Starting from a young age, Americans and many other
Westerners internalize Gekko's belief until many feel too ashamed to cry. In
human minds and bodies, "the relationship between physical and emotional
pain goes beyond semantics," and the cultural rule against crying to show pain
applies to both (Frazzetto 117). Literary critic Robyn Warhol points out that
those who "allow themselves to cry" seem effeminate, and effeminacy points
to "the sexual role of one who is penetrated" (Warhol 10). Warhol invokes the
cultural premise that people weeping publicly *choose* to cry, a belief that may
not hold true in every case. Supposedly, a person who cries has let something
or someone "get to her." She has been punctured, and cultural contempt for
the penetrated runs deep.[1] Besides being despised for effeminacy, people who
cry before witnesses seem to violate a social pact that others struggle to uphold.
Metaphorically, this pact involves emotional hygiene: one should keep one's
harmful emotional germs to oneself so as not to infect others. But this cultural
contempt for tears also suggests an underlying hatred of weakness. Gordon
Gekko serves as the perfect spokesman for a culture that bans expressions
of pain.

This chapter analyzes emotion metaphors from films and scholarly studies,
from 1995 to 2015. The works examined reveal the power of cultural pressures
to suppress negative emotions. In the twenty-first century United States, what
discourages a person from expressing pain publicly and pointing to an external
cause? In the age of the Internet, Dante's association of anger with darkness

and filth lives on, and Bunyan's allegory depicting fear, doubt, and despondence as a bog is thriving in self-help parables. Accusations of "wallowing in self-pity" are likely to silence all but the most confident voices. Hogs wallow; people don't—and who wants to be stripped of her humanity and called a hog? Such metaphors for self-pity reveal the intense cultural forces working to ensure that pain stays hidden and private. This rule of privacy suits those whom the current social system serves best. But it stifles the voices of those being crushed, who need to call attention to their pain.

Crying to Send a Message

Crying involves more than tears, and scholars rarely mention the red eyes, runny nose, careening voice, and ragged breaths so essential to the experience. The tight focus on water-drops suggests the distance between theories of crying and the embodied experience of sobbing. Tears figure among human beings' most powerful communicative tools, but adults who use them don't earn much respect (Frazzetto 115). Maybe crying to send a message is so disliked because it communicates pain in such a strident way. Historian Tom Lutz finds that in human confrontations, tears offer "an irrefutable argument" (Lutz 25). "Most crying has a reason, and usually it is obvious," claims art historian James Elkins (Elkins 23). Tears work like early radio broadcasts: they rivet the attention, but their messages are fuzzy (Lutz 298). Crying can indicate anguish, sorrow, joy, anger, frustration, or a whirling rush of emotions the crier can't define.

Cultural representations of crying often emphasize the manipulative possibilities of tears. Working from the dubious premise that crying can be controlled, they reveal contempt for those who weep to influence others. In *Crying: The Natural and Cultural History of Tears*, Tom Lutz traces twin Western views of tears, one regarding them as merely "physical," and hence inviting exploitation; the other, as "moral," conveying profound feeling (Lutz 31–32). Lutz challenges these categories and questions the presence of any boundary between them. "Physical" and "authentic" categories of tears are connected because only belief in the crier's sincerity makes manipulation possible.

Lutz questions the link of tears to "emotional authenticity," since crying can mean so many different things (Lutz 54). James Elkins points out that "crying can be ostentatious, a show of grief for everyone to witness . . . ," and the performance may be dissociated from inner pain (Elkins 26). Lutz examines legends of "crocodile tears" that cause unwary sympathizers to be devoured (Lutz 21). These false tears—often associated with women—aim "to ensnare, to confuse, to extort, to deceive" and are regarded as "a breach not just of etiquette but of ethics" (Lutz 24, 21). In cultural stereotypes, crying is frequently represented as "an underhanded way to get what one wants," especially in depictions of women (Lutz 56). When used to force others to enact one's will, crying can become "emotional blackmail" (Lutz 57, 225). "If you don't do what

I want, you're hurting me," runs the logic. "See how you're hurting me!" Lutz notes that although women supposedly use crying to manipulate, men commit emotional blackmail just as often by using other emotions such as rage (Lutz 57). Historian Ute Frevert cites research indicating that compared with men, women are more likely to cry to express anger because they have been trained not to act in more aggressive ways (Frevert 97–98, 141).[2] To keep people from learning to control others through tears, behavioral psychologists used to teach parents to ignore their babies' crying so that their children wouldn't become "tyrants" (Lutz 134). Those who held power in families had to ensure that their influence wasn't usurped through crying.

Scholars of literature, history, and culture have noticed that people who cry are rarely those who make the rules. Tom Lutz calls tears "the weapons of the oppressed" and "the weapon of choice for those who feel themselves to be vulnerable" (Lutz 57). Literary scholar Franco Moretti asserts that "tears are always the product of *powerlessness*" (Moretti 162, original emphasis). Based on his analysis of "moving" novels, Moretti hypothesizes that readers shed tears when they see how the world needs to change, but they know that this change will never happen (Moretti 162). Moretti acknowledges a certain truth in stereotypes that depict tears as hypocritical. In his view, crying involves doublethink because readers acknowledge reality while remaining true to ideals that oppose the status quo (Moretti 180). Tears seem to show surrender, but not a permanent defeat. With them comes hope that "the reality of defeat has not entirely extinguished the desire for revenge . . . ," so that those oppressed will continue to dream of victory (Moretti 180). There are reasons that crying can be received as a challenge to authority.

Despite—or maybe because of—this perceived threat, cultural stereotypes depict tears as an alternative to action. Stereotypes are notorious for contradictions, and in the case of crying, tears are represented as both manipulative and ineffective. Crybabies wail instead of fighting back, arousing disgust in their schoolmates. Supposedly, tears of "private emotions" such as self-pity leave people "luxuriating in the emotions themselves," so that people take "no action beyond feeling them" (Lutz 246). Expressing one's anguish to the world does not necessarily mean fighting what caused the anguish (Lutz 249). Crying may offer a false promise that tears will change an unjust situation without the need for other action (Lutz 240). Moretti notes that crying blinds one temporarily, screening off a world too painful to see (Moretti 179). By reputation, crying turns one inward rather than outward, and tears can be an "indulgence in self-pity, rage, or self-loathing" (Lutz 23, 115). James Elkins, however, challenges the separation of crying from productive thought. He follows twenty-first-century neuroscientists such as Antonio Damasio in arguing that emotion and reason are interdependent: "we think while we cry, and we feel while we think" (Elkins 213).[3] Culturally, however, crying to show one's pain remains associated with childishness, weakness, and cowardice.

It would seem that to act effectively in the world, one must learn not to weep. Lutz points out that most people cry instinctively; the skill they acquire through practice is *not* crying (Lutz 128). Many cultures worldwide, not just Western ones, teach that preoccupation with one's feelings is "narcissistic and childish" (Lutz 54). Lutz concludes his natural history of tears with an appeal not to suppress crying, but to move through and beyond it: "To cry together is to create community, to recognize each other, and to then stop crying is to forge ahead with that community. . . . Learning not to cry . . . is often a matter of learning how to feel something else" (Lutz 290). In these assertions, Lutz draws on the popular Western metaphor of linear, progressive motion. One is reminded of Travis Bradberry's and Jean Greaves's advice in *Emotional Intelligence 2.0* to "move toward the emotion, into it, and eventually through it" (Bradberry and Greaves 68). Supposedly, crying holds one back when one urgently needs to "forge ahead." But if Elkins is right that people think when they cry, weeping may enable thoughts on the direction in which to move. As an art critic, Elkins challenges academic and cultural prohibitions against discussing the emotions evoked by art. "Our tearless condition is our chosen state," he asserts. "We're in a prison . . . of our own making" (Elkins 208–09). Viewing tears as obstructive restricts human experience in ways that can hinder the most vulnerable human beings.

The Least Loved Emotion

There are no neuroscientific studies of self-pity, which most laboratory researchers would regard as a compound, subjective feeling. There are few psychological analyses, since not only would it be hard to recruit participants—it would be challenging to get the research funded. The few recent studies that use the term "self-pity" have been conducted mainly by humanities scholars. Unsurprisingly, they denounce the emotion in ardent and creative ways.

In twenty-first-century English-speaking cultures, "self-pity" works as a stigmatizing label. The views of anyone to whom it can be stuck are invalidated, since that person is perceived as socially noxious. People who feel sorry for themselves arouse contempt because supposedly, they have stopped contributing to society. They have suffered the same sorrows as everyone else, but they have shut themselves down in protest. Labels like "self-pity" are used more as weapons than descriptions, and they are rarely defined. For the purpose of this study, I will define self-pity as believing for a significant length of time that one has suffered unjustly, that one deserves comfort and compensation, and that one's suffering should be acknowledged by others.

Literary scholar Eric P. Levy offers a psychological narrative that challenges a self-pitying person's claim for reparations. Levy draws on psychoanalytic theory and self psychology, and his account has creative flair. According to Levy, the self-pitying person lives between two mirrors, one of which represents the eyes of her rejecting parents; the other mirror, her own, self-loving gaze:

> Consider the child crying alone before the mirror of parental judgment, staring at the one thing which makes him unworthy of love: his own reflection; his

inadequacy as reflected in his parent's eyes. . . . How he yearns for an impossible state where he could feel loved and valued, yet never have to be seen; for such exposure could only mean inevitable rejection. How he yearns to perform forever for approving company—yet never lose the safety of total withdrawal. The only way to do that is with a second mirror: in particular, the mirror of self-pity. (Levy 18)

The self-pitier aims to win love without exposing herself to rejection, and between the two mirrors, she finds a safe place (Levy 18). The greater a person's feeling of inadequacy, the less likely she is to leave the confining, protective shelter she has constructed (Levy 21). Rather than engaging a world that can cause pain, the self-pitier tries to merge with her own, sympathetic reflection (Levy 19). Levy suspects that despite apparent low self-esteem, self-pitiers are driven by "aristocratic vanity": "Can there be misery . . . loftier than mine?" they ask themselves (Beckett 2; qtd. in Levy 27).

In Levy's scenario, the self-pitier seeks love but is unwilling to pay the price. Genuine love demands ongoing responses and inevitable risks of rejection. Instead, the "false self" of the self-pitier defines itself through fantasy and shuns "responsibility, resolution, fortitude, self-sacrifice" (Levy 25–26). Rather than seeking to end suffering, the sympathetic self in the mirror tries to prolong it. "Life immerses one in change," observes Levy, but change is the last thing the self-pitier wants (Levy 23). If the self-pitier took real steps to end her pain, her reflection would no longer be needed (Levy 20). "The renunciation of weakness," writes Levy, "imposes the responsibilities of strength . . ." (Levy 28). Levy argues that people who pity themselves don't want to become strong enough to end their pain.

Critiques of late twentieth-century poetry also represent self-pity as abhorrent weakness. Joseph McElrath excoriates poets who "whine out the pains their tender, so sensitive, oh so sensitive souls have felt" (McElrath 65). He is particularly hard on Rod McKuen, "poor Rod, . . . alone in his room, picking his scabs, opening the wounds that life has given him, whining for a down-and-out generation" (McElrath 60). McElrath contrasts poets who focus on their own emotions with the social activists of the late 1960s, who used their emotions to engage the world. Literary critic Robert Peters treats the "Self-Pity Poem" with equal contempt and singles out poet Charles Wright. In Peters's view, the "blubbering and hopeless" Self-Pity Poem "requires no definition"—he knows one when he sees it (Peters 39). Peters finds "claustrophobic and depressing narcissism" in Wright's poetry and argues that because Wright focuses on his own pain, he creates "an 'I' too petty and self-absorbed to assume the cosmological" (Peters 40–41). All poets need to be attuned to their feelings, but to create valuable art, they must "transcend the snivel" (Peters 41). In a culture known for fostering individuality, dwelling on one's own pain is unacceptable.

The metaphors of these literary scholars who analyze self-pity reveal the cultural assumptions feeding their contempt. First and foremost, they depict self-pity as withdrawal. McElrath recalls his urge to "break out of the truly walled enclosure of the self," commenting, "one could suffocate in there . . ." (McElrath 54). In a study of Alexander Payne's film *Sideways* (2004), film critic Natalie Reitano describes the protagonist Miles's retreat "into the citadel of self-pity" (Reitano). As a metaphoric source, a citadel associates self-pity with a timid choice to live behind walls when one should be out fighting battles. Levy's metaphors depict the self-pitier's fear of life as a feeble ego's terror of being devoured. He compares the false self to an "anxious gardener who stifles growth because he fears being overrun by his plants" (Levy 26). According to Levy, the self-pitier imagines fulfillment in a real relationship as a "voracious snake that would swallow and absorb his identity" (Levy 26). Together, these metaphors suggest that self-pity's reigning element is fear.

But self-pity metaphors also recall the isolation of Dante's angry sinners bubbling in the mud. Many of these metaphors convey the filth associated not just with fear but with rage. Levy speculates that the protected space between mirrors becomes a coffin when viewed up close. In this sarcophagus, the self-pitying person "looks like a mummy, with one long ancient filthy bandage wound continuously around his body from head to toe" (Levy 20). The self-pitier has muffled herself too tightly to move, and her protective wrapping is dirty. In Levy's metaphoric logic, the mummified self feeds on filth, "gorging on garbage," so that she can then vomit and purge (Levy 25). In the closed system that self-pity creates, no nutritious food can enter from the outside. Metaphors for self-pity emphasize the poor hygiene that comes with shutting oneself in.

Metaphors for this unloved emotion also imply that angry sufferers work to keep their wounds fresh. Just as McElrath depicts Rod McKuen fingering his scabs, Reitano notes that in *Sideways*, Miles is picking "at the scabs of his broken heart" (Reitano). According to this metaphoric logic, emotional injuries have caused wounds that the sufferers won't allow to heal. Healing would mean that the episode has ended—without anyone paying for the pain or appreciating how greatly the victim has suffered. Picking at the crust of a wound means maintaining control, even if it causes fresh bleeding. It takes emotions other than fear to open a wound so that onlookers can see the blood.

Metaphors for self-pity depict the complex emotion as a compound of fear, anger, and pleasure. Joseph McElrath asks writers whether they want to take action or go for "a delicious swim in a pool of self-pity" (McElrath 59). It's unlikely that such an emotional mess is universally human, and understandably, laboratory studies of emotion focus on self-pity's more basic components. Cultural metaphors suggest that fear is the main one. Probably inspired by John Bunyan's Slough of Despond, McElrath calls self-pity a "modern swamp" (McElrath 58). In Bunyan's allegory, the Slough represents doubt, and fear causes a struggling sinner to fall in. But the mud of self-pity also resembles Dante's river-slime, which engulfs sinners sent to hell for anger.

It is no coincidence that so many self-pity metaphors focus on the skin, which forms scabs, needs bandages, or luxuriates in water. Self-pity involves a response to pain, and it focuses on the relationship between "inside" and "outside." Metaphors of confinement, filth, and reopened wounds represent self-pity as the *wrong response* to pain; it is cowardly, self-indulgent, and immature. But the appropriateness of this emotion depends on where one locates the pain's cause. If it is outside, one may need protection, and one may have a right to be angry.

Not Sorry for Herself

In Ridley Scott's *G. I. Jane* (1997), Master Chief Urgayle walks among his recruits, misquoting D. H. Lawrence's poem, "Self-Pity":

> I never saw a wild thing
> sorry for itself.
> A bird will fall frozen dead from a bough
> without ever having felt sorry for itself. (Lawrence 58; Scott 00:20:24–38)[4]

Urgayle means to intimidate the would-be Navy Seals, who stand as rigid as Lawrence's heroic bird. He inculcates them with his philosophy, of which "Self-Pity" forms the core. No one who pities herself can belong to his elite unit. No one focused on her own pain can be trusted to perform jobs in which other people's lives depend on her actions. Urgayle pauses before Jordan O'Neil, the first female officer to attempt Navy Seal training. In this film about enabled movement, O'Neil triumphs because she agrees with Urgayle. She never dwells on the wrongs she has suffered and instead works to strengthen herself in every sense. Film scholar Linda Ruth Williams argues that *G. I. Jane* depicts a "war with . . . personal weakness" (Williams 182). O'Neil's intense bodily training—and abuse—conveys the emotional training that goes along with it. Her journey recreates Dante's *Inferno* and Bunyan's *The Pilgrim's Progress* because while slogging through hell, she is fighting her way toward salvation.

O'Neil undertakes this journey to gain "advancement" (Scott 00:12:24). She wants to move up, and she wants to move forward, but she is being held back. As a Naval Intelligence Officer, she sees men with less time in rank being promoted over her because they have combat experience, and she doesn't. When O'Neil applied for active duty, she was rejected because submarines lacked female bathrooms. Film scholar Sarah Hagelin has discussed the cultural context in which *G. I. Jane* appeared: the Tailhook scandal (1991), the Shannon Faulkner case at The Citadel (1995), and the military's Don't Ask Don't Tell policy (1993) (Hagelin 88, 91, 74). In 1990s popular culture, it seemed that biologically based sex differences would require "special treatment" for female soldiers (Hagelin 91). In Scott's film, however, O'Neil enters Seal training to advance her career rather than to win attention. If she wants to create future opportunities for women, it will be by example, not through a media campaign.[5] "I'm just not interested in being some poster girl for women's rights," she tells her boyfriend, a fellow Naval Intelligence Officer (Scott 00:11:22). O'Neil wins a chance to break a barrier when powerful Texas Senator Lillian

DeHaven chooses her as a test case. If O'Neil can "go the distance" and survive Navy Seal training, she can participate in combat and rise to the rank that she deserves, and other women may gain the same opportunity (Scott 00:10:06).

As depicted in the film, Seal training works physically and psychologically to build team spirit and crush self-involvement. It brings searing pain to test worthiness, and recruits who dwell on their own suffering fail. From the outset, the film depicts O'Neil as someone with the right attitude toward pain. "I expect a certain amount of pain," she tells her commanding officer (Scott 00:15:36). In the course of her training, she is waterboarded, forced to eat garbage, and beaten until blood runs between her teeth. She is likely to win viewers' sympathy not just through her endurance of pain but through her responses to it. O'Neil never tattles or complains, even when invited to do so. Instead, she "offers her body for punishment like a man's" (Hagelin 96).[6] Instinctively generous, she shares the food she has snatched and invites team members to step on her back to scale a wall. It is easy to like her when after twenty-four hours of grueling training, she bites into a hoarded biscuit and writes about "Why I Love the U. S. Navy," as the dim lights and opera music Urgayle has ordered lull other recruits to sleep. O'Neil takes control of her training and demands that her special treatment end. She shaves her head, bunks with the male recruits, and works in her free time to overcome her lack of upper body strength, about which Urgayle taunts her. No matter what her training brings, she never feels self-pity, which can emerge when people attribute their suffering to external causes. O'Neil is less interested in changing a system than she is in changing herself.

Within the context the film creates, this attitude impresses her teammates and helps her survive. At first, the male trainees vary in their responses to O'Neil. Cortez drops her in training after she has enabled team members to climb a wall. McCool, who is African American, accepts her, recalling his grandfather's mistreatment in the navy of the 1940s. The base commander openly expresses his disgust that O'Neil is being forced on him by politicians. Only Master Chief Urgayle unflinchingly gives O'Neil the equality that she demands (Hagelin 99). In training designed to prepare Seals for capture and torture, Urgayle beats her senseless and threatens to rape her, as might happen in an actual capture. He punches her just as he would a man to prove that the threat of integration lies not in women's weakness but in men's responses to female suffering. "She's not the problem. We are," he tells the officer who assisted him with the "interrogation" (Scott 01:18:45).[7] When attacked by Urgayle, O'Neil fights back, breaking his nose with a kick and rasping "Suck my dick!" (Scott 01:17:40). Rather than protest, she uses what remains of her voice to urge her teammates not to talk.

O'Neil could quit the Navy and take her sufferings to the press, but in the film's vision, "a strong woman (a real feminist) doesn't complain . . ." (Hagelin 101). O'Neil's real enemy isn't Urgayle but DeHaven, who arranges to have O'Neil removed from Seal training in order to save five Texas military bases and her Senate seat.[8] O'Neil's commander offers her a desk job, and she is furious.

She began her journey at a console, and her forward motion would be checked if she had to "drive a desk" (Scott 01:25:51). When O'Neil learns of DeHaven's betrayal, she quits Navy Seal training. She is willing to undergo any level of pain but will not function as an object controlled by others. By the film's logic, Urgayle shows O'Neil more respect than DeHaven does because he challenges her directly. O'Neil responds to DeHaven as she did to Urgayle, with a blow that could "deface" her opponent. O'Neil threatens to go to CSPAN, not to voice her sufferings to but expose foul play. Defeated, the Senator arranges for O'Neil to return to the Seals, where she successfully completes her training. In Scott's film, advancing requires more than enduring pain: it means defeating skilled enemies and escaping traps.

The film's ending suggests that like O'Neil, Master Chief Urgayle has grown emotionally. Despite his increasing admiration for his trainee, he fails to trust her in combat, and rather than letting her take on a Libyan foe, he sets off a firefight in which he is wounded. O'Neil proves herself by dragging him to safety, something he had earlier doubted she could ever do. After graduation, O'Neil finds a gift from Urgayle: the Navy Cross he once earned, marking "Self-Pity" in a book of D. H. Lawrence's poems. Literary scholar Mike Chasar reads the return of "Self-Pity" as a sign of Urgayle's changed perspective (Chasar). Whereas initially, Urgayle saw uncomplaining animals as superior, Scott's shot of the circled, unmarked poem at the film's end suggests a new understanding of emotions he has learned through his interactions with O'Neil (Chasar). Whether or not Urgayle has changed, the film stands firm in its rejection of self-pity. O'Neil survives her training because she moves forward in a journey of self-improvement rather than dwelling on how others have hurt her.

In its imagery, Ridley Scott's *G. I. Jane* shows its concern with motion. "Move, move, move!" shout the officers at the exhausted recruits (Scott 00:36:16). The film abounds with shots of soldiers running, jeeps rolling, and boats cutting waves. In its most memorable images, the film depicts O'Neil grimacing through pushups, gaining strength as she forces herself upward with one arm. This self-directed transformation of her body suggests a transformation of her entire being. Mud and water abound in her journey through hell, and Scott's camera invites the viewer to share her suffering. Like Dante's sinners and Bunyan's pilgrim, O'Neil gets dirty, and she gets wet. Her physical and emotional strength grow synergistically as her ambition drives her to train harder, and her increased strength leads her to attempt more. When she fails, she looks only to herself, showing a tough survival instinct and pure devotion to her team. *G. I. Jane* depicts no possible gain from self-pity because it aims to celebrate strength more than to criticize a social system.

Enchained

In the emotional climax of Paul Feig's *Bridesmaids* (2011), Annie Walker sits weeping on her mother's couch. "Wilson!" she sobs, mourning with Tom

Hanks in *Castaway* (2000) as his companion soccer ball bobs off on the waves (Feig 01:29:55). The film within the film conveys Annie's feelings of isolation and abandonment. Suddenly Megan bursts in with nine puppies and noisily refutes Annie's claim that she has no friends. "I don't think you want any help," challenges Megan. "I think you want a little pity party. . . . I am life, and I'm going to bite you in the ass!" (Feig 01:31:05–23). In a bizarre sequence that recalls Dante's *Inferno*, Megan wrestles with Annie and bites her just as threatened (Figure 3.1). Megan is pleased to see Annie hit back and tells her, "I'm trying to get you to fight for your shitty life. . . . Now, you've got to stop feeling sorry for yourself, okay, because I do not associate with people who blame the world for their problems. Because you're your problem, Annie, and you're also your solution" (Feig 01:31:31–01:33:11). If Jordan O'Neil responded the right way to pain, Annie Walker has been responding wrong. She has been attributing her losses to an unfair world rather than to her own mistakes. In the couch scene, widely excerpted on the Internet as an inspirational "tough love" talk, Megan practices the pedagogy of Dante. When physically attacked and bitten, Annie instinctively fights back—and learns that she must fight her way through life rather than regard herself as life's victim.

In many ways, *Bridesmaids* is a progressive film. It depicts women seeking sexual pleasure and physically expressing their anger. Motherhood comes across as . . . something other than an ideal state for which women long. In the outrageously funny bridal fitting scene, women explode in bursts of vomit and diarrhea from the designer dresses stitched to contain them. Although the film

FIGURE 3.1 Megan (Melissa McCarthy) orders Annie (Kristen Wiig) to fight for her life in Paul Feig's *Bridesmaids*. © 2011 Universal City Studios LLC. Courtesy of Universal Studios Licensing LLC. All rights reserved.

doesn't focus on race, it presents loving marriages and friendships between people of different races as ordinary and expected. But *Bridesmaids* is also a didactic film, showing the victims of economic downturns how to act.[9] In the film's ideology, one can't control life, but one can control one's reaction to hardship. Rather than brooding over how one has been wronged, one should ask, "What have I done wrong?" and change one's ways. In its representation of self-pity as self-induced paralysis, *Bridesmaids* locates blame in individuals, discouraging criticism of the socioeconomic system in which they live. The film's ideology emerges through its central metaphors of enchainment and arrested movement.

Annie has made mistakes, and when one traces the steps that led her to her mother's couch, the trail isn't hard to follow. Annie lost her bakery in the economic crash of 2008, and along with it, her money, her apartment, and her boyfriend. The graffiti that has transformed her bakery's sign from "Cake Baby" to "Cock Baby" might be read in several ways. It may be a patriarchal jeer, indicating that Annie should be giving men pleasure rather than running a business, but it also shows her emotional stagnation. Figuratively, the "Cake Baby" was Annie's child, the living product of her creative energy. Since its "death," she has been dissipating her energy in a demoralizing, purely sexual relationship and an unfulfilling job. In her career and in her love life, she has stopped moving and has gotten stuck.

Bridesmaids follows Annie's disastrous choices as her best friend Lillian's maid of honor. In hilarious sequences, she competes with Helen Harris III, the wife of Lillian's fiancé's boss, to make Lillian's wedding extraordinary. For the bridal fitting luncheon, Annie chooses a dubious restaurant that leaves the bridesmaids retching—and worse—in an elegant bathroom. Annie's fear of flying, which reflects her emotional fear of movement, leads her to mix alcohol with pills and wreck the bridesmaids' trip to Las Vegas. Unsurprisingly, Lillian asks Helen to replace Annie as her maid of honor. As Annie's anger grows, she loses her job for verbally abusing a customer who believes a girlhood friendship will last forever. Annie fails to repair her dying car's taillights, so that she is stopped by the highway patrolman Nathan Rhodes. Warm-hearted Nathan expresses serious interest in Annie and urges her to bake again. Her worst mistake may be rejecting him after just one passion-filled night. As he points out, her emotional siege mentality is causing her to endanger others. "Your problem is that you just don't understand that you hurt people," says Nathan, who serves as a figurative as well as a literal highway patrolman and might be compared with Help in *The Pilgrim's Progress* (Feig 01:26:24). Like *G. I. Jane*, *Bridesmaids* implies that a person focused on her own pain is socially irresponsible because she is ignoring other people's needs.

Despite her blunders—or more likely, because of them—Annie may win a viewer's sympathy. In some ways, her competition with rich, groomed Helen brings to mind Sianne Ngai's analysis of *Single White Female* (Ngai 151–73). Envy plays a role in both films, and both focus on white women's class differences (Ngai 170–71). In *Bridesmaids*, however, the audience shares Annie's perspective rather than that of the envied character. Although Annie would love to have Helen's money, she doesn't want to emulate Helen. The desire to have never collapses into the desire to be (Ngai 139), although envy permeates Annie's hatred of Helen. The film's shots of Milwaukee, with its Harley Davidson factory, bring to mind Laverne and Shirley, the working-class friends of the late 1970s. Here Annie and Lillian grew up together, and Annie's humble shower gift to Lillian (a box of her favorite Milwaukee treats) comes across as more genuine than Helen's offering, a prepaid trip to Paris. The audience may groan but still root for Annie as she demolishes the Parisian bridal shower Helen has crafted. One can see no good reason why Helen is rich, and Annie is poor. Despite Annie's blunders, the difference between her income and Helen's seems to come from more than their actions.

Annie, however, has one serious flaw: she is resistant to change. She may have learned to dig in emotionally from her mother, who still calls her ex-husband's wife "that new whore" after the two have been married for twelve years (Feig 00:15:25). Annie has also picked up her mother's habit of maintaining fictions, since her mother attends Alcoholics Anonymous (AA) meetings although she has never drunk. In the situation the film presents, lived fantasies and emotional stubbornness work against the constant change that life demands. In a confrontation early in the film, Helen argues that people change with time, and Annie, that they don't. "I wish that things were the way they used to be," Annie tells Nathan. "After I went under, I just kind of stopped, I guess" (Feig 01:08:09–11). Annie rejects Nathan because his efforts to help her are making her feel like an object. "I don't need you to fix me!" she says (Feig 01:11:31). *Bridesmaids* represents self-pity and withdrawal as self-destructive, since to survive, one needs to keep moving as the world moves.

Annie's "cure"—after Megan's motivational bite—involves admitting her mistakes, taking responsibility for her life, and reaching out to others. Its logic follows that of AA, which so fascinates her mother. Rooted in religion, the Twelve Steps of AA call for "a searching and fearless moral inventory" of oneself and a vow to "make amends" to all the people one has wronged ("Twelve Steps"). Once awakened, Annie gets her taillights fixed and tells her mother that she loves her. She introduces her mother to a friendly mechanic and helps her to progress emotionally, just as Annie is doing. Annie even bakes Nathan a carrot cake, although his wounds prove hard to heal. On the morning of Lillian's wedding, Annie helps Helen to find the bride, who has withdrawn into her old apartment. Horrified by the expensive spectacle her wedding has become, Lillian moans, "everything's going to change" (Feig 01:45:34). Annie, who has needed help for most of the film, now rallies to motivate Lillian: "Things are going to change, but they'll be better. . . . I'm going to be fine. You need to blaze the trail for me and then report back and tell me what's coming" (Feig 01:45:51–01:46:39). With these thoughts, the reunited friends embrace the wedding. Each has helped the other to resume her journey down a "trail," a linear representation of life.

In the metaphoric logic of *Bridesmaids*, Annie must free herself from emotional bonds before she can move forward. Through an inspiring song, the film represents these undesirable emotions as chains. Unbeknown to Lillian, Helen has arranged for Lillian's favorite girlhood singing group to perform. At the wedding reception, the band Wilson Phillips sings its 1990 hit song, "Hold On."[10] The buoyant song's lyrics drive home the film's message that people who respond to life's "bites" with fearful, angry withdrawal are causing their own pain. After a socioeconomic and emotional jolt, feeling self-pity—dwelling on one's pain and its external causes—is tantamount to chaining oneself up. Feeling sorry for oneself means immobilizing oneself at a time when movement is vital. Metaphorically, people who pity themselves have stopped moving because they are bound up, but they, not the world, have forged their chains. One can quickly grow used to confinement and dirt, which may begin to feel like a pleasant, protective shell. Unchaining oneself requires changing one's attitude more than fighting injustice because the real cause of one's problems is oneself. At the same time, Wilson Phillips's lyrics metaphorically represent survival as a fierce, determined grip. Surviving in a world that could "bite" one at any time demands both the willingness to move and the tenacity to hold fast. Only one voice disrupts this metaphoric logic: that of Lillian's African American father. "I am not paying for this shit," he says (Feig 01:48:49).[11] Apparently, not everyone is convinced.

Empowering Tears

Not every scholar in the humanities and social sciences views crying and self-pity as emotional fetters. Miriam Elson, a clinical social worker at the University of Chicago, argues that self-pitying people need empathy and support rather than commands to grow up. In her textbook, *Self Psychology in Clinical Social Work* (1989), Elson advocated applying psychoanalyst Heinz Kohut's approach in clinical settings ("Miriam Elson"). In the 1960s, Kohut introduced self psychology as a method that would try to understand patients' lives from their own perspectives rather than imposing standard psychoanalytic narratives ("Self Psychology Psychoanalysis"). Literary scholar Eric P. Levy drew on self psychology when he described self-pity as a life between mirrors (Levy 28, note 2). Elson, a clinician, valued her patients' well-being and sought a strategy that would help them heal. Based on her interactions with suffering people, she came to regard self-pity as the only feeling available to people who had never received the emotional responses they needed (Elson 5). Elson noted that babies whose needs are ignored show "contentless crying" (Elson 7). Children whose parents have never empathized with them develop weak selves whose structures require reinforcement (Elson 6). As adults, such people seek validation from others and sometimes use manipulative tears to evoke the responses they crave (Elson 4–5). In popular culture, these individuals tend to be described contemptuously as "needy" and "clinging."

Elson argues that being made to feel ashamed of self-pity does not help people heal. Despite its poor cultural reputation, self-pity shows a person's "awareness of . . . a phase-appropriate but unmet need . . ." (Elson 12). Elson describes one patient who "supplied through her self-pity the missing empathy of others" (Elson 8). Elson doesn't recommend self-pity as a permanent emotional state, but she doesn't think therapists should condemn it. A patient who feels sorry for herself is showing "a primitive form of empathy" (Elson 13). Rather than reproof, such a patient deserves credit for resourcefulness, since she has supplied "soothing not forthcoming from appropriate sources" (Elson 13). In such cases, a therapist should validate the patient's feelings and free her from trying to extract empathy from people who respond only with contempt. Rather than stamping out self-pity, clinicians should guide patients through it as a step toward developing "mature empathy" (Elson 13). According to Elson, self-pitying patients are trying to help themselves and need to be encouraged, not reproached.

In her descriptions of self-pity, Elson uses metaphors to depict the kind of therapy she wants to give. She writes that a person denied support "retreats to self-pity," implying withdrawal into a fortress and the abandonment of forward motion (Elson 5). Elson calls one patient "clinging and dependent," although she applauds the woman's therapist for offering guidance rather than ridiculing her as a "baby" (Elson 7). Following Kohut, Elson offers alternate metaphors of restoration and repair. Both Elson (born in the United States in 1909) and Kohut (born in Austria in 1913) experienced World War II as adults, so that rebuilding weakened structures worked for them as a powerful metaphoric source ("Miriam Elson"; "Heinz Kohut"). Elson describes psychological development as "structure building," and she characterizes patients whose needs have gone unmet as having "a deficit in psychic structure" (Elson 5). In her judgment, the aim of therapy is "structure repair, rebuilding, or renewal," so that a patient can resume developing on her own (Elson 6). In Elson's clinical experience, self-pity indicates strength in weakness: the resourcefulness to give oneself what one has never received.

If physiology forms the "entire fund and capital" of emotion, as William James argued, then crying is self-pity's cash flow (James 458). A body that feels sorry for itself does more than weep, but crying works as self-pity's most visible manifestation. For people who want to show the world their pain, crying offers a powerful form of communication—one that few people want to see. In Having a Good Cry, literary scholar Robyn Warhol uncovers cultural assumptions underlying contempt for some people's crying, and for certain types of crying. Like Tom Lutz, Warhol questions any sharp boundary between "authentic" feelings and physical signs of emotion evoked by manipulative means (Warhol 23). She sees prejudices about gender and social class in this split, which implies that a person who cries at Hamlet has been moved by universal human emotions, but one who cries at Stella Dallas has been conned by a tearjerker (Warhol 33). Behind the cultural forces working to separate "authentic" from "inauthentic" emotion, Warhol detects a privileging of high over low culture, and of masculinity over femininity. Regarding "some feelings as more genuine, more fully human than others . . ." insinuates that people whose emotional life differs must be something other (or less) than human (Warhol 20). People whose emotions are considered "genuine" tend to be well-educated white men, and derogatory labels such as "tearjerkers" and "weepies" privilege the emotional experiences of elite viewers (Warhol 35). Warhol hears a resonant harmony in condemnations of effeminacy and popular art forms, since mass culture has long been linked to women (Warhol 31). "Who is to judge," she asks, "whether the woman sobbing at a melodramatic movie is experiencing a 'sincere,' 'authentic,' 'real' emotion, or whether she is 'merely' being 'manipulated' by sentimentalism?" (Warhol 23). Belittling the emotions of those who hold less social power discourages them from using their emotions to gain more.

Why do readers actively seek out books that make them cry? Both Lutz and Warhol question the long-held view that crying is cathartic. Lutz calls the reference to purging "pity and fear" in Aristotle's *Poetics* "the most often debated sentence in the history of aesthetics" (Lutz 117). Every therapist Lutz interviewed for his study thought that crying helped patients because of its cathartic effects (Lutz 119). But despite widespread agreement among health care workers, there are few or no clinical or experimental findings indicating that crying benefits people by letting them purge painful emotions (Lutz 120).

Warhol draws on Zoltán Kövecses's studies of emotion metaphors to reveal the metaphoric basis of catharsis theories. Sigmund Freud's discussions of hysteria and sexuality, she shows, rely on the traditional concept of emotion as a liquid in a container (Warhol 16–17). Freud and Aristotle, who have had such enormous influence on Western cultural understandings of emotion, theorized within the cultures of their times. As Lutz and Warhol argue, their ideas about emotional purging can't simply be dismissed as wrong, but as the products of past cultures, they need re-examining.

Warhol's research suggests that people who read to cry are seeking affirmation, not catharsis. She describes the "good cry," which involves "not the cathartic experience of tragedy, but the affirmative, triumphant, feminine 'tears of joy'" (Warhol 27). Sentimentalism, she finds, is anything but cathartic because it "encourages readers to rehearse and reinforce the feelings it evokes" (Warhol 18). Warhol's view comes close to Moretti's, which encourages respect for tears that flow when the readers of "moving" literature realize the world doesn't match their notions of justice (Moretti 162). Warhol attacks the assumption that crying immobilizes a thinker.

In what sense can crying be "affirmative"? Like Lutz, Warhol views it as a way to reinforce bonds with fellow human beings. The "good cry" shows "the affirmation of community, the persistence of hopefulness and of willingness, the belief that everyone matters . . ." (Warhol 55–56). Warhol doesn't follow Lutz in urging readers to move beyond tears to achieve social action and responsible adulthood. She avoids studying isolated individuals and emphasizes the ways that oppressed people find strength in crying together.

Neither Lutz nor Warhol, who have undertaken the two most thorough, recent cultural studies of tears, has a positive word to say about self-pity. But societies are composed of individuals, and if "everyone matters," then everyone's suffering counts. One person's troubles are rarely unique. More often, they reflect wide-reaching social issues: a single parent abandoned by a partner; a "downsized" employee; a person despised for her appearance. When these people weep, they are accused of self-pity, but they could be crying for us all.

Forbidding Tears

Together, popular films and cultural studies of tears suggest reasons that nobody likes a crybaby. In the United States and other Western cultures, frequent crying is associated with weakness, effeminacy, immaturity, and social inadequacy. Crying that forms the "fund and capital" of self-pity tends to be the most despised (James 458). Prolonged weeping may be regarded as "an indulgence in self-pity, rage, or self-loathing" (Lutz 115). These economic metaphors depict crying and self-pity as bad investments: they may feel good in the short-term, but in the long-term, they can lead to emotional and moral bankruptcy.

Representations of self-pity associate this emotion with an alarming number of deadly sins. In attributing pain to external sources, the self-pitier is angry and out for compensation. Self-pity also involves pride because people who experience it may ask, "Can there be misery . . . loftier than mine?" (Beckett 2; qtd. in Levy 27). "Indulge" conveys the luxurious aspects of self-pity, the "delicious swim" that feels good against the skin (McElrath 59). Annie on her mother's couch suggests self-pity's tendency toward filth and sloth. As Megan points out, Annie badly needs a shower. Above all, those who feel sorry for themselves are depicted as *not moving*. In metaphors of motion versus stasis, emotional, spiritual, and economic thinking converge with basic bodily experiences.

If one imagines life as a journey to salvation or prosperity, the worst one can do is stand still. Bunyan's Slough of Despond represents the hesitation caused by fear and doubt as a filthy bog sucking travelers down. Popular calls to "move on" play on cultural assumptions that moving forward is good. Commands to "let go" are closely related, since one can't progress without releasing one's grip and liberating one's hands to reach for new things. This pattern of metaphors implies that it is emotionally healthy to move forward, stay clean—and buy. The journey model drives consumerism because one socially sanctioned way to move on is to shop: to throw away everything associated with the past and buy a cartload of goods. Shopping, moving, starting a business—all these actions suggest progress, whereas reflecting on one's emotions does not. If life is a pilgrimage, then self-pity is a dirty, sticky trap.

In this metaphoric system, a person who balks appears to be letting others down. In war, one person's weakness can cause the death of a whole squad, so military training like that shown in *G. I. Jane* emphasizes team loyalty and tries to end emotional indulgence. Life will always bring pain, runs the logic, and although one can't control life, one can control one's response to it. Protesting about the external causes of pain wastes time, as does crying to draw attention to one's suffering. Publicly expressing pain and pointing to its causes are the *wrong responses* to life. The right ones are looking to oneself for the causes of one's suffering, correcting one's ways, and marching on.

But need we see life as a journey? Metaphors that figure life through progressive motion discourage pauses to reconsider the direction, pace, and purpose of one's march. Representing life as a linear trek toward a goal encourages conformity rather than than creative experiments. Conformity doesn't mean maturity or fulfillment, and although the march-to-salvation model can inspire, it can serve intolerance. Commands to "let go" and "move on" tend not to nourish thought. As the work of emotion researchers is showing, it is worth thinking about how one feels, and why. Reflecting on one's emotions and their causes can lead to a more fulfilling, productive life (Goleman x–xiii).

Honest thought about one's situation, from multiple perspectives, may confirm one's initial impression that one has been unjustly hurt. In this case, publicly expressing one's pain may help others who are being similarly mistreated. Dismissing those who protest injustice as crybabies ensures that abuses will continue.

Supposedly, no one likes a crybaby because she breaks the rules: she indulges in behavior that the more tractable have stifled. Socially, few people receive more blame than those who act out other people's secret wishes, and one of the most widespread human desires is to show the world how much one hurts. When people refuse to stifle their emotions, social complications arise. For those who hold relatively less social power, half-suppressing one's emotions—or conspicuously suppressing them— can serve as a protest tactic. Physically manifesting one's unhappiness can undermine the vulnerable happiness of those more privileged. Perhaps for this reason, descriptions of socially undesirable emotions such as self-pity often convey the perspective of "winners" who don't want to listen to "losers."

Notes

1. In *El laberinto de la soledad,* Octavio Paz analyzes Mexican cultural contempt for people who open themselves ("que se abren") sexually or metaphorically (Paz 26–27).

2. Frevert cites Ann M. Kring, "Gender and Anger," and Elizabeth M. Messner, "Emotionale Tränen."

3. Damasio does not claim that people think while crying, but in *Descartes' Error,* he argues that emotions play a vital role in decision-making. Just as bodies and minds are interdependent, reason and emotion should not be understood as opposed (Damasio 248).

4. Urgayle misquotes the third line of Lawrence's poem, which reads, "A *small* bird will *drop* frozen dead from a bough" (Lawrence 58, emphasis added). Urgayle quotes the rest of the poem accurately.

5. Williams argues that *G. I. Jane* depicts one individual's body-oriented "female self-overcoming" rather than a struggle to open the way for future female Seals (Williams 173).

6. Sarah Hagelin believes that *G. I. Jane* re-educates audiences to see violence against women in military training as potentially empowering rather than annihilating (Hagelin 89).

7. According to Sarah Hagelin, Scott's film implies that the "insidious condescension" of gender norming is the real threat to equality and to the military, not the advent of female soldiers (Hagelin 89).

8. Although *G. I. Jane* avoids a full confrontation with homosexuality, it raises the issue of lesbianism. DeHaven's staff members take photographs that falsely suggest a relationship between O'Neil and the female base doctor. In a subtler way, the film hints that DeHaven herself is attracted to O'Neil. Studying the photographs in O'Neil's file, she calls the young officer, "top drawer . . . with silk stockings inside" (Scott 00:07:45). Clad in a loose dress, Dehaven meets with O'Neil at night in her Senate office. Sipping whiskey, Dehaven tells O'Neil that the dark office is starting to remind her of "an old whorehouse" (Scott 00:09:23). Presumably DeHaven wants a conventionally attractive test candidate who doesn't look like a stereotypical lesbian, as Sarah Hagelin contends (Hagelin 91), but Dehaven may also be following her own inclinations.

9. In "Gendering the Recession," Diane Negra identifies *Bridesmaids* as one of several recent films that suggest how women should respond to the 2008 crash. Some of these films show salvation through a return to traditional women's crafts, such as cupcake-baking.

10. HOLD ON. Words and music by Carnie Wilson, Chynna Phillips, & Glen Ballard. ©1990 EMI Blackwood Music Inc., Smooshie Music, Universal Music Corp., and Aerostation Corp. The lyrics of "Hold On" could not be reproduced in this book, but I encourage readers to listen to the song with special attention to its metaphor of enchainment.

11. Lillian's father speaks this line before the band starts singing, and he is later shown dancing and enjoying the music with the other guests. Earlier in the film, he also expressed a wish that Lillian and Doug would marry quickly and avoid a big, expensive wedding, which Lillian worries that he can't afford. His main concern seems to be financial, but it is significant that he offers the one resisting voice in the film's final spectacle.

CHAPTER 4 | The Sound and Smell of Suffering

I don't pity myself . . . I pity . . . other people . . . more.

—VIRGINIA WOOLF, *Mrs. Dalloway*

IN THE TWENTY-FIRST CENTURY, to accuse even a literary character of self-pity can provoke outrage. So negative has this label become that people who have survived almost any ordeal need to show they are free from self-pity to prove themselves worthy of being heard. This chapter examines the emotion metaphors associated with two conspicuously suffering female characters: Charlotte Bartlett in E. M. Forster's *A Room with a View* (1908) and Doris Kilman in Virginia Woolf's *Mrs. Dalloway* (1925). This chapter returns to the first historical period considered, 1864 to 1925, to show that manifesting one's suffering, which has never been popular in Anglo-American cultures, was not always as great an offense as it is today, and that in people who lack social rights, it can serve as a protest tactic.

Forster's and Woolf's novels emerged in decades when traditional class and gender roles were shifting in Great Britain and elsewhere in the Western World. The Industrial Revolution, the availability of office jobs, and the loss of more than 37 million soldiers (more than three million of them from the British Empire) loosened rules about who could perform what sort of work (Royde-Smith et al.). Not until 1918, however, did British women aged thirty or older win the right to vote, and only in 1928 was this right extended to all women over the age of twenty-one ("Woman Suffrage"). In early twentieth-century Great Britain, it was no longer certain (although it was still likely) that someone born into a social class would remain there all her life, or that a woman would devote her life to marriage and childrearing. This environment of unpredictable mobility and often unfulfilled hope made life emotionally hard for society's less privileged members.

E. M. Forster's and Virginia Woolf's metaphors for Charlotte Bartlett's and Doris Kilman's emotions deserve attention for several reasons. First, these writers created complex, well-developed characters. If Charlotte and Doris feel self-pity, they feel a hundred other emotions as well. By presenting these three-dimensional characters in social contexts and networks of relationships,

Forster and Woolf suggest that Charlotte's and Doris's pains have causes that lie beyond their troubled psyches. A second reason to focus on these characters' emotions is that Charlotte and Doris share features beyond their tendencies toward martyrdom. Both are single, middle-aged women drawn to other women, and both are relatively well-off, though not as independent as they would like to be. By examining the ways that Forster's and Woolf's emotion metaphors coincide and differ, one can weigh the roles of culture, biology, and individual artistry in the depiction of emotion. A third reason to examine Woolf's and Forster's emotion metaphors is that these master writers have created art from cultural conventions. Their metaphoric vehicles (light and darkness; frozen, flowing, or boiling water) resemble Dante's, Bunyan's, and those of the "folk" model Zoltán Kövecses has identified, but they glow with originality (Kövecses, *Emotion Concepts* 144–48). With Charlotte's sighs and Doris's odor, Forster and Woolf have created their own ways of representing suffering that many people would rather not perceive. For readers, Woolf and Forster make Doris's and Charlotte's emotions feel real.

The words with which skilled authors describe characters' emotions call out to a reader's senses. Socially undesirable emotions such as bitterness (itself a metaphor), spite, and self-pity tend to be represented through unpleasant sensations.[1] Research in cognitive science and cognitive literary studies indicates that readers activate memories of their own sensory experiences in order to simulate (imagine, or mentally elaborate) those of fictional characters. Psychologist Lawrence Barsalou's research has shown that "we represent other people's minds using simulations of our own minds" (Barsalou 623). When reading well-written stories, as in ordinary life, people draw on their diverse memories of sensations so that they can feel what the characters are feeling, both physically and emotionally. Literary scholar Patrick Colm Hogan has found that "simulation remains closely interconnected with emotion systems" (Hogan, *How Authors' Minds Make Stories* 25). Because each reader has had different experiences, each will create unique simulations in response to a descriptive passage. Within a given culture and even across cultures, these simulations will coincide to a degree. Within cultures, readers learn to associate words and ideas with sensations and emotions; across cultures, readers share at least some physiological experiences, such as an increase in heart rate when they feel angry or afraid. It would insult any reader's intelligence, however, to predict how she will respond to a complex character. Charlotte and Doris annoy their novels' protagonists, but Forster and Woolf have given them such depth that many readers may object to descriptions of them as self-pitying.

If readers enjoy these irritating characters, it may be because, in expressing their suffering, Charlotte and Doris sigh for people besides themselves. These unhappy women find ways to express their discontent in a society where female virtue demands stifling one's frustration. Created two decades apart by two mutually acquainted British authors, Charlotte and Doris play vital roles in emotionally rich novels. As minor characters, they draw attention to the emotional erasure threatening the female protagonist of each novel. The metaphoric patterns from which their emotions grow have roots extending to the heart of each work. Created from biology and ideology, Forster's and Woolf's metaphors suggest how emotional experiences acquire meanings.

Charlotte's Sighs

Forster narrates *A Room with a View* with free indirect discourse, and his third-person narrator slips so subtly between characters' viewpoints that readers may barely notice the shifts.[2] His choices of which perspectives to favor affect readers' responses to the characters, but Forster avoids calling attention to his narrative strategy. Most of the time, he offers the viewpoint of Lucy Honeychurch, a young, upper-middle-class English woman encountering Italy for the first time. Lucy's older, unmarried cousin Charlotte Bartlett accompanies her as a companion and chaperone. Although Lucy is engaged to Cecil, she develops feelings—of which she is hardly aware—for George Emerson, a passionate, lower-middle-class young man whom she meets in her Florentine pension. Meanwhile, Charlotte bonds with novelist Eleanor Lavish, to whom she describes the romance she is overtly thwarting. Forster's novel centers on the question of which path Lucy will choose. Will she marry patronizing Cecil; will she stay single and guard her independence; or will she follow her emotions and marry George, who comes across as her natural partner? Forster's choice to enter most of his characters' minds, but to favor Lucy's, affects the way that he represents emotion. Readers get to know Charlotte *as Lucy experiences her*. Through Forster's rich metaphoric descriptions, however, he reveals the depth of this conflicted character on whose actions his novel hinges.

To convey the force of human emotions, Forster uses three closely related metaphoric patterns. The first involves water, free-flowing or contained, especially the rushing water of the Arno River.[3] In many ways, this depiction of emotions through confined or flowing water fits the liquid-in-a-container model described by linguist Zoltán Kövecses (Kövecses, *Emotion Concepts* 144–48). Forster's second metaphoric pattern, which contrasts light with darkness, recalls Dante's depiction of prolonged anger as a perverse rejection of daylight (Alighieri, *Inferno* 105).[4] Forster brings original variations to both patterns by cross-connecting the metaphoric sources (vehicles), for instance, by describing light in terms of water. Forster also alters the targets (tenors) of these metaphors by associating unrestricted light and water with love; and darkness and containment, with lovelessness. Forster's third pattern of emotion metaphors differs from the first two by using more modern, technological "vehicles": electric trams. These three families of intermingling metaphors show the force of the characters' emotions by engaging the readers' senses.

Water surges everywhere in *A Room with a View*, especially in the novel's most emotionally charged scenes. Forster's descriptions of the Arno River invite readers to imagine its sights and sounds. In the opening scene that gives the novel its title, Lucy and Charlotte are longing for a view of the Arno. Beside the "gushing" river (Forster 42), Lucy and George bond emotionally after witnessing a murder, which causes Lucy to faint. Recalling the feel of George's arms around her, Lucy contemplates "the River Arno, whose roar was suggesting some unexpected melody to her ears" (Forster 42). The music of the Arno inspires melancholy George to live, and by the next morning, the river is "a lion . . . in strength, voice and color" (Forster 44). Expressing the force of life, the Florentine river even gets the last word in the novel. George and Lucy, now married, listen to "the river, bearing down the snows of winter into the Mediterranean" (Forster 196). With this conclusion, Forster leaves readers with an image of emotional flow. His final reference to transformed snows emerges from a conversation in which George and Lucy make a joint discovery. Rather than stopping them, "dreadful frozen Charlotte" has actually allowed them to come together (Forster 194). George declares that Charlotte "is not frozen," and the final image of flux, a few lines later, suggests that even the most rigid person may be capable of emotional movement (Forster 196).[5]

Forster's use of flowing water to represent emotion illustrates the way a writer can vary and develop metaphors to make art, much as a composer develops variations on a theme. Metaphorically, one could say that Forster's plot is about enabling impeded flow. Charlotte has a different relationship with water than have Lucy and George. They like to swim naked in a pond, whereas she wants fluids to stay in their containers and feels anxious when her boiler is replaced.[6] Mrs. Honeychurch observes that "water preys upon one's mind," and she is right in many senses (Forster 129). The perceptive clergyman Mr. Beebe predicts that when Lucy lives as passionately as she plays Beethoven, "the watertight compartments in her will break down" (Forster 86).

Together, these suggestive references to water illustrate how emotion metaphors can emerge when physiology and culture combine. Human emotion concepts may be "influenced by certain universal properties of the human body," but "feeling states are also, in part, culturally determined" (Kövecses, *Metaphor and Emotion* 146, 187). Forster's references to containers in danger of bursting invoke the "folk understanding" of emotion as a confined fluid (Kövecses, *Emotion Concepts* 144). As a metaphoric source (or vehicle) for emotion, water offers all the complexity for which philosopher Max Black could hope. Depending on the form of water selected, a metaphoric water source can emphasize different aspects of emotion and can structure understanding in different ways. Water can roar with unstoppable force; it can freeze; and it can leak. Whether confined, trickling, or gushing, it demands attention and can't be ignored.

Forster's references to light and darkness also emphasize emotion's enclosure or free flow. His metaphoric family representing emotion through light resembles the one that figures it through liquid because both metaphoric groups privilege movement over blockage, and both depict dynamic systems. As the second part of Forster's novel opens, water has turned to sunlight. The curtains in Lucy's English home work like "sluice-gates" holding back a "sea of radiance" and admitting a "rivulet of light" (Forster 77). Like the free-flowing water of the Arno, this brilliant sunlight suggests the force of emotions one should not block. Forster associates light with George and his father, the novel's two most open characters. Mr. Emerson urges Lucy to "pull out from the depths those thoughts that you do not understand, and spread them out in the sunlight and know the meaning of them" (Forster 25). Forster relies on the Platonic metaphor representing knowledge in terms of light, but the knowledge he invokes is emotional. Forster uses sunlight as a metaphoric source so that its heat matters as much as its enabling of sight. When George wants to "stand for all he [is] worth in the sun," he relishes its warmth against his skin (Forster 145). By appealing to vision and touch at once, Forster invites readers to imagine George's love of life.

In Forster's metaphoric pattern associating love with light, darkness represents not just ignorance but the willful suppression of knowledge. Whereas George often appears in outdoor scenes, Cecil avoids the sun, and Lucy can envision him only in a room. When she ends her engagement with Cecil and he withdraws upstairs, "the shadows from the bannisters passed over his face like the beat of wings" (Forster 162). Literary critic Elaine Scarry has observed that in writing, "getting mental pictures to move is everything" (Scarry 81). She has noticed that skilled writers often describe one image moving across another, as though cuing readers to move the first image against a background in their minds (Scarry 108). Forster's description of Cecil through Lucy's eyes does emotional work by allowing readers to picture him behind prison bars. This fascinating image sets up one of the novel's most powerful passages. Vowing never to marry, Lucy puts out a lamp, and the narrator responds with horror:

> She gave up trying to understand herself, and joined the vast armies of the be-nighted, who follow neither the heart nor the brain, and march to their destiny by catchwords. The armies are full of pleasant and pious folk. But they have yielded to the only enemy that matters—the enemy within. They have sinned against passion and truth, and vain will be their strife after virtue. As the years pass, they are censured. Their pleasantry and their piety show cracks, their wit becomes cynicism, their unselfishness hypocrisy; they feel and produce discomfort wherever they go. . . . The night received [Lucy], as it had received Miss Bartlett thirty years before. (Forster 162–63)

According to this metaphoric logic, emotionally benighted people have extinguished their own lamps. Those who live in darkness are lying to themselves about what they feel. Having freed herself from Cecil, Lucy is unsure what to do, and one option is a lifetime of denial. The narrator points to Charlotte to show the results of three decades of night.

Lucy, however, is a twentieth-century woman, not a younger version of her cousin Charlotte. In Florence, Lucy wanted "something big, and she believed that it would have come to her on the windswept platform of an electric tram" (Forster 37). To convey Lucy's desire, Forster employs a modern metaphoric vehicle: a noisy, crowded electric train. Like water and sunlight, this vehicle *moves*, so that here again, Forster cross-connects the qualities of his metaphoric sources. In Lucy's first view of Florence, an "overflowing" tram "came rushing" under her window, sounding like the Arno beyond it (Forster 14). The periodic, insistent trams remind Lucy of the "big" thing she wants in life but can't identify. On a drive with Charlotte and the Emersons, a tram comes "squealing" up the road—and after Lucy's kiss with George, the tram's wire is struck by lightning (Forster 56). Like the metaphoric families of water and light, this group of electrical metaphors suggests unpredictable forces that can be controlled only in part.

Together, these three metaphoric patterns characterize Charlotte as benighted but unfrozen, and capable of movement. In Forster's hands, she is a complex character, emotionally vigilant enough to nip other people's emotions in the bud but conflicted enough to spare a few.[7] The first line of the novel—which is hers—reveals her longing for a Florentine view. Her negotiations leave her with the larger room, which supposedly can't go to Lucy because it was George's. Initially, Charlotte opposes Mr. Emerson's offer to trade rooms, but she later negotiates and supervises the move. Forster black-boxes the Florentine scene in which Charlotte confronts George, so that readers hear only his "heavy, tired breathing" and receive assurance that "the chaperon [*sic*] had done her work" (Forster 73). Charlotte's actions to that point suggest that she reproached and threatened George, but while doing the work her culture demands, she may have conveyed an insufficiently suppressed wish. After hearing George denounce Cecil and declare his love for Lucy, Charlotte first exclaims, "What an awful man!" but then "essay[s] the roguish," asking, "Well, it isn't everyone who could boast such a conquest, dearest, is it?" (Forster 156). In such moments, Charlotte seems human enough that readers may wonder what she was like before the night received her, and what heartbreak might have driven her there.

Although unloved, Charlotte often gets what she wants, and in doing so, she drives the plot. As Lucy grows in emotional awareness, she thinks, "It sometimes seemed as if [Charlotte] planned every word she spoke or caused to be spoken" (Forster 135). Charlotte plays a central role in many of the novel's coincidences, which viewed in retrospect are less coincidental than they seem.[8] Charlotte "just happens" to see George and Lucy kiss, and then to tell Eleanor Lavish about it (Hinojosa 91). Charlotte's self-recriminations after George and Lucy kiss make Lucy promise not to tell her mother. When Lucy discovers a description of her and George kissing in the novel of Eleanor Lavish, Lucy angrily reproaches her cousin, since only Charlotte could have told Eleanor about it. Charlotte acts "absolutely helpless," and when Lucy decides to confront George herself, she realizes, "this was what her cousin had intended all along" (Forster 152–53). By the end of the novel, George's inkling that "she fought us on the surface, and yet she hoped" seems plausible (Forster 195). Forster's plot depends on the emotional depth of an unhappy woman who expresses her discontent in creative ways.

Scholarly studies of *A Room with a View* rarely mention how funny Forster's novel is. Charlotte's scenes can be hilarious because of the way she uses her suffering to impose her will on others. Through years of practice, she has learned to stage her misery with a director's eye. With masochistic tendencies, she creates many of her own problems to evoke the pity she claims not to seek. Ostensibly muffled but clear, her expressions of pain combine culturally imposed self-renunciation with self-serving skill. As a poor cousin, she has mastered the art of manipulating others to enact her wishes.

Charlotte's technique—if it can be called that—is to put herself down, conspicuously sacrifice her desires, and urge others to carry out theirs instead. The result, especially in women of Edwardian Britain, is guilt for selfishly imposing one's will on Charlotte. Readers first experience Charlotte in action in the conflict that gives the novel its name: " 'Any nook does for me,' Miss Bartlett continued, 'but it does seem hard that you shouldn't have a view.' Lucy felt that she had been selfish" (Forster 3). When those around Charlotte carry out their wishes, she indicates that they are making her suffer. Lucy, on her first day in Florence, wants to go out, but "Miss Bartlett was, after all, a wee bit tired, and thought they had better spend the morning settling in" (Forster 15). Charlotte insists on accompanying Lucy but makes sure that Lucy knows the sacrifice Charlotte is making: "She was determined to take Lucy herself, her head not being so very bad" (Forster 15). So effective is Charlotte's unselfishness that Lucy ends up begging Charlotte to do what Charlotte wants. Rather than visit the Torre del Gallo, Lucy runs errands with Charlotte, and Charlotte relishes her small triumph: "Look, Lucia! Oh, you are watching for the Torre del Gallo party. I feared you would repent you of your choice" (Forster 44). Charlotte makes sure not only that others do what she wants, but that they know they are doing so.

The emotional metaphors of *A Room with a View* reveal Charlotte's soul by divulging her fears. Water, above all, threatens her, and she seeks protection from it. Lucy, whose sympathy her cousin aims to stir, fears that "poor Charlotte will be sopped" in a rainstorm:

> The expedition was typical of Miss Bartlett, who would return cold, tired, hungry, and angelic, with a ruined skirt, a pulpy Baedeker, and a tickling cough in her throat. On another day, when the whole world was singing and the air ran into the mouth like wine, she would refuse to stir from the drawing-room, saying that she was an old thing, and no fit companion for a hearty girl. (Forster 30)

In a novel where water and light carry emotional force, Charlotte is no friend of the elements. The day of wine and singing, imagined by Lucy and the narrator, holds no place for her. She seems to want to hurt herself so that she will be noticed at all.

Charlotte's self-deprecation approaches masochism, but her ingenuity in obtaining her wishes suggests rich veins of self-worth. Rooted in her shifting personality, her manipulation grows on unstable ground. On some level, at least in momentary glimmers, she believes that she deserves more than she has. She wants protection, for example, from the wetness she fears will damage her health. In an extremely funny scene, Charlotte drives Lucy to George by sacrificing a mackintosh square:

> The ground will do for me. Really I have not had rheumatism for years. If I do feel it coming on I shall stand. Imagine your mother's feelings if I let you sit in the wet in your white linen. . . . Even if my dress is thinner it will not show so much, being brown. Sit down, dear; you are too unselfish; you don't assert yourself enough. . . . Now don't be alarmed; this isn't a cold. It's the tiniest cough, and I have had it three days. It's nothing to do with sitting here at all. (Forster 61)

As this scene emphasizes, Charlotte's suffering tends to focus on small illnesses caused by exposure to the elements. By this time, readers will be familiar with her ways, and her message could not be clearer: if you take the square, you are being selfish and causing me to suffer. After five minutes, Lucy flees in exasperation and ends up in George's arms. Apparently, Charlotte has won protection from nature by exposing Lucy to nature—except that an encounter between George and Lucy may be just what Charlotte wants.

Readers may have trouble discerning Charlotte's motives, since Forster's narrator so rarely enters her mind. When he does, he reveals only that her back hurts, and that "for all her diplomacy, she felt that she was growing old" (Forster 70). Diplomacy is the word for Charlotte's game of revelation and concealment, since she covertly communicates the pain she feels. At night in the pension, she sighs "into a crack in the partition wall" so that Lucy cannot miss her wordless protest (Forster 72). As Charlotte convinces Lucy to leave Italy, the narrator breaks loose, voicing a thought more in his own voice than the protagonist's: "Miss Bartlett assumed her favorite role, that of the prematurely aged martyr" (Forster 71). If readers can believe him and the other characters, Charlotte has few aims in life beyond performing her suffering.

Humor resists analysis, and it is hard to say what makes Charlotte's martyrdom so funny. She doesn't enjoy the small victories she wins, perhaps because pleasure would smack of selfishness. Forster's narrator claims to readers that "unselfishness with Miss Bartlett had entirely usurped the functions of enthusiasm" (Forster 61). Maybe, by masking desire with sacrifice on a petty level, she is unmasking the self-interest of a whole "unselfish" society.

Charlotte Bartlett's tactics are not often practiced by a society's most powerful members. Forster builds sympathy for this sighing spinster by showing the social forces that have shaped her as well as her subtle resistance to them. First are the social expectations of her gender, which she seems largely to have internalized. Lucy recollects a speech by Charlotte outlining women's proper role:

> It was not that ladies were inferior to men; it was that they were different. Their mission was to inspire others to achievement rather than to achieve themselves. Indirectly, by means of tact and a spotless name, a lady could accomplish much.

But if she rushed into the fray herself she would be first censured, then despised, and finally ignored. (Forster 37)

Charlotte, however, is not living to inspire a man and children; she prefers exploring Florence with a female novelist. Forster's narrator seems to sense the unstable emotional ground underlying her professed views. As if unable to stand what he reports, the narrator follows this passage with an ironic paragraph on how this medieval ideal of womanhood "grows degenerate" and has developed "strange desires" (Forster 37). Such comments, along with remarks from Mr. Emerson, make it clear that Forster's novel challenges this ideology associated with Charlotte. The narrator's irony grows bitterer when Charlotte, "like a great artist," paints for Lucy "the complete picture of a cheerless, loveless world in which the young rush to destruction until they learn better" (Forster 72). Here again, the narrator intervenes. With a dash, he jabs this thought attributed to Charlotte and adds: "a shamefaced world of precautions and barriers which may avert evil, but which do not seem to bring good, if we may judge from those who have used them most" (Forster 72). The narrator and most of the characters reject Charlotte's feeling that "life contains nothing satisfactory," and it is unclear whether Charlotte believes this herself (Forster 124).

Although the narrator resists a medieval notion of womanhood, other characters show the strength of the patriarchal forces acting on and through Charlotte. The lowest assessments of womanhood come from Lucy's fiancé, Cecil, who believes that "a woman's power and charm reside in mystery, not in muscular rant" (Forster 93). Cecil can understand no relationship between a man and a woman other than "protector and protected," and he regards Lucy as his "little thing" (Forster 143, 110). If Lucy marries Cecil, it is clear what awaits her. The suppression of her spirit begun by her chaperone will be completed by her husband.

The view of woman as a nurturer of men also comes from Lucy's cheerful, down-to-earth mother. Mrs. Honeychurch hates "literature in the hands of females" and "inveigh[s] against those women who (instead of minding their houses and their children) seek notoriety by print" (Forster 128). At a time when the suffragette movement was most active (Brown 284–85), Mrs. Honeychurch explodes at Lucy's desire to share a flat with a girl in London:

> And mess with typewriters and latchkeys. . . . And agitate and scream, and be carried off kicking by the police. And call it a Mission—when no one wants you! And call it Duty—when it means that you can't stand your own home! And call it Work—when thousands of men are starving with the competition as it is! (Forster 180–81)

Significantly, after this tirade, Mrs. Honeychurch says that Lucy reminds her of Charlotte Bartlett. With all of the forces acting on her, Lucy doesn't know what she wants; she asks for more independence, then withdraws her request. *A Room with a View* is no feminist novel and suggests that a woman's fulfillment lies not in independence but in finding love with a respectful, emotionally honest man. Charlotte's presence gives Forster's story complexity because she reveals the conflicts underlying women's voiced desires. In a culture where saying and doing what one wants are condemned as selfish, many women surprise themselves by blurting out their wishes, only to apologize and take them back.

Charlotte resists socioeconomic restrictions more than she does those imposed by gender. The difference between her income and the Honeychurches' evokes more staged suffering than the deprivations of Edwardian women. On her own, Charlotte couldn't afford a trip to Italy, but as Lucy's chaperone, she is enjoying tourism funded by Lucy's mother. Compared with most early twentieth-century Britons, Charlotte is well off: she can maintain her own household, and she doesn't have to work. Relative to Lucy's family, however, she is poor, a fact of which she continually reminds them. The Honeychurches' high social position resulted from Lucy's father's work as a solicitor, plus a fortunate mistake. Newcomers to their area "mistook [them] for the remnants of an indigenous aristocracy" but continued to like them even after learning that they had earned their wealth (Forster 102). On many levels, Forster's novel conveys the arbitrariness with which social positions are established. George Emerson and his father, who are learned and intelligent, rank below the Honeychurches on the social scale, and Forster's plot relies on this difference. Charlotte's irritating expressions of gratitude merge with the novel's subversive questions about why some people are worth more than others.

On the very first page, Forster's narrator mentions that Charlotte "made many a tactful allusion" to the Honeychurches' generosity (Forster 3). "My own wishes," Charlotte tells Lucy, "are unimportant in comparison with yours . . . when I am only here through your kindness" (Forster 10–11). When the relationship between George and Lucy convinces Charlotte to flee to Rome, she mourns, "[I have] failed in my duty to your mother. She has been so generous to me" (Forster 71). With Mr. Beebe, Charlotte is more direct, describing Lucy's unhappiness with her when "all the time I felt that I was spending her mother's money" (Forster 174). Supposedly, these calculated allusions express gratitude, but they create a different effect. With a mosquito's insistent whine, they ask, "Why are you rich when I'm not?"

Charlotte differs from Mr. Emerson, who cares about social inequities on a broad scale. Although she seems to believe she deserves more money, she relishes her social position with snobbery that may repel some readers. When malicious Reverend Eager calls Mr. Emerson "the son of a laborer . . . a mechanic of some sort himself . . .," Charlotte seems to share his view: " 'How wonderfully people rise in these days!' sighed Miss Bartlett, fingering a model of the leaning Tower of Pisa" (Forster 49). Charlotte's sigh, by now a leitmotif, conveys her general discontent with the order of things. Her suggestive fingering indicates gladness of her superiority to lower-middle-class men. Charlotte learns that George's profession is "the railway," and from within her mind, the narrator gives her response: "She was very sorry that she had asked him. She had no idea that it would be such a dreadful answer" (Forster 60). As a complex character, Charlotte both parrots and questions her culture's ideology. To reassure herself of her superiority to others, she reproduces class prejudices, but she challenges them when they imply that others are superior to her. With these very human contradictions, she can't be categorized as either a subversive or a snob.

In one more way that the novel scarcely dares to mention, Charlotte is being shaped by social forces. Mr. Beebe suspects that Charlotte may "reveal unknown depths of strangeness" when he notices her close friendship with Eleanor Lavish (Forster 31). From the first, Charlotte is drawn to the confident, eccentric novelist pursuing adventures in Italy. Charlotte considers Eleanor a "really clever woman" and actively seeks her out (Forster 46). The two develop an intimacy that has profound effects on the plot. Since the posthumous publication of *Maurice* (1971) and the revelation of Forster's homosexuality, critics have studied the homoeroticism of *A Room with a View* and have read George and Lucy as a disguised gay pair.[9] Few have responded to hints that Charlotte and Eleanor are pursuing forbidden pleasures. In the late nineteenth century, "strange" could imply homosexual, and Mr. Beebe would be one to know. The Reverend is "from rather profound reasons, somewhat chilly in his attitude towards the other sex" (Forster 31). When Eleanor's cigarette case turns up in an armchair, he quips, "A good fellow, Lavish, but I wish she'd start a pipe" (Forster 32). The intimacy between Charlotte and Eleanor may not be sexual, but for Charlotte, it creates enough fun to produce guilt. When she asks Lucy for forgiveness, Charlotte moans, "What right had I to make friends with Miss Lavish?" (Forster 72). At this point, the reader doesn't yet know that Charlotte has told Eleanor of Lucy's kiss, or that Eleanor will write about it in her novel. Charlotte begs forgiveness for daring to pursue pleasures that include unspecified intimacy with another woman.

Because conflicting emotions heave in Charlotte, she is always trying to erase her words and deeds. To the other characters, her requests for forgiveness become as irritating as her actions and their consequences. In Florence, when Charlotte asks for Lucy's pardon, "Lucy was on her guard at once, knowing by bitter experience what forgiving Miss Bartlett meant" (Forster 71). The narrator doesn't explain, but Charlotte's pleas to be forgiven show that she is asking for absolution before her act and its consequences are known. Charlotte's misdeed promises to be bad enough that there can be no pardon. In all Charlotte's references to forgiving herself, she calls attention to the conflicts within her. As an aging, unmarried woman in a society that requires women to suppress most desires, she acts awkwardly and indirectly because each thought emerges from warring forces. Each wish must be rationalized through roundabout logic; each impulsive act canceled by a pardon. Her contradictory behavior typifies that of people struggling in a society whose rules deny their inner nature.

It is easy to miss Charlotte's subtle resistance to social forces because most of the other characters experience her as oppressive.[10] Forster appeals to all of a reader's senses to show why they feel constricted by her. To convey

Charlotte's force, Forster often relies on tactile imagery, and her fingering of the Leaning Tower model reminds readers of her controlling hand.[11] When Charlotte discovers the question mark George has pinned over his washstand, perhaps as a message to Lucy, Charlotte takes it down and places it between two pieces of blotting paper.[12] Once engulfed, George's question settles under Charlotte's sigh, which closes the paragraph and the chapter. It is no wonder that when Lucy learns of Charlotte's intended visit in Part Two, she protests, "we're squeezed to death as it is" (Forster 129). As George Lakoff and Mark Johnson might say, Forster represents Charlotte's "handling" of Lucy in an oppressively grounded way.

Charlotte's restrictive nature focuses on Lucy, whom she has been sent to Italy to protect. In an unforgettable multimodal image, Mr. Beebe describes Lucy as a kite whose string is being held by Charlotte (Forster 87). The clergyman fantasizes about the string breaking so that Lucy can fly free. Readers who have flown kites may recall the ripping sounds and the pull and burn of the string against the hand. Anyone who has felt these combined sensations must have imagined how it might feel if the kite broke loose. Through this visual, auditory, and tactile imagery, Forster helps readers to imagine how Charlotte affects the people around her.

Visually, Forster tends to depict Charlotte as obscuring and obstructive. He describes Lucy's and George's kiss in a colorful setting, a hillside with violets running "down in rivulets and streams and cataracts" (Forster 63). At this vital moment, Charlotte's sudden appearance creates a disruption in two sensory modalities. Not only does she break "the silence of life"; she stands "brown against the view" (Forster 63). Charlotte emerges like a blot on a painting, as though sent by Forster to wreck a simulated visual tableau. For much of the novel, her purpose seems to be to keep things from happening, and Forster depicts her so that readers can see, hear, and feel the way that Lucy experiences her psychologically.

As a chaperone, Charlotte reproduces and benefits from her society's ideology; as a single woman, she resists it through conspicuous suffering. Forster may have depicted her contradictions so tellingly because his life gave him so many opportunities to study the psychology of middle-aged women. Life never explains art, but Forster's experiences provide an essential context in which to read A Room with a View. As an only child who lost his father as a baby, Forster maintained a close relationship with his mother, Lily, and he loved his maternal grandmother, Louise Whichelo (Herz 145). An £8000 legacy from his great aunt, Marianne Thornton, allowed him to study at Cambridge and to live as a writer without having to support himself through other work (Saunders 26). In 1901–1902, after completing his degree, Forster spent a year traveling through Italy with his mother (Saunders 11; Sampaio 898). According to some scholars, Forster's mother "dominated" him (Goldman 121) and had "an infantilizing effect" on Forster (Saunders 12). Lily accused her son of absentmindedness and said, "I never saw anybody so incapable" (Saunders 12). Soon afterward, Forster sprained his ankle on the pension stairs and broke his arm on the steps of St. Peter's, so that he couldn't wash or dress without her help (Saunders 12). *A Room with a View* emerged from his notes taken during this trip, and Forster's diaries and letters indicate "tensions" between him and his mother (Brown 298). Charlotte Bartlett, who swirled up from his Italian experiences, may embody at least some of the mother washing and scolding him.[13] Forster claims to have modeled Charlotte on his Aunt Emily, but like his novel, Charlotte probably reflects all of his experiences with women up to that time (Brown 298). Between 1902 and 1908, *A Room with a View* developed slowly, and Forster could not have helped but hear the spreading debates about women's roles.[14]

Forster's relationships with women offered rich material for the creation of repressed, oppressive characters that in sudden impulses resist social rules. As a homosexual man starting a novel less than ten years after Oscar Wilde's trial, Forster understood the frustration of crushing one's desires as well as the danger of not doing so. He also knew that people can't easily be sorted into the oppressors and the oppressed. Women could be overbearing, omnipresent, and suffocating. In 1930, Forster wrote, "If women ever wanted to be by themselves all would be well. But I don't believe they ever want to be . . . their instinct is never to let men be by themselves" (qtd. in Rahman 50). The forced squelching of one's wishes doesn't make for pleasant emotions or stable, serene personalities. With her manipulative, half-revealed suffering, Charlotte sighs at the culture oppressing her.

Doris's Scent

One night, Forster and Virginia Woolf got drunk and "talked of sodomy, and sapphism, with emotion" (Woolf, *Diary* 3: 193).[15] According to Woolf, Forster "said he thought Sapphism disgusting: partly from convention, partly because he disliked that women should be independent of men" (Woolf, *Diary* 3: 193). Woolf and Forster knew each other well and respected each other's writing— to a point.[16] Although they shared concerns about the social laws crushing women, Forster remained uneasy about what lifting those laws might mean. "I always feel him shrinking sensitively from me, as a woman, a clever woman, an up to date woman," Woolf wrote in 1919 (Woolf, *Diary* 1: 263). Forster once infuriated Woolf by telling her that the London Library Board (of which he was a member) had agreed not to accept women because "ladies are impossible" (Woolf, *Diary* 4: 126). The creator of George Emerson, who said, "this desire to govern a woman—it lies very deep, and men and women must fight it together . . . ," did not think like his character (Forster 155). In his ideas about what women should do and feel, Forster seems to have been as muddled as Charlotte Bartlett.

To understand the ways that metaphors shape understandings of discouraged emotions, it pays to compare Charlotte with Doris Kilman, a character integral to Woolf's *Mrs. Dalloway*. Like Charlotte, Doris is unmarried, middle-aged, attracted to women, and irritating to the protagonist. Social injustice has left Doris with a lasting grievance, and she asserts herself more than Charlotte in making her suffering known.[17] Forster and Woolf represent their characters' emotions with distinct metaphoric patterns because their creative aims and techniques vary. Whereas Charlotte fears leakage or invasion by water, Doris feels stuffed, boiling, and ready to burst. She lacks creative tasks to busy her strong hands, and she emits an unpleasant odor. Unlike Forster, Woolf grants access to her tormented character's mind. Three years before many British women could vote, Woolf invited readers into the mind and body of a frustrated, unhappy woman.

Woolf's innovative narration differs from Forster's free indirect discourse. Forster's narrator moves so smoothly from character to character that a reader may not consciously note the shifts in point of view (Heath 419). *Mrs. Dalloway*, in contrast, is *about* consciousness and narration in a way that *A Room with a View* is not. Woolf's narrative loops through many of her characters' minds, revealing their complex relationships and distinct perspectives. In one key scene, the narrative dwells in Doris's consciousness to reveal some culturally disdained emotions, but many impressions of Doris come from the central character, Clarissa Dalloway. Wealthy Clarissa has an ordinary mind, and her attempts at profound thought fizzle owing to her lack of analytical skill. As a middle-aged woman, Clarissa competes with Doris for the favor of Clarissa's increasingly independent daughter, Elizabeth, whom Doris tutors. Even Clarissa realizes that the "brutal monster" disturbing her sleep is only her mental representation of Doris (Woolf, *Mrs. Dalloway* 12; Primamore 128). Woolf makes sure readers know Clarissa is projecting by offering them Doris's contrasting viewpoint.

Forster's readers hear very little about Charlotte Bartlett's body. She seems not to want to know that she has one, and Forster structures his narrative so that the notion of inhabiting Charlotte's body to share her feelings would be as comic as it is absurd. Woolf, in contrast, reveals Doris's emotions through embodied metaphors that show her conflicts. Doris feels (and tries not to feel) a "violent grudge against the world which had scorned her, sneered at her, cast her off, beginning with this indignity—the infliction of her unlovable body which people could not bear to see" (Woolf, *Mrs. Dalloway* 126). Doris's evangelical minister has helped supply the words for this thought, but long before Doris developed a close relationship with God, her resentment of injustice focused on her body.

Woolf describes Doris's emotions in visceral terms that encourage readers to feel her rage in their bellies. Doris turned to religion because she felt "bitter and burning," and "hot and turbulent feelings . . . boiled and surged in her" (Woolf, *Mrs. Dalloway* 121). Fat and awkward, she eats for comfort, and in her key scene with Elizabeth in the Army and Navy store tearoom, she resents a child for eating a cake: "Could Miss Kilman really mind it? Yes, Miss Kilman did mind it. She had wanted that cake—the pink one. The pleasure of eating was almost the only pure pleasure left her, and then to be baffled even in that!" (Woolf, *Mrs. Dalloway* 127). In a culture that demands unselfishness from women, resenting a child is taboo. Doris may be self-righteous, but she is also honest, admitting a feeling most women would have denied. In this scene, Doris feels acute hunger in many senses because she notices Elizabeth withdrawing. Like Charlotte with her Leaning Tower, Doris sits "fingering the last two inches of a chocolate éclair" and feels as though she is "about to split asunder" (Woolf, *Mrs. Dalloway* 128). When Elizabeth leaves, the girl seems to be "drawing out . . . the very entrails in [Doris's] body, stretching them as she crossed the room . . ." (Woolf, *Mrs. Dalloway* 129). Doris experiences the world's efforts to deprive her as a cruel campaign to tear her guts out. To Doris Kilman, a life without love or intellectual recognition feels like being eviscerated, boiled, and stuffed.

Elizabeth, whose point of view Woolf also gives, perceives her tutor as an "unwieldy battleship" (Woolf, *Mrs. Dalloway* 127). In context, the pupil's metaphor makes sense: in the wake of a world war, she and Doris are going to drink tea in the Army and Navy stores. Elizabeth's comparison also confirms Doris's perception of herself as an oversized thing filled with explosive power. Big and hard to steer, Doris doesn't belong in a public place crammed with attractive goods. Like a gunship, she has the intellectual and emotive force to blast her environment to bits, but in the narrow channels her society offers her, she can barely maneuver. She gives the impression of a battleship stuck in a Venetian canal.

To indicate the force of Doris's thwarted will, Woolf focuses on her hands. Hand movements are a classic Western metaphoric source for acts of will, and self-help books such as *Who Moved My Cheese?* make frequent use of them to urge emotionally "paralyzed" people to act (Johnson 53). In Woolf's tragicomic tearoom scene, Doris's hand movements work as a leitmotif. As Elizabeth tries to leave, Doris's "large hand opened and shut on the table" (Woolf, *Mrs. Dalloway* 128). As Doris senses Elizabeth's withdrawal, the tutor's "thick fingers [curl] inwards" (Woolf, *Mrs. Dalloway* 129). Her strong, empty hands craving useful work suggest her mind's desperation to exert itself. Woolf's description shares ground with Forster's images of blocked flow, but it focuses on a rejected woman's body. With a metaphor that evokes vision as well as touch, Woolf invites readers to feel Doris's impotence and the excruciating emotions that accompany it. Woolf's depiction of Doris's misery seems designed to make readers feel her frustration in their own hands.

When Doris expresses her discontent, her tactics carry greater force than Charlotte's sighs. With comic, self-defeating fury, Doris uses her body to make her feelings perceptible to every sense. Insistently, though maybe not consciously, she asserts herself by reminding people, "I am here!" Like Charlotte, Doris seems drawn to waterproof fabrics, and because she wears a green mackintosh coat all year round, she sweats. There are few more effective ways of asserting one's presence than making sure that others breathe one's odor. The tactic, which may have evolutionary roots, is guaranteed to win attention, if not love. Doris enters Woolf's novel when a smell brings her to Clarissa's mind.[18]

Although the narrator doesn't say so directly, Doris makes a strong olfactory impression.

Visually, Doris proves equally imposing because she does "not, after all, dress to please" (Woolf, *Mrs. Dalloway* 120). This thought comes not from Clarissa but from Doris, in a moment of defiance as Elizabeth stands poised between her mother and Miss Kilman. Doris doesn't want to fit into a picture and fade into pleasant invisibility. To have her feelings acknowledged, Doris would rather live as a brown blot than a pretty violet on a hillside. Doris fumes that she "[can]not help being ugly," but Woolf's novel suggests that she can (Woolf, *Mrs. Dalloway* 126). She can't afford clothes like the ones Clarissa wears, but she might take off her mackintosh.[19] She might eat fewer cakes. But Miss Kilman refuses to "make herself agreeable" to any sense (Woolf, *Mrs. Dalloway* 122). For those thriving in the social system that thwarted her, she will not make life easy. She wants everyone who benefits from the system that crushed her to know how badly she has been hurt.

Doris Kilman has a legitimate grievance. The reader first learns of her troubles from Clarissa, then from Doris, and although Mrs. Dalloway can't fathom poverty, their accounts harmonize. Clarissa admits that:

> [Doris] had been badly treated of course; one must make allowances for that . . . Year in year out she wore that coat; she perspired; she was never in the room five minutes without making you feel her superiority, your inferiority; how poor she was; how rich you were; . . . all her soul rusted with that grievance sticking in it, her dismissal from school during the War—poor embittered unfortunate creature! (Woolf, *Mrs. Dalloway* 11–12)

In recalling the source of Doris's problems, Clarissa focuses on how the tutor makes her feel. As a result of this technique on Woolf's part, readers who have become involved in Clarissa's emotions may imagine Doris as a self-righteous martyr. Doris's account of her suffering coincides with Clarissa's, but its tone differs:

> She had been cheated. . . . Just as she might have had a chance at Miss Dolby's school, the war came; and she had never been able to tell lies. . . . It was true that the family was of German origin; spelt the name Kiehlman in the eighteenth century; but her brother had been killed. They turned her out because she would not pretend that the Germans were all villains. (Woolf, *Mrs. Dalloway* 120–21)

During World War I, Doris fell victim to wartime propaganda that fanned hatred of anyone German (Levenback 4). Because of her ancestry, but mainly because of her honesty, Doris lost her chance at a good secondary education (Primamore 126). Despite her expulsion from a prestigious school, Doris educated herself, and if readers can believe Doris, "her knowledge of modern history was more than respectable" (Woolf, *Mrs. Dalloway* 129). The tutor's claim is plausible because she focuses so intensely on the past.

Woolf's diaries indicate that as her draft of *The Hours* evolved into *Mrs. Dalloway*, Doris developed with Woolf's choice to integrate the war's effects into her novel (Levenback 3). The most obvious reminder of the war's human cost is Woolf's character Septimus Smith, the traumatized veteran who commits suicide. But Woolf also wanted to include a victim who lives on, less violent and more tenacious in her response. A diary entry by Woolf on 9 April, 1918 suggests that Doris was inspired by Louise Matthaei, who was forced to leave Newnham College, Cambridge, because of her father's German background.[20] Moved by her meeting with Matthaei, Woolf wrote:

> It is easy to see from her limp, apologetic attitude that the cloud has sapped her powers of resistance . . . as if a dog used to excessive beating, dreaded even the raising of a hand. . . . She has to earn her living. . . . She is a lanky gawky unattractive woman, about 35 . . . dressed in her best, which was inconceivably stiff and ugly. But she has a quick mind, and is an enthusiast; said she loved writing. (Woolf, *Diary* 1: 135–36)

Although Matthaei's defeated attitude bothered Woolf, she sympathized with British citizens of German origin, some of whom had lost their livelihoods due to collective hate and fear (Levenback 4). Matthaei, however, was only one starting point for a character that never stops protesting her mistreatment.[21]

For one more vital reason, Doris feels more like a monkey wrench than a cog in her society's machinery. Her desires include an attraction to Elizabeth, which exceeds that of tutor to student. Woolf's novel offers no evidence for sexual involvement between the women, but it indicates desire on Doris's part. According to Clarissa's husband Richard, his seventeen-year-old daughter is just undergoing a phase "such as all girls go through" (Woolf, *Mrs. Dalloway* 11). Clarissa, who has experienced this phase herself, thinks, "It might be falling in love. But why with Miss Kilman?" (Woolf, *Mrs. Dalloway* 11). Whether or not Doris and Elizabeth are lovers, the two have lately become "inseparable" (Woolf, *Mrs. Dalloway* 11). Under Doris's influence, Elizabeth has been taking Communion and ignoring her appearance. The girl's dark, inexplicably Asian looks suggest her tenuous relationship with her fair mother, who cares about manners and dress. Doris, who despises Clarissa's "smattering of culture," wants to be foremost in Elizabeth's mind, but she is also drawn to her pupil's body (Woolf, *Mrs. Dalloway* 120). In a moment of self-pity, Doris reflects that her ugliness means "never meeting the opposite sex," but it is doubtful she wants to (Woolf, *Mrs. Dalloway* 126). The more significant consequence of her looks is that "never would she come first with anyone," and her next thought is of Elizabeth (Woolf, *Mrs. Dalloway* 126). "Except for Elizabeth," she reflects, "her food was all that she lived for, her comforts; her dinner, her tea; her hot-water bottle at night" (Woolf, *Mrs. Dalloway* 126). Her comparison of Elizabeth to warm, comforting sensations suggests a physical attraction. Doris's visceral agony when Elizabeth leaves conveys a ruptured bond stronger than that of teacher to student.

The fact that Woolf prolongs their tragicomic parting in the Army and Navy stores shows how much Doris's emotions matter to the novel. Doris describes herself as "a wheel without a tire (she was fond of such metaphors), jolted by every pebble" (Woolf, *Mrs. Dalloway* 127). In this embodied metaphor, the cushion of rubber and air represents happy people's ability to absorb shocks, a capacity Doris claims to lack. When she reflects that she is "fond of such metaphors," one senses her intelligence, her ability to think on a meta-level.

If Doris does feel sorry for herself, *Mrs. Dalloway* implies that she has the right to do so. If this multiperspective novel supports anything, it is an individual's right to her inner life. When Doris tells Elizabeth she doesn't feel self-pity, she indicates just the opposite: " 'I don't pity myself,' she said. 'I pity—she meant to say 'your mother' but no, she could not, not to Elizabeth. 'I pity other people,' she said, 'more' " (Woolf, *Mrs. Dalloway* 129). Woolf's many interruptions of this sentence convey the warring mental forces that produced the thought. Doris does pity herself, and she can't stand Elizabeth's mother. But she doesn't want to *be* like rich, slim Clarissa Dalloway. By revealing Doris's reflective mind, Woolf shows that Doris wants to be herself but enjoy the privileges Clarissa has arbitrarily been given.

The triangle of Elizabeth, Clarissa, and Doris reveals the tutor's integral role in *Mrs. Dalloway*. Emotionally, Doris also bears a close resemblance to the desperate veteran, Septimus Smith, since supposedly, both suffer from emotions "out of proportion" to the events that caused them (Levenback 3). Both Doris and Septimus are emotionally isolated, and both receive ideological coaching: Doris, from her minister; and Septimus, from his uncomprehending doctor, Sir William Bradshaw, whose name brings to mind railway schedules. Worshipping "proportion"—an undefined, insipid sense of normalcy—Sir William forces his patients to relinquish all resistance to their expected social roles (Woolf, *Mrs. Dalloway* 97). The doctor's bullying response to his patients' question, "Why live?" precedes Doris's and Elizabeth's Army and Navy store scene, and Septimus's suicide occurs soon afterward (Woolf, *Mrs. Dalloway* 99). Sir William's recollections of his sessions with patients read as though he were talking to Doris. To Bradshaw's assertion that life is good, they reply, "to us . . . life has given no such bounty" (Woolf, *Mrs. Dalloway* 99). Sir William responds that they lack a sense of proportion. They have no right to feel sorry for themselves.

So finely rooted is Doris in *Mrs. Dalloway* that without her, the novel might not work. As the story unfolds, readers may begin to suspect that her unsavory emotions reflect everyone's. In some ways, fleshy Miss Kilman serves as an "alter ego" of Clarissa by embodying the demands of the flesh Clarissa has denied.[22] The two are close in age; each has lost a sibling; and they compete for the love of a seventeen-year-old girl (Moon 276). In her youth, Clarissa first desired her lively friend Sally; then, passionate, hapless Peter. Finally, she sacrificed her physical and emotional needs for a stable, prosperous life with Richard Dalloway (Moon 278). Big, smelly Doris may be poor, but she has followed her urges to eat, to develop herself intellectually, and to be close to another woman. Along with Peter's reappearance, Doris's presence provokes thoughts that have been disturbing Clarissa for years. In a novel in which none of the characters are happy, Doris Kilman fits right in (Primamore 132).

By expressing her misery more vividly than others do, the angry tutor plays a special role. Like Charlotte Bartlett, Doris reveals the forces acting on the protagonist so that readers can imagine their long-term consequences. On August, 30, 1923, Woolf wrote in her diary: "I dig out beautiful caves behind my characters: I think that gives exactly what I want; humanity, humor, depth. The idea is that the caves shall connect, and each comes to daylight at the present moment" (Woolf, *Diary* 2: 263). An exploration of the cave behind Doris leads to the consciousness of every character in Woolf's novel. If Doris feels insignificant, then so does Clarissa; if Doris is wondering, "Why live?" then so is Septimus. To Clarissa, Doris is *persona non grata*, and readers who like the protagonist may find Doris obnoxious. Others may prefer Doris's stink to Clarissa's mediocrity. But Clarissa Dalloway *is* like Doris Kilman—as are most of the characters, as are most readers. Comically assertive and tragically repulsive, she is unmistakably human (Primamore 135–36).[23]

Making Suffering Perceptible

In their encounters with Charlotte and Doris, readers may feel a constrictive stickiness. If they do, it may be because metaphorically, Forster and Woolf associate these women with darkness, restricted flow, confinement, and body odors. These single, middle-aged women protect themselves with waterproof fabric and bring to mind stuffy rooms and tight containers. How do readers know this? Because articulate narrators lead them through the minds of Lucy, Clarissa, and other characters who perceive Charlotte and Doris as musty. But Forster and Woolf show that there is more to these suffering women by depicting them in shifting contexts and, in Doris's case, by granting access to her mind.

Life has disappointed Doris and Charlotte, although their hardships differ in scale. Forster's narrator reveals no single event that relegated Charlotte to darkness, and relative to most women in early twentieth-century Britain, she is privileged and prosperous. Her diffuse unhappiness emerges in sighs like an ill-smelling gas produced by a culture that demands suppression of the female self. Viewed predominantly from outside Charlotte's mind, her confused, stunted emotions emerge through metaphors of darkness and obstructed flow. Doris, in contrast, has a specific grievance, and Woolf's narrator draws readers into her thoughts. Some of Woolf's metaphors for Doris's feelings involve pent-up forces, and they are more violent, visceral, and grounded than Charlotte's. In Doris's case, an oversized, awkward body conveys the anguish of a soul ready to explode.

What these characters share is that they feel the wrong emotions—according to more privileged people in their society. Rather than cheerfully accepting their lots, they feel anger that they are forced to swallow. In Charlotte, this anger is almost entirely suppressed; in Doris, somewhat less so. In these complex characters capable of generosity and kindness, resentment wrestles with benevolence. Their physical awkwardness conveys the anguish of mental worlds in which each move emerges from conflict. They are casualties of a sort, but they are walking wounded who manage to communicate their views.

With their sighs, smells, and minor collisions, they broadcast an unmistakable message: "I am suffering! I am unhappy! Look at me!" Charlotte and Doris manifest pain likely to impress the senses of any potential witness. In a society that offers them no sympathy, they evoke and garner it themselves. Their visible, audible, and olfactory expressions of pain are self-asserting in a culture that forbids female selfishness and anger. If one cannot achieve fulfillment through work and is forbidden to resent this fact, one can still convey publicly, "I hurt!"

For those who have love and money, suffering spinsters can be a nuisance. In novels about quests for meaning and fulfillment, they maintain a subversive presence, reminding readers of all the people obstructed from living satisfying lives. Charlotte and Doris are hardly revolutionaries, and like most people, they are driven by conflicting impulses. Through their half-stifled suffering, they convey that all is not well in the fictional worlds they inhabit, or in the cultures that inspired them.[24]

Notes

1. Sianne Ngai has pointed out the metaphoric quality of the term "irritable," which compares phenomena that bother a person emotionally to those that irritate the skin (Ngai 184).

2. Jeffrey Heath has observed that Forster's narrator "slides like a chameleon" into Lucy's mind (Heath 419).

3. Paraphrasing an argument of James McConkey in *The Novels of E. M. Forster*, Tarir Rahman calls Forster's water references in *A Room with a View* "an expanding symbol" that "develops in significance at every occurrence" (Rahman 56).

4. Jeffrey Heath notes that Forster called Dante's *Divine Comedy* one of his three "great books" and asserts that, "It is through Dante . . . that we reach to the heart of Forster's world view" (Heath 414–15). Judith Scherer Herz points out that Forster was "reading Dante while writing" *A Room with a View* and that in November 1908 he gave "a lecture on Dante at the Working Men's College" (Herz 146).

5. Judith Scherer Herz believes that Forster's reference to "a love more mysterious" describes "the strange, unconscious impulse that led Charlotte Bartlett to allow for the fateful conversation with Mr. Emerson" (Herz 146).

6. Jeffrey Heath comments on Forster's water imagery and its relation to Charlotte, who "heats her bath water in a boiler, and has her water cut off by the plumbers" (Heath 407).

7. Lynne Walhout Hinojosa, who associates Charlotte with medieval (a code word for Victorian) ways of thinking, believes that Charlotte has a "deep self" (Hinojosa 91). Richard Keller Simon, who calls Charlotte a "villain," later reflects that in *A Room with a View*, "there are really no villains" (Simon 211).

8. Lynne Walhout Hinojosa lists the many coincidences in which Charlotte plays a role and reflects, "It might be an aging spinster who has the power to direct history . . ." (Hinojosa 91).

9. Tony Brown describes the influence of gay activist Edward Carpenter on Forster (Brown 279). A. A. Markley offers a detailed reading of *A Room with a View* as a camouflaged homosexual love story (Markley 268-69).

10. Some critics find Charlotte oppressive as well. Richard Keller Simon calls her "boorish," "prudish," and "unlikeable" and labels her a "laughter-hater," and a "villain" (Simon 203, 211, 218).

11. Jeffrey Heath comments on Charlotte's attraction to the Leaning Tower, writing that "she carries [it], with its tilted and winding interior, like an emblem of her psyche" (Heath 423). Charlotte's control of the miniature tower replica also suggests that she wants to keep any threatening phallus well in hand.

12. Jeffrey Heath notes that Charlotte "flattens George's menacing question mark . . ." (Heath 397).

13. Tony Brown writes that "some of [Charlotte Bartlett's] more irritating characteristics seem to have been derived from Forster's mother" (Brown 285). Judith Scherer Herz believes that Lily Forster was "an improbable combination of Charlotte Bartlett and Mrs. Honeychurch" (Herz 139).

14. The published novel, *A Room with a View* (1908), represents Forster's third draft. The first ("Old Lucy") and the second ("New Lucy") were set aside while Forster wrote *Where Angels Fear to Tread* (1905) and *The Longest Journey* (1907) (Brown 285; Herz 139–40). Richard Keller Simon calls Forster's first three related novels "a carefully structured set of variations on a common theme" (Simon 199).

15. Woolf describes this evening in her diary entry of August 31, 1928.

16. Jane Goldman writes that Forster's "warm, constructive appreciation of Woolf is tempered by abhorrence of her feminism, which he finds to disfigure her writing" (Goldman 122). Woolf thought Forster's writing was "flawed" because readers could distinguish its realistic from its symbolic aspects (Goldman 130).

17. In a passionate defense of Woolf and her character Doris Kilman, Elizabeth Primamore writes that "Kilman's presence is a constant reminder of the unfairness of the social system" (Primamore 129). Primamore challenges John Carey, who charges Woolf with classism and offers her apparently negative portrait of Miss Kilman as evidence. Primamore emphasizes Kilman's virtues but does not discuss the humor and irony with which Woolf depicts her. Primamore is right, however, that through Kilman's presence, Woolf reminds readers of social injustice. This complex character is fully human in her angry, ugly response to unfairness.

18. Clarissa does not think of Doris's smell directly, but of the scent of tar associated with Elizabeth's dog, Grizzle. Clarissa's thoughts continue, "Still, better poor Grizzle than Miss Kilman; better distemper and tar and all the rest of it than sitting mewed in a stuffy bedroom with a prayer book!" (Woolf 11).

19. Reginald Abbott writes that in the commodity culture of London, Doris's inability to buy fashionable clothes "reinforces her social nonstatus" (Abbott 207). Woolf may have enjoyed the irony of setting Doris's key scene in a department store.

20. Karen L. Levenback proposes that Woolf "used as a model for Doris Kilman the situation and appearance of Louise Matthaei without endowing Miss Kilman with her passivity" (Levenback 4).

21. Molly Hoff has traced some figures from classical mythology that may have contributed to Doris Kilman. These include "the Lemnian women" (punished by Aphrodite by being permeated with a bad smell), "the centaur Chiron" (a tutor), and "the gorgon Medusa," whom people cannot stand to see (Hoff 149).

22. Kenneth Moon illustrates the many ways in which Doris Kilman mirrors Clarissa Dalloway, reminding Clarissa of the desires she has repressed (Moon 278).

23. Elizabeth Primamore reads Doris Kilman as "a representation of humanity, in all its awkwardness, trying to find a place in a world" (Primamore 135–36).

24. Elizabeth Primamore writes that "Kilman's presence is a constant reminder of the unfairness of the social system" (Primamore 129).

CHAPTER 5 | Making Suffering Visible

> When the world offers one no options, there is suffering. . . . We are hurt,
> and want everyone to know it.
>
> —PAT SANBORN

ASSERTING ONE'S IDENTITY THROUGH suffering requires witnesses, but not all witnesses have equal value. Most satisfying are those who have caused one's pain, at least, according to one's own view. If people can't assert themselves any other way, forcing more privileged people to see their suffering can console their wounded selfhood. Metaphorically, attempts to show pain may appeal to any sense, but the fiercest efforts focus on vision. The sighs, scents, and fingerings of Charlotte Bartlett and Doris Kilman communicate their frustration subtly. The three angry male characters examined in this chapter act more aggressively to show that their humanity has been denied.

This chapter spans the historical periods 1864 to 1925 and 1995 to 2015 because the tendency to manifest pain visually occurs in both. In a century and a half, the urge evolves, however, as the concept and the stakes of vision change.[1] Fyodor Dostoevsky's *Notes from the Underground* (1864), Franz Kafka's *The Metamorphosis* (1915), and Michael Haneke's film *Caché* (2005) all present frustrated characters who appear when unwanted and use their bodies, sometimes in extreme ways, to remind others of their suffering. The central metaphors of these works share some features: the existence of unseen spaces from which socially unappreciated people watch those more privileged; and the insistent emergence of excluded people to show that they are humans, not vermin. These works vary in the perspectives they offer and in the power they associate with visualization. Dostoevsky's and Kafka's novellas present the viewpoints of rejected men in ironic but sympathetic ways. Haneke's film comes from the perspective of a privileged man who feels menaced by a marginalized one he has wronged. In Dostoevsky's tale, visualization involves crashing a dinner party; in Kafka's, crawling out from under a sofa. In Haneke's story of twenty-first century media, the stakes are much higher because the visual recordings used in the characters' fight for power could potentially be seen by the whole world. All three of these works engage the world in the sense that they represent one unhappy person's emotions in a way applicable to many more. Through its metaphors, Dostoevsky's story brings to mind Russian serfdom; Kafka's, anti-Semitism; and Haneke's, European colonialism and its legacy. Metaphorically, each work represents socially discouraged emotions in a way that reaches beyond its own story.

Through metaphors that appeal strongly to vision, Dostoevsky, Kafka, and Haneke created characters that confront people who look away from pain. The greater their denial, the more insistent and violent these manifestations become. The metaphors for these characters' emotions may begin with traditional dirt and darkness, but they do not end there. These wounded men venture out into the daylight so that people enjoying a brighter life have to see their suffering—and know that they are being watched.

The Underground

Small and angry, Dostoevsky's Underground Man is one of literature's most lovable, awful characters. Dostoevsky constructed *Notes from the Underground* so that readers encounter the Underground Man's dank philosophy in Part I, then learn (in Part II) of the actions that made him the man he is. In a work that conveys the value of emotion and compassion, this structural choice has profound effects.[2] After forming an initial response, readers may alter their judgments of the protagonist—perhaps for the worse—when they learn the context of his life. Sixteen years earlier, when the incidents of Part II occurred, a craving for contact led the Underground Man to seek a former classmate and invite himself to a dinner for Zverkov, a schoolmate he despises. There he gets drunk and annoys the guests, but they won't take his insults seriously. When he follows his classmates to a brothel, he comes closer than ever in his life to a reciprocal human encounter. Drawn to Liza, a prostitute, he harangues her and tries to break her emotionally so that she will leave her degrading life. When Liza comes to see him, he breaks down himself, but rather than forming a bond with her, he rejects her by offering her money. Since this emotional exchange with Liza, whom he never saw again, the Underground Man has withdrawn into his metaphorical hole (Anderson 414). As a forty-year-old retired civil servant, he is now seeking attention in other ways.

As the protagonist and first-person narrator, the Underground Man doesn't speak for Dostoevsky, but his persona emerged from pain in his creator's life. If Part I of *Notes from the Underground* occurs in 1864, when the novella was published, then the incidents with Zverkov and Liza happened in 1848, during a year of revolutions across Europe. In that year, Dostoevsky joined the meetings of the socialist, Western-looking Petrashevsky Circle (Frank 222). A year later, he was arrested for his political activities, traumatized by a mock execution, and sent to a Siberian work camp. Together, Dostoevsky's imprisonment and forced military service took ten years of his life (Katz 93).

Dostoevsky risked his life to fight injustice because in 1848, most Russians were living in slavery. His hatred of serfdom comes through in Zverkov's bragging about the two hundred souls he has inherited: "not a single girl in his village would escape his attention . . . and . . . if the peasants even dared protest, he'd have them all flogged . . ." (Dostoevsky, *Notes* 42–43).[3] The Underground Man detests Zverkov for good reason. In 1848, the Underground Man's feeling of invisibility was shared by most people in tsarist Russia.

In a letter to his brother Mikhail, Dostoevsky wrote that he "conceived of [*Notes from the Underground*] during my years of imprisonment, lying on a bunk bed, at a painful moment of grief and disintegration."[4] Ten years of physical and psychological abuse had worn away his belief in rationality and inborn human goodness (Fortin 234). Travels to England and France in 1862 had alarmed him because the poverty he saw there seemed caused by the Western belief in an autonomous, self-seeking individual (Lunt 491). Dostoevsky doubted that Russian social problems could be solved with European philosophies, and he worried about intellectuals who uncritically embraced them (Frank 206).[5] In the spring of 1864, Dostoevsky wrote *Notes from the Underground* in a "race against death" as his wife Marya and his brother Mikhail were dying (Astell 187). "Yesterday Marya Dmitrievna suffered a decisive attack," he wrote to Mikhail. "Blood gushed from her throat, and began to flood into her chest and suffocate her."[6] Emotionally, Dostoevsky wrote under agonizing conditions, but he promised his brother that his new work would be, "a powerful and candid piece; it will be the truth."[7] *Notes from the Underground* emerged from physical torment and despair, and its representation of emotions has visceral sources.

As a conflicted character, the Underground Man seizes so much attention that readers may miss Dostoevsky's satirical aims (Frank 207). His complex portrait created with irony and humor offers a nightmarish response to N. G. Chernyshevsky's *What Is to Be Done?* (1863), a utopian novel that promoted science and reason as solutions to Russian social problems (Frank 204). Dostoevsky hoped that *Notes from the Underground* would offer Russians a "'new' path" strikingly different from Chernyshevsky's vapid utopia (Jackson 182). The socialist visionary had claimed that once people learned what works to their best advantage (i.e., making sacrifices for others), they would act rationally, in their own best interest. As a fully realized, tormented human being, the Underground Man shows the naïveté of Chernyshevsky's claim (Frank 215). The epigraph to Part II of *Notes from the Underground*, taken from a poem by N. A. Nekrasov, offers a cliché of the 1840s: the narrative of a young man "saving" a prostitute. Dostoevsky's quashing of the poem with "Etc., etc., etc." shows that he thought it was drivel. Like the Underground Man's lecture to Liza, it consists of language divorced from complex emotion (Frank 223–24). In contrast, both the Underground Man's spite and Liza's empathy—despite his abuse of her—are messily, palpitatingly human.

Through *Notes from the Underground*, Dostoevsky hoped to convey how rarely people *do* act in their own best interest, although they remain capable of impulsive kindness and love. Rejecting the Western notion of autonomous selfhood, Dostoevsky wrote in *Winter Notes on Summer Impressions* that "voluntary, completely self-conscious, and totally unconstrained sacrifice of one's entire self for the good of everyone is . . . a sign of the highest development of individuality."[8] Censors deleted his passages on "the necessity of faith and Christ," so that his representation of human complexity had to rely on his characters' actions.[9] Maybe because the Underground Man isn't a role model, he is oddly appealing to many readers. His self-pity, spite, and self-loathing feel familiar and real, as do his contradictions. Under different circumstances, he might act less cruelly and loathe himself less . . . or he might not. In an "underground" note, down below the main text, Dostoevsky claimed that his character "not only may, but actually must exist in our society" (Dostoevsky, *Notes* 3). Probably the author wrote this note with a sad half-smile, and with the utmost irony.

As the central metaphor of Dostoevsky's work, the underground suggests the protagonist's social and emotional state. The Russian word in the title, "podpol'ya," means literally "under the ground" or "under the floor," as in a dark cellar.[10] To some degree, Dostoevsky's underground draws on Dante's classic metaphor of angry souls bubbling alone in fetid mud. But the ironic "Notes" scratched by this spiteful soul create more complex relationships among dirt, darkness, isolation, and the emotions they supposedly represent. Dostoevsky's protagonist loves and hates the underground, the self-created space where he chooses to live. When the incidents of Part II occurred, this hidden darkness was already developing within him. He suspects that even then, when he engaged alone in petty vices, he was "carrying around the underground in [his] soul" (Dostoevsky, *Notes* 33). In Part I, this metaphorical underground of Part II has become literal, physical, and entrapping. Like the sinners in Dante's *Inferno*, the Underground Man is corporeally experiencing in an "afterlife" what his soul once enacted in the world.

As a metaphoric source, the underground offers a dark spectrum of qualities for the Underground Man to map onto the target, his life. As Max Black indicates, creative metaphors make meaning by selectively aligning aspects of the source and target so that both can be understood in new ways (Black, "Metaphor" 291–92). Characterizing himself as an underground creature lets the Underground Man define himself defiantly and ironically. As George Lakoff and Zoltán Kövecses have shown, metaphors can make meaning through systems of entailments, in which certain qualities of the sources and targets align and begin to dance (Lakoff and Johnson 96; Kövecses, *Metaphor and Emotion* 148). As a source of meaning, Dostoevsky's underground offers much more than a dark and dirty space.

Dostoevsky broadens his metaphor's possibilities by never specifying what the underground represents. As a fiction writer, he accomplishes more by inviting readers to *feel* the underground and imagine its range of meanings. "Podpol'ya" may offer a way of conveying all the humiliations and failures of the protagonist's life.[11] Even during the time of Part II, he recognized the underground as an essential part of his being. He describes his first indulgences in "petty vice" (probably visits to other women like Liza) as sinking into "dark, subterranean, loathsome depravity" (Dostoevsky, *Notes* 33). His harangue to Liza involves two descriptions of dark cellars that show his affinity with the prostitute. Both he and Liza are trapped, and his emotional attack on her mirrors his tormenting of himself. He begins by describing a coffin carried "up from an underground cellar" and ends by placing Liza in this space: "they'll shove you into the filthiest corner of the cellar—into darkness and dampness; lying there alone, what will you think about then?" (Dostoevsky, *Notes* 61, 70). The Underground Man could be talking to himself, which—given his lack of awareness of other people—he probably is. When he rejects the chance to form a human bond with Liza, he moves into this dark space for good. In the moment when he might have reached out to her, he thinks, "I wanted to remain alone in my underground" (Dostoevsky, *Notes* 86). The tragedy of his life is that he has received his wish.

Besides offering dank, gloomy shelter, the underground hosts a realm of lowly creatures. Dostoevsky makes creative use of this metaphorical entailment by having his Underground Man identify with vermin because he is sure people see him as subhuman. His emotions emerge from his body, and no doubt, his small size plays a role. He describes himself as a tiny test-tube man who "honestly considers himself not as a person, but a mouse" (Dostoevsky, *Notes* 8). This dusky little mouse lives in a hole and feels unable to avenge itself against larger creatures. Most of the time, the Underground Man compares himself to even simpler organisms. He describes his apartment as "my shell, my case," suggesting that he is a mollusk or an insect (Dostoevsky, *Notes* 77). He assures his listeners that he "couldn't . . . become an insect," although he "wished to become an insect many times" (Dostoevsky, *Notes* 5). He implies that he can't be as "low" as people treat him, but whether he projects his low self-esteem onto others or internalizes their disgust, he sees himself as verminous. At the dinner celebration, Zverkov examines the Underground Man "as if [he] were an insect," mirroring the Underground Man's assessment of Zverkov as "a little insect" (Dostoevsky, *Notes* 52, 43). The Underground Man thinks people see him as a fly, a creature that moves through the air but settles on unclean surfaces. He feels humiliated that he is "a fly in the eyes of society, a disgusting, obscene fly" (Dostoevsky, *Notes* 36). The Underground Man's schoolmates pay as little attention to him as if he were "some sort of ordinary house fly" (Dostoevsky, *Notes* 42). As entailments of the underground, the despised creatures to which he compares himself offer an intriguing range of metaphoric qualities. The vermin loathed by humans live close to their larger neighbors, out of sight and eager for human droppings. The Underground Man claims to despise the humans above ground, but he also lives off of them. For years, he has been "listening to all [their] words through a crack" (Dostoevsky, *Notes* 27). Through these metaphoric entailments, *Notes from the Underground* reminds readers that from behind walls and under floorboards, unwanted creatures are watching and listening to people who wish that they weren't there.

The Underground Man feels toward his metaphoric home everything that he feels toward his emotional life. His descriptions of his living space and his way of inhabiting it apply equally to his consciousness. The hypothetical test-tube man who buries himself alive in a "disgusting, stinking underground" is one of his representations of himself (Dostoevsky, *Notes* 8). The Underground Man lives in a "nasty, squalid" room "on the outskirts of town" with a spiteful, foul-smelling female servant, who would probably characterize him the same way (Dostoevsky, *Notes* 5). As the only literate inhabitant of this space, he exerts narrative control, which might be compromised if he interacted with others.[12] Aware of what he has gained and lost, he celebrates and loathes the underground. Within the space of one paragraph, he writes, "Long live the underground!" and "To hell with the underground!" (Dostoevsky, *Notes* 26). To preserve some autonomy and human dignity, he has tried to withdraw from people who won't respect his humanity as he defines it.

As a metaphor for his emotions, the "underground" suggests why he can't fulfill his desires, and it illustrates his response to that failure. He can't get what he wants because he lives underground, and he stays there because he can't ful-fill his wishes. Typically, he expresses his aims negatively, so that readers learn about him by hearing what he doesn't like. He can't stand living as an "organ stop," a mechanical part worked by another person's hand (Dostoevsky, *Notes* 17). He needs to show that he has his own will—that he can think and initiate actions. When people treat him as an object, their actions confirm his fears that he is just a thing controlled by nature.[13] His former schoolmates regard him as "insignificant" and as a "nonentity" (Dostoevsky, *Notes* 43). Zverkov claims that the Underground Man can't insult him, because the thoughts of a nonentity don't matter. The emotions he develops toward confident people have the same aim as his humiliating behavior: he wants to prove to them and to himself that he exists as a human being.[14]

Perhaps for this reason, the Underground Man's narrative focuses on insults he has received and his emotional responses to them. All his life, he has been "the first to be blamed for everything," but he claims always to have been "the innocent victim" (Dostoevsky, *Notes* 7). In an ironic passage, he describes an acutely conscious mouse, a creature that "almost always feels of-fended" (Dostoevsky, *Notes* 8). The Underground Man is describing himself, of course, and Dostoevsky, who had called an earlier 1861 novel *The Insulted and the Injured*, had been thinking about the emotions of injured people for some time.[15] The Underground Man is aware of his sensitivity and even tells Liza he is ashamed of it. "It's as if the skin's been stripped away from my body," he confesses, "so that even wafts of air cause pain" (Dostoevsky, *Notes* 83). In this description, he sounds as vulnerable as Doris Kilman, who compares herself to "a wheel without a tire" (Woolf, *Mrs. Dalloway* 127). Life has hurt the Underground Man, and he describes his emotional pain through metaphors of bodily anguish.

The Underground Man's mix of emotions suggests his humanity, not just to readers but to himself. Almost every claim he makes about his feelings, he later contradicts. Looking back on his bullying lecture to Liza, he thinks, "artifice goes along so easily with feeling" (Dostoevsky, *Notes* 64). Once the Underground Man builds narrative momentum, he rides his emotional logic, regardless of the direction it is taking. For readers, not just the reversals, but the time scale of his emotions, may be striking. Recalling an officer who shoved him aside, he writes, "I stared at him with malice and hatred, and continued to do so for several years!" (Dostoevsky, *Notes* 35). Rather than fading with time, his emotions appear to gain strength. To prove that he exists, the Underground Man writes about his feelings to reinforce and develop them.

Through his emotions, the Underground Man tries to assert the humanity his injurers have denied. When he describes himself, "spite" is the word he most often uses. "I am a spiteful man," he declares in the opening line (Dostoevsky, *Notes* 3). To show that he is not a passive victim, he garners and nourishes memories of small insults and plans miniscule retaliations. A few paragraphs into the story, he tells readers that he has lied: he is not spiteful or embittered, but he has "lied out of spite" (Dostoevsky, *Notes* 4). Impulses heave in him that are anything but spiteful, but he refuses to acknowledge them. His ensuing narrative only complicates this first knot of contradictions.

The inward spirals of this loner's thoughts hold a reader's attention with their recursive quality. More compelling than the Underground Man's reports of spite are his feelings about the way he feels. In a "self-pitying but strongly critical tone," he examines himself relentlessly (Sanborn 207). Most often, he expresses shame about his feelings—much more than about his actions. He is "shamefully aware" that spite and bitterness form only a part of his inner being (Dostoevsky, *Notes* 4). Tellingly, his feelings of shame often coincide with his feelings of superiority (Anderson 423). Another metaphorical entailment of the underground is dirt, itself a classic metaphoric source for self-pity. "In the dirt I consoled myself knowing that at other times I was a hero," reflects the Underground Man, "and that the hero covered himself with dirt; . . . an ordinary man would be ashamed to wallow in filth, but a hero is too noble to become defiled; consequently, he can wallow" (Dostoevsky, *Notes* 39). In his inner turbulence, he feels both proud and ashamed to wallow in his emotions.

To show that he is more than an object, the Underground Man hurts himself emotionally and socially. To act against one's own interest, he argues against Chernyshevsky, is quintessentially human, which one can prove only by behaving in unpredictable ways. His determination to show his agency applies equally to his inner and outer worlds. He feels trapped in natural and social systems to whose laws he knows he is subject, and he struggles to oppose them to prove that he is human. His desires emerge most clearly in the story's emotional climax, when he tells Liza, "They won't let me . . . I can't be . . . good!" ("Mne ne dayut . . . Ya ne mogu byt . . . dobrym!") (Dostoevsky, *Notes* 84; Russian qtd. in Fortin 237). His formulation, with its shift from compulsion to agency, reveals the quandary in which he lives. He wants to be "good" on his own terms, to live up to the ideals he has forged. At the same time, he wants to be "good" in a social sense and have his goodness recognized by others. People won't let him be good because their notions of goodness differ from his. He is left with only his emotions to prove his humanity, but his need to be perceived is so strong, he forces himself on people anyway.

One of his chief motives, as a writer and a submerged person, is to make people aware of his pain. In less subtle ways than Charlotte Bartlett, he hurts or humiliates himself, then manifests the results to prove that he exists. As the Underground Man reveals himself, he and his readers discover the pleasure he finds in his pain. He gnaws at himself until "the bitterness turn[s] into some kind of shameful, accursed sweetness," which he calls "the pleasure . . . from the overly acute consciousness of one's own humiliation" (Dostoevsky, *Notes* 6). As the Underground Man paces drunkenly at Zverkov's dinner, he thinks with pleasure of how he'll treasure the memory of this indignity. After intense pain, burying oneself in the underground to savor it can lead to a "strange enjoyment" (Dostoevsky, *Notes* 9). The pleasure may come from knowing one is soothing oneself, taking control by becoming one's own witness.

Dostoevsky's novella suggests, however, that greater delights lie in forcing others to perceive one's pain. The Underground Man claims that even toothaches can be enjoyable because it is humiliating to succumb to natural laws. The pleasure of a toothache comes not from hurting but from producing moans for days and nights on end. The sufferer knows that her moans are useless, but she thinks, "You won't sleep; you too must be aware at all times that I have a toothache" (Dostoevsky, *Notes* 11). Broadcasting one's pain to all who can hear it can feel immensely satisfying. In Russian, two families of words can represent pleasure: "slad," denoting sweetness; and "vol," meaning the freedom to act at will (Sanborn 202). In the previous passages, Dostoevsky uses variations on "slad," implying a cloying sweetness (Sanborn 205–06). The Underground Man may never have learned what true pleasure and freedom are.

Broadcasting one's pain requires an audience, and the central contradiction of the Underground Man's life may be his simultaneous need for and rejection of people. His descriptions of his schoolmates make it easy to believe that he detested them and was despised in turn. His hatred often involves anticipation: he hates others because he is sure they will loathe him—and he is often right. Because he was different, his schoolmates treated him with "spiteful and pitiless jibes," and he responded by withdrawing into "wounded and excessive pride" (Dostoevsky, *Notes* 46). *Notes from the Underground* offers no reference point outside the Underground Man's mind, but within his narrative, his classmates' actions support his characterization of them as shallow, materialistic, and mean. It would be wrong to say that he envies them, especially their charismatic leader, Zverkov. Since school, they have acquired wealth and social skills that he lacks, but as in many people accused of envy, he doesn't want to *be* like more privileged men. He wants to have the opportunities that these less intelligent, less sensitive people have unfairly been given.

With real human beings, the Underground Man lacks the control he maintains in his narratives, so that he is "numbed by paralysis" (Dostoevsky, *Notes* 41). As an office worker, he despised his colleagues but also feared them and saw them as superior. The same mix of hate and intimidation marked his feelings toward his self-righteous servant, Apollon, whom he couldn't seem to fire. Unable to relate to the hostile aliens around him, he thinks, "I'm alone, and they are *everyone*" (Dostoevsky, *Notes* 31, original emphasis).

Since no one seems to notice his humanity, the Underground Man tries to assert it himself. He does so not just by recalling his slights but by avenging himself against those who have slighted him. With a pungent mix of shame and glee, he describes his responses to people who have insulted him. No one knows better than he does how ineffectual his revenge plots are. "I couldn't be revenged on anyone for anything," he explains, "because, most likely, I would never have decided to do anything, even if I could have" (Dostoevsky, *Notes* 7). Out of a sense of loyalty to himself, the Underground Man refuses to forgive. If someone insults him and he just accepts it, how can he value himself? Yet his perceptive, analytical consciousness prevents him from taking action.

In only one case, the funniest in the story, does he avenge himself against an evil-doer. One night on a walk, the Underground Man sees a bar patron thrown out a window and envies him—probably because the man is getting so much attention. When the Underground Man enters the bar, an officer moves him aside as if he were an object. Outraged, he recalls how the officer "took hold of me by the shoulders and without a word of warning or explanation, moved me from where I was standing to another place . . ." (Dostoevsky, *Notes* 33–34). The officer shifts him just as a musician's hand might pull an organ stop. The officer causes offense by "entirely failing to notice me," by ignoring the Underground Man's consciousness, his sentience, his feelings (Dostoevsky, *Notes* 34). Rather than protesting on the spot, the Underground Man withdraws spitefully and spends years planning his revenge. He fantasizes about a duel, then about a passionate friendship, until he finds a solution that feels right: he will bump the officer on Nevsky Prospect, shoulder to shoulder, as an equal. The Underground Man splurges on a new beaver collar so that he'll look like a peer, and after one aborted attempt, he jolts the offender. The officer pretends not to notice—and probably doesn't—but for a little while, the Underground Man feels triumphant. He has "publicly placed [him]self on an equal social footing with him" and proved that he is no object (Dostoevsky, *Notes* 38). Soon afterward, he feels nauseated because he knows that the expensive bump has accomplished nothing. His anger and resentment stem not just from class inequities. His vengeful urges come from his desire to be recognized as a unique person, and he stays underground, unsatisfied.

Dark, dirty, and crawling with vermin, the emotional underground offers protection at a price. It brings secure shelter, since few people would want to invade it, but it makes its denizens invisible. It grants the Underground Man the autonomy he craves without satisfying his desire to be seen and heard. Like many people, he longs to talk about his pain and probably to be comforted. He seeks a compromise by recording his emotions in a safe place, but his narrative anticipates readers. Originally, Dostoevsky called his novella *A Confession*, and a confession needs a listener (Bakhtin 146; Fortin 234).[16] Dostoevsky may have changed his title because calling his work *Notes from the Underground* opens new degrees of freedom for understanding the character and his purposes. Rather than a confession, the Underground Man's narrative comes across as a disastrous, chaotic lecture. He writes to analyze his emotions, but just as his narrative troubles notions of confession, it parodies the lecture genre. His motives show themselves most clearly in his denials, of which his confessional lecture is full. He doesn't want forgiveness; he isn't ashamed; he isn't trying to justify himself; he doesn't need any readers; and he won't grovel for attention—but attention is what he most desires. Simultaneously, he seeks autonomy and recognition.[17] His quandary is how to control his life and still find witnesses to affirm it.

On a conscious level, the Underground Man has trouble understanding his attraction to other people. In his metaphors to explain his attachment, he sounds like the mechanical part he is trying not to be: "I'd already latched on and wouldn't let go" (Dostoevsky, *Notes* 44). His reliance on other people to establish his identity comes through most clearly in his writing. His *Notes* anticipate listeners' reactions to such an extent, they are more a dialogue than a monologue (Bakhtin 146). One could say that the Underground Man writes as he lives, claiming not to care what others think, but letting expected responses shape his thoughts. His attitude toward himself depends greatly on other people's attitudes toward him (Bakhtin 150). Through this mesh of interwoven thoughts run his tough fibers of self-assertion. In his efforts to be perceived, the Underground Man aims "to annoy the other person" (Bakhtin 151). If others won't let him be good, and he has only pain and spite to prove his humanity, then they will have to listen to him moan.[18] His toothache will keep the whole world awake. If no one will acknowledge his feelings or his will, then they must see and hear his pain.

The Vermin

Notes from the Underground may be about becoming visible, but Dostoevsky reveals little about the Underground Man's looks other than his shabby clothes and small size. The brooding man keeps mainly to the underground, and the St. Petersburg residents seem glad of this. The Underground Man is a voice, a mind, whose appearance the reader must construct from the character's self-perceptions and other people's responses. Kafka's *Metamorphosis*, on the other hand, is all about Gregor Samsa's visual appearance and its effect on others. From the first sentence when Gregor awakens "transformed . . . into a gigantic insect" ("zu einem ungeheuren Ungeziefer verwandelt"), readers will want to know what he looks like, perhaps even more than what he thinks (Kafka, *Metamorphosis* 67; *Verwandlung* 6).[19]

Critical interpretations of Kafka's story have often focused on what Gregor's transformation "means." Is his metamorphosis into a monstrous vermin a metaphor, and the tale an allegory, or should the story be taken at face value? With its rich irony and humor, Kafka's novella works on both literal and metaphorical levels.[20] *The Metamorphosis* may not convey anything more than the instability of all things and their tendency to turn into something else. The practical, matter-of-fact tone that makes the story so funny supports literal readings by emphasizing details. As a giant bug, Gregor is more worried about how to get out of bed and get to work than about how his transformation will affect him long-term. He narrates like a person in shock, attending to small, material matters rather than the big issue of his transformed body. Among the critics who have warned against facile allegorical readings of Kafka's works are Vladimir Nabokov, Walter Benjamin, and Theodor Adorno.[21] Kafka's descriptively rich *Metamorphosis* can be read literally, and Gregor's transformation need not work overtime as a metaphorical source.

Despite Kafka's attention to material details, he rejected any complete visual depiction of his protagonist. His third-person narration offers mainly Gregor's perspective, and, like most people, Gregor perceives himself one part at a time, usually the part that hurts most.[22] No one who sees Gregor offers a full, systematic description, and he never looks in a mirror. Readers have to assemble him piece by piece based on the visual and tactile information Kafka provides. On October 25, 1915, Kafka begged his publisher, Kurt Wolff, not to include a picture of Gregor on the title page: "Not that, please, not that! . . . The insect itself cannot be drawn. It can't even be shown from a distance" (Kafka, *Briefe* 2: 145, my trans.).[23] As a result, readers must enlist their own memories to read Kafka's text, and they see the vermin that they create. By withholding a complete visual representation of Gregor, Kafka opened the way for metaphorical readings.

By his own account, Kafka struggled with metaphors, although he admired those that resonated. On December 6, 1921, he wrote in his diary, "Metaphors are one thing among many that drive me to desperation in writing" (Kafka, *Tagebücher* 3: 196, my trans.).[24] It troubled him that writing didn't "live in itself" and always referred to something else (Kafka, *Tagebücher* 3: 197, my trans.).[25] Metaphors increased this distance by adding another level of referral. At the same time, Kafka respected intelligently constructed figures. Reportedly, he told Johannes Urzidil:

> To be a poet means to be strong in metaphors. The greatest poets were always the most metaphorical ones. They were those who recognized the deep mutual concern, yes, even the identity of things between which nobody noticed the slightest connection before. It is the range and the scope of the metaphor which make one a poet. (Urzidil 22)

If Kafka found it challenging to create good metaphors, it was probably because he rejected hackneyed or misaligned comparisons.

Gregor's transformation may represent something beyond itself, and some readers have no doubt that his metamorphosis is a "magnificent metaphor" (Leadbeater 169).[26] If the changes in Gregor point toward a meaning beyond themselves, what is their metaphorical target? I see this target as near rather than far: Gregor's transformation corporeally manifests *the way things already are*. Gregor has no control over his metamorphosis, but in a way, it fulfills a wish. Gregor's human desires have always inconvenienced his family, and his new appearance forces them to confront what they don't want to see. Gregor has turned into a huge, hideous inconvenience from which they cannot look away. The metaphor, if there is one, works visually and involves a resonance between the way Gregor looks and the way he feels.[27] Having been seen as a bug, Gregor has become what people have perceived in order to reflect their perceptions back at them.[28] Like the Underground Man, Gregor wants to reveal his humanity because he is being treated like a bug.

Kafka's story suggests that Gregor has been living as a vermin for some time. He feels injured and insulted because no one is recognizing his life's value. Since his father's business collapsed five years ago, the family has lived on Gregor's labor, and his job dehumanizes him. He mentions "old debts" that his parents owe his employer, for whom he works as a traveling salesman (Kafka, *Metamorphosis* 76). He expects it will take him five or six years to pay these debts, since he is supporting his family while saving money. Kafka's third-person narrative from Gregor's point of view conveys his conflicting feelings about his work. On the one hand, Gregor earnestly wants to help his family. His aging father no longer seems fit to work; his mother suffers from asthma; and his sister is seventeen. His family has been accustomed to a high standard of living, and Gregor feels "great pride in the fact that he had been able to provide such a life for his parents and sister in such a fine flat" (Kafka, *Metamorphosis* 89). Despite their reduced circumstances, they employ a cook and a serving girl and seem used to being waited on. For years Gregor has been supporting the family, and all of them, Gregor included, have "simply got used to it" (Kafka, *Metamorphosis* 95).

On the other hand, Gregor has become completely fed up with this state of things. Mentally and physically, he is being turned into a bug by his exhausting work. Kafka conveys Gregor's longing to be human partly through his desire to move freely. As a textile salesman, he travels busily about, but rather than directing his own moves, he flies back and forth like an organ stop pulled by a musician's hand. He rises at 4 AM and at night "throw[s] himself down, tired out, on damp bedding" in small hotels (Kafka, *Metamorphosis* 111). When he has the luxury of sleeping at home, he reads railway timetables or busies himself with a jigsaw doing fine, insect-like carpentry. "If I didn't have to hold [myself back] because of my parents," he admits, "I'd have given notice long ago" (Kafka, *Metamorphosis* 68–69).[29] Gregor can regain his humanity only if he asserts himself and makes those around him acknowledge his needs.

Intimidated and conflicted, however, he suppresses his anger and drudges on. His authoritarian father maintains control of the household finances, despite his own failure at business. In the mornings when Gregor goes off to work, the old man lies "wearily sunk in bed" (Kafka, *Metamorphosis* 108). His father then lingers for hours over breakfast, reading the newspapers that affirm his authority. In the afternoon, he reads the paper "in a loud voice" to his wife and poses as the disseminator of knowledge (Kafka, *Metamorphosis* 88). Gregor, too, reads newspapers at night, but he can't wrest his father's hold on power.

Just as Dostoevsky's suffering affected his portrayal of the Underground Man's emotions, Kafka's own feelings toward his parents helped him to mold Gregor's. Kafka had little trouble portraying a son who became an image of the way he was treated, then showed himself to his oppressors.[30] "I have always experienced my parents as persecutors," he wrote to his friend Felice Bauer in November 1912. "All parents want to do is drag one down to them, into the old times out of which one wants to rise up and breathe" (Kafka, *Briefe* 1: 253, my trans.).[31] As in *The Metamorphosis*, Kafka represents emotional oppression through physical oppression. Parents restrict one's movements by pulling one down when one is trying to rise, and squeezing one when one is struggling to breathe. In these metaphors, Kafka draws on the Western tradition that associates brooding with restricted motion and self-assertion with free movement. In *The Metamorphosis*, Gregor's confinement in a vermin-body conveys his emotional entrapment, somewhat as the mud does Dante's hell and Bunyan's bog.

To represent Gregor's complex emotions, Kafka relies on two supporting metaphors. First, Gregor dreams of quitting his job when he has paid his parents' debts, vowing, "I'll cut myself completely loose then" ("Dann wird der grosse Schnitt gemacht") (Kafka, *Metamorphosis* 69; *Verwandlung* 10). He fantasizes about cutting himself free as though he were tethered to a post. In German, Kafka shows Gregor's internal bondage by casting his sentence in the passive voice. Literally, he boasts to readers, "then the great cut will be made"— but he does not say how or by whom. "Making the great cut" reinforces the metaphorical link between bondage and chronic anger developed since the days of Dante.

Kafka's second metaphor for Gregor's emerging emotions comes from his sister: "Gregor's broken loose" ("Gregor ist ausgebrochen") (Kafka, *Metamorphosis* 107; *Verwandlung* 80). In the scene in which she exclaims this, Gregor has broken out literally and figuratively, as though rupturing the walls of a confining cell. As an emotion metaphor, "breaking loose" brings to mind the liquid-in-a-container pattern identified by Zoltán Kövecses (Kövecses, *Emotion Concepts* 144–48). When Gregor's mother and sister try to remove his furniture, he exerts his will by showing himself. Rather than hiding, he crawls agitatedly about, making himself horribly visible. Although he isn't happy, he has achieved the real aim of his vermin life. More than anything else, Gregor wants to be *seen* in every sense.

As a literary creator, Kafka wants his readers not just to visualize Gregor but to share every sensation he feels. He aims to put readers into Gregor's body, and his ingenious strategies for doing so affect the way his story makes meaning. Kafka's writing almost begs readers to simulate life as a bug.[32] He tries to make readers see through Gregor's low-lying eyes, revealing, for instance, that Gregor is, "dumbfounded at the enormous size of his [father's] shoe soles" (Kafka, *Metamorphosis* 108). Yet vision alone doesn't suffice to describe the world from a vermin's perspective. Gregor is also shocked by his new voice, which has "a persistent horrible twittering squeak behind it like an undertone" and which no one but he can understand (Kafka, *Metamorphosis* 70). Because Gregor's vision and hearing remain largely human, Kafka takes greater pains describing Gregor's less familiar visceral and tactile sensations. A full meal swells him so that "he was so cramped he could hardly breathe. Slight attacks of breathlessness afflicted him and his eyes were starting a little out of his head" (Kafka, *Metamorphosis* 92). This description seems designed to make readers recall the sensation of being stuffed. After Gregor has been battered for revealing himself the first time, he takes inventory of his strange, hurting body: "His left side felt like one single long, unpleasantly tense scar, and he had actually to limp on his two rows of legs. One little leg, moreover, had been severely damaged . . . and trailed uselessly behind him" (Kafka, *Metamorphosis* 88). This is the closest Gregor comes to taking stock of himself, since he never studies a visual reflection. Kafka forbade his publisher to show Gregor for a reason: his story is about what it *feels like* to be Gregor.

Kafka devotes such fierce energy to describing Gregor's body because readers won't understand Gregor's emotions unless they can imagine life under a vermin's shell. The linchpin of Kafka's central metaphor is *feeling*, which applies equally to emotions and bodily sensations. To place readers in Gregor's vermin body, Kafka calls attention to Gregor's least familiar parts. Most of all, he writes about his legs, whose movements horrify Gregor at first because he can't consciously control them. "His numerous legs . . . [wave] helplessly before his eyes," until he has to shut them "to keep from seeing his struggling legs . . ." (Kafka, *Metamorphosis* 67–68). Kafka doesn't specify how many legs Gregor has because the transformed man doesn't know himself. He relies on visual rather than proprioceptive feedback, since he can't interpret what his new legs are telling him. Bewildered, he can only watch "his little legs struggling against each other more wildly than ever" (Kafka, *Metamorphosis* 72). The mismatch between his mind and body is tragic, and it seems to have a long history.

Gregor's memories indicate that like his creator, he has never felt good in his body.[33] Kafka suffered from insomnia, and he often wrote at night. In a diary entry of October 2, 1911, he describes awakening "as if I had stuck my head into a wrong hole," and he remembers awakening from a night of deep sleep "as if I were locked inside a nut" (Kafka, *Tagebücher* 1: 42, my trans.).[34] The latter sensation suggests Gregor's unpleasant discovery on awakening from "uneasy dreams" (Kafka, *Metamorphosis* 67). Inside his new body, as in his emotions, he feels horribly ill at ease. Also like Kafka, who died of tuberculosis at forty, Gregor has lungs that have "not been very dependable," and many of his visceral descriptions involve breathing or breathlessness (Kafka, *Metamorphosis* 109).[35] His body feels itchy, awkward, and strange, and readers may sense that his shame of it predates his transformation. When Gregor "scuttle[s] under the sofa, where he [feels] comfortable at once," he re-enacts a move he has been making for years (Kafka, *Metamorphosis* 90). Whereas he used to conceal his emotions and longings, he now tries to hide his body.

As Gregor learns how to use his new body, the reader learns with him. Because his main means of discovery is pain, the reader shares his wounds and aches. When Gregor bumps his bed, "the stinging pain he felt informed him that precisely this lower part of his body was . . . probably the most sensitive" (Kafka, *Metamorphosis* 72). Kafka devotes much of Part I to Gregor's bodily experiments, many of which cause damage. Gregor hits his head when he falls out of bed and "rub[s] it on the carpet in pain and irritation" (Kafka, *Metamorphosis* 75). The worst pain he experiences comes from an attack, and Kafka calls on readers to suffer it with him. As the apple hurled by Gregor's father sticks in his back, "Gregor wanted to drag himself forward, as if this startling, incredible pain could be left behind him; but he felt as if nailed to the spot and flattened himself out in a complete derangement of all his senses" (Kafka, *Metamorphosis* 109–10). In this moment of annihilating pain, Kafka helps readers to feel Gregor's shock by describing what his body is doing. Kafka's depiction invites active responses in which readers can consult their own memories of pain.

In Gregor's transformed body, many of his thoughts involve food, and his hunger suggests all his unfulfilled longings. His sister takes over his feeding, since his parents have never wanted to know about his desires, emotional or physical: "not that they would have wanted him to starve, of course, but perhaps they could not have borne to know more about his feeding . . ." (Kafka, *Metamorphosis* 92). As a bug, Gregor hides this literal hunger just as he has suppressed his other desires. He hopes desperately that his sister will bring him some food, but "he would rather starve than draw her attention to the fact, although he felt a wild impulse to dart out from under the sofa, throw himself at her feet and beg her for something to eat" (Kafka, *Metamorphosis* 91). In moments, Gregor's emotions burst forth as he demands that his human needs be fulfilled.[36] As his sister's attentions wane, he is "filled with rage at the way they were neglecting him, and . . . he would make plans for getting into the larder to take the food that was after all his due . . ." (Kafka, *Metamorphosis* 114). In his verminous body, his suppressed rage over his hunger becomes easier to see.

Not all of Gregor's bodily experiences bring pain, and learning about his new self also creates pleasure. He feels "physical comfort" and "joy" when his legs find "firm ground" and are "completely obedient" (Kafka, *Metamorphosis* 84). Gregor likes to hang from the ceiling, where the sensation of being surrounded by air suggests the freedom he seeks. Kafka's story is so tragic in part because just as Gregor is learning to appreciate his body, it fails.

In readers who have entered Gregor's body, its deterioration may evoke anguish. Kafka deftly shows its decline without Gregor's full awareness of what is happening. After his father pierces his back with the apple, Gregor "creep[s] across his room like an old invalid" (Kafka, *Metamorphosis* 110). Frustrated by the charwoman who calls him a dung-beetle, he "[runs] at her, as if to attack her, although slowly and feebly enough" (Kafka, *Metamorphosis* 116). When he withdraws for the last time and is "amazed at the distance separating him from his room . . . ," some readers may cry (Kafka, *Metamorphosis* 126). Gregor's death is devastating because Kafka has worked to make readers' identification with him visceral, emotional, and total.[37]

Kafka leads readers to Gregor's emotions through his sensations because simply reporting his emotions wouldn't work. Describing a character's inner world in an abstract way rarely promotes identification, especially when the character is locked in conflict. Much as Gregor longs to "break loose" and thrive as a human being, he has internalized people's low opinions of him and is eager to redeem himself by being "good." Seeing himself as a vermin, inside and out, has shaped his perception of the world around him. Gregor's new body corresponds to his inner life in that it may offer a hidden means of escape, accessible to instincts he hardly knows he has. If he is a beetle, he has wings folded under his shell, but he doesn't know how to use them (Durantaye 323). Instead, Gregor restricts his movements, so fully has he internalized his father's rule. He crouches by his door to show his father "that his son had the good intention of getting back into his room immediately and that it was not necessary to drive him there . . ." (Kafka, *Metamorphosis* 107). Gregor's most vermin-like feature may well be his fear.

Opposing this sense of learned worthlessness is Gregor's need to form human bonds. For years he has hungered to be free to form relationships outside his family group. With his constant travel, he has been able to make only "casual acquaintances that are always new and never become intimate friends" (Kafka, *Metamorphosis* 68). His references to young women are poignant and sad: "a chambermaid in one of the rural hotels, a sweet and fleeting memory, a cashier in a milliner's shop, whom he had wooed earnestly but too slowly" (Kafka, *Metamorphosis* 114). One senses that Gregor's relationships have come to naught because he believes he is verminous. He has settled for a stand-in of a loving woman, a framed magazine ad of a pretty girl in fur. The picture sparks one of his most human responses when he literally sticks to it to prevent its removal from his room. Only after he has turned into an insect does he begin to fight for his humanity.

Like the Underground Man, Gregor wants to be human and to be "good," but on his own terms. His desires to form relationships and to suppress himself clash, and their combination gives him psychological depth. On the one hand, Gregor feels attracted to other people, above all to his family. It relieves him to know they've sent for a locksmith to open his door, since he feels "himself drawn once more into the human circle" (Kafka, *Metamorphosis* 80). When Gregor hears voices, he runs "to the door of the room concerned and press[es] his whole body against it" (Kafka, *Metamorphosis* 93). His visceral loneliness reaches the reader through a shared sense of touch. Gregor values integration into a family as an essential feature of humanity.

On the other hand, Gregor has become so used to hiding his emotions that crushing them has become automatic. His anger pushes up from below in barely perceptible heaves. When Gregor learns that his father has been reserving money from Gregor's earnings, he thinks, "True, he could really have paid off some more of his father's debts to the chief with this extra money, and so brought much nearer the day on which he could quit his job, but doubtless it was better the way his father had arranged it" (Kafka, *Metamorphosis* 96). Not only has his father ensured that Gregor's drudgery will continue; his father has declined to tell him, denying him his most basic rights. Even transformed, Gregor can rebel only in his thoughts. It takes other people to see his subdued aggression, since he often cannot. On one occasion, his sister spies him and jumps back, so that "a stranger might well have thought that he had been lying in wait for her there meaning to bite her" (Kafka, *Metamorphosis* 99). As a hideous creature, Gregor can express his anger simply by showing himself.

Gregor doesn't transform himself by choice, and his *Verwandlung* isn't his idea. As a fantasy, however, his metamorphosis can be read as a protest, even an act of revenge. An unknown force has externalized his feelings, and if he looks like a vermin, it is because he has been forced to regard his emotions that way for most of his life. Gregor's new body screams to everyone who sees it, "Look what you've done to me! See how you're making me feel!" The chief clerk—who has not yet seen Gregor—voices his employee's wish to be seen when he accuses him of "making a disgraceful exhibition of yourself" (Kafka, *Metamorphosis* 77). Both the original German, "mit sonderbaren Launen zu paradieren" (Kafka *Verwandlung* 24, literally, "parading about with strange moods") and the translation convey Gregor's wish to show his rage, his loneliness, his sexuality. Gregor wants to "show himself" to the clerk, and he is "eager to find out what the others . . . would say at the sight of him" (Kafka, *Metamorphosis* 78). His transformation may be a fantasized act of self-exposure driven by an angry will to live.

If *The Metamorphosis* is a fantasy on Gregor's—or Kafka's—part, fear drives it as much as desire. With a certain glee, the story shows what might happen if Gregor revealed himself, along with the frightful consequences. Once Gregor makes his family see him as an emotional, hurting being, they want to remove him from their midst. With his earning power gone and his body broadcasting his feelings, he becomes an unwanted object. "We must try to get rid of it. We've tried to look after it and to put up with it as far as is humanly possible," says his sister, with a telling choice of words (Kafka, *Metamorphosis* 124). It is Gregor's humanity they want to expulse, his emotions, his sexuality, his will. Gregor the hard-working insect is welcome; Gregor the hurting human is not. Just as Gregor has always suspected, once his family knows that he is *not* a bug, they want to kick him out.

Kafka's use of language to show Gregor's predicament suggests relationships extending far beyond the Samsa family. Whether or not Gregor's new status as an "ungeheures Ungeziefer" is metaphorical, Kafka's famous phrase for an angry son links Gregor to the author, his friends, and European Jews in 1915. The double negation ("un-" "Un-") suggests a nonbeing or "something indeterminate" that can't be described in words (S. Ryan 7). Kafka seems to have been thinking about "Ungeziefer" for some time, since in fragments of a story mixed with a diary entry of July 1910 ("To Be Unhappy," later called "The Little Inhabitant of Ruins"), a character describes himself as creeping about underground, "not better than a vermin" ("nicht besser als ein Ungeziefer") (Kafka, *Tagebücher* 1: 21–22).[38] In Kafka's famous, undelivered letter to his father, he describes his father's way of battling him as the "struggle of a vermin that not only stings, but also sucks the blood in order to support its life" (Kafka, *Brief an den Vater* 59, my trans.).[39] Kafka also reproached his father for comparing his friend, the Jewish actor Jizchak Löwy, to an "Ungeziefer" (Kafka, *Brief an den Vater* 13). The vermin metaphor links Kafka's three *Die Söhne* stories, which depict the suffering of demoralized sons (M. P. Ryan 80).[40] Kafka's use of "Ungeziefer" for Gregor ties his protagonist to a greater circle of humiliated, injured people.

Among these were Kafka's fellow Jews, referred to in anti-Semitic writings of Kafka's day as mice, moths, lice, cockroaches, and other vermin—"Ungeziefer der Menschheit" (Gilman 31, 80). Kafka showed his awareness, perhaps even his internalization of these metaphors, when he confided to his friend Max Brod that Jewish writers "wanted to write in German; but with their little hind legs they remained stuck in the Jewishness of their fathers and with their little front legs they were finding no new ground" (qtd. in Sokel 843–44).[41] If Gregor's new appearance represents a wish to show himself, he is revealing his suffering to more people than his father. The anti-Semitism of those who saw Kafka as a vermin doesn't "explain" *The Metamorphosis* any more than Dostoevsky's years in Siberia account for *Notes from the Underground*. But it would be wrong to claim that these works were fully independent of their creators' social contexts, or of the authors' emotional responses to them. These artworks grew from painful ground and arose to develop their own life. With deep irony, these stories depict fictional protests that express themselves visually. What should remain hidden to suit some people's convenience breaks out to expose hideous pain. Each novella depicts a humiliating world from the perspective of a man trying to reveal himself. Visual exhibits of hidden pain carry the greatest force when perceived by those who don't want to see them.

The Cut

Caché differs from *Notes from the Underground* and *The Metamorphosis* by offering the viewpoint of a privileged character challenged by an injured one. All three of these works depict characters communicating their pain by showing it, and all rely to some degree on the Western metaphor that represents knowledge through vision. As a twenty-first century filmmaker, however, Michael Haneke uses strategies unavailable to Kafka and Dostoevsky to subvert the equation of seeing with knowing. While depicting a man who visually demonstrates his pain, *Caché* (which means "hidden") repeatedly shows that one cannot trust what one sees, and that the mass media designed to reveal suffering hide as much as they expose (Celik 70).

Like Dostoevsky's and Kafka's works, Haneke's tale of a fight for visibility can be read literally or metaphorically. As with *Notes from the Underground* and *The Metamorphosis*, it would do *Caché* an injustice to read it *just* allegorically because it is a rich, revealing study of individual minds. But Haneke's film points toward a situation extending beyond his main characters, Georges and Majid. Through the story of these two men, *Caché* suggests a whole population struggling to be seen in a society trying to hide them.

Weeks after the release of *Caché* in October 2005, riots broke out in the suburbs of French cities, where people of African descent live in poverty. Even though *Caché* is set in France, Haneke's film suggests that the conditions shaping these characters' lives extend beyond French borders. The television screen glowing in Georges's apartment offers visual representations of conflicts abroad. When Georges turns on his television, its images of pain don't disturb him; if anything, they provide a soothing narrative (Seshadri 44). Georges's television depicts violence and its aftermath, but the device designed to transmit images around the world presents them in ways that make them invisible (Celik 70). The suffering of the people depicted doesn't register emotionally in the characters. Although widely disseminated in visual forms, people's anguish remains hidden.

Even more than *The Metamorphosis*, Haneke's *Caché* is about vision. Through the way it establishes its point of view, the film leads viewers to identify with Georges Laurent, the host of a television talk show about literature.[42] As a screenwriter and director, Haneke takes measures to ensure that his viewers will see themselves in this Parisian intellectual with a murky past. Haneke describes his film, which brought him the best director prize at Cannes, as "a tale of morality dealing with how one lives with guilt" (Toubiana, qtd. in Celik 59). From the outset, audiences realize that Georges has much to hide, and emotionally, *Caché* may hurt to watch.[43] Haneke's film creates agonizing tension because when confronted with suffering that he doesn't want to see, Georges does everything he can to look away.

Cinematically, Haneke warns the viewer that what one sees can be judged only in context. Georges, his wife Anne, and their twelve-year-old son Pierrot live on the rue des Iris, whose name suggests not the flower but the eye.[44] Haneke's long opening shot, which seems to show a quiet street, may frustrate viewers because nothing is happening (Seshadri 44). Really, a great deal is going on: voices break in, and the image dissolves to reveal that the audience has been watching not an actual street but a video that Georges and Anne are viewing. The tape, which depicts hours of surveillance of their house-front, has been delivered to their door along with a drawing of a boy spitting blood. Georges receives another such picture at work, and Pierrot finds one at school saying, "pour Pierrot, de la part de son Papa" ("for Pierrot, from his Dad") (Haneke 00:19:10).[45] When the doorbell rings during a dinner party at Georges's, the audience may jump. Georges leaves his guests to confront what appears to be a stalker. "Montrez-vous, espèce de lâche! Montrez-vous et dites ce que vous voulez!" ("Show yourself, you coward! Show yourself, and say what you want!"), he yells into the empty street (Haneke 00:25:36). A new tape and drawing have arrived, this one depicting a bloodied rooster. Georges reveals his and Anne's troubles to his guests, saying, "Je n'ai rien à cacher" ("I have nothing to hide") and claiming that the family is "sous surveillance" ("under surveillance") (Haneke 00:28:11–33). An unknown person is watching them and wants to make sure that they know.

In these early scenes, viewers may sympathize with Georges, who feels violated and stalked. Emotionally, Haneke relies on this initial sympathy, which will create conflicts if viewers' feelings toward Georges change. The new tape depicts a rainy drive to a place Georges calls "la maison de mon enfance" ("the house where I grew up") (Haneke 00:29:09). He goes to visit his aging mother, who still lives there, and their tense exchanges reveal a family tradition of concealment and denial. Georges knows very well who probably sent the tapes, but he won't tell his family or the viewers. His mother repeatedly asks him what's wrong, but he answers "rien" ("nothing") (Haneke 00:31:06). Georges enquires about a boy named Majid, whom his mother at first seems not to recall. When pressed, she tells Georges that the matter of Majid is "un mauvais souvenir" ("an unpleasant memory") (Haneke 00:33:36). Haneke then places the viewer in a dream of Georges's, somewhat as the director seated the audience before Georges's video in the first scene. One recognizes the courtyard of Georges's childhood house—but from the perspective of a rooster. When the animal is struck with an axe, viewers may feel the brutal cut. The camera retreats to six-year-old Georges's point of view as he watches the decapitated, bleeding creature toss itself around the courtyard. A dark boy with a bloody face looms up, wielding the fatal axe, and Georges awakens, gasping for breath. If this is Majid, and Majid is watching Georges's family, Georges seems to have good reason to be scared.[46] But the emotional tone of the scene with his mother suggests there is more to the story.

By now viewers may suspect who—besides Haneke—is filming Georges's life, but Georges won't reveal his knowledge. As the audience comes closer to Georges in its awareness, it may withdraw from him emotionally. Once again, Haneke offers a sequence that turns into a videotape viewed by Georges. By this time, viewers may begin to think that *every* new shot is a tape so that they will not be fooled again (Seshadri 45). The new video depicts a long, dark hallway in a vast housing project on Avenue Lenine. Physically, this apartment doesn't lie far from Georges's, but as the street names suggest, aesthetics and politics separate the homes. Georges and Anne fight about whether Georges should go to Avenue Lenine, which she insists is too dangerous. He tells Anne that he suspects who is sending the tapes, and she is furious that he refuses to confide in her. Out of curiosity, viewers may want Georges to go because like Anne, they may be getting frustrated that he will reveal nothing of Majid.

In the first confrontation between Georges and Majid, Haneke establishes the contrast between them visually before their main dialogue begins. The audience already knows Georges's salon, with its modern furniture and walls of books. The printed and recorded texts on Georges's shelves speak of his education, his experiences, his developed mind. Among his books are tapes of his literary show and a television offering the images to which he devotes his life.[47] Georges's living room looks like the set of his show, where a wall of pseudo-books conveys his critical authority (Seshadri 40). Majid's apartment, in contrast, displays his poverty because of what it doesn't hide. Without being dirty or disordered, it is a space of ugly functionality. Two patterns of tacky wallpaper clash behind a cheap, enamel-topped table. Wash hangs in a corner, and shelves contain stacked dishes and cleaning supplies. No doubt Georges owns more expensive versions of these items, but on the rue des Iris, they are out of sight. They are stashed in the kitchen, bathroom, bedroom, or closets where the bourgeois guests and Haneke's camera don't go. Majid's minimal space serves his physical needs; he speaks with Georges in his kitchen because he has no salon. In the twenty-first century, the Underground has become a cubicle in a suburban high-rise built to keep unwanted people out of sight.

In their first encounter since childhood, Majid calls Georges "tu," but Georges initially addresses Majid as "vous."[48] Majid recognizes Georges at once, but Georges reacts more like "the droll dog of a thief who declined to know the constable."[49] Majid is soft-spoken and polite and invites Georges to enter and sit down. Georges, in contrast, acts aggressive and demands to know what the middle-aged French-Algerian man wants. In Georges's dream, Majid dwarfed six-year-old Georges, but Georges the adult stands taller than Majid. Haneke has filmed the scenes between them to show not just how tall these male characters are, but how tall they *feel*. Haneke envisioned their first adult confrontation as a response to media stereotypes of dark radicals bullying white victims (Toubiana, qtd. in Celik 73). In Georges' and Majid's first adult encounter, Georges plays the bully; Majid comes across as a man battered by life, and his soft, weary voice conveys anger as well as resignation. In Majid's claim that he did not expect to see Georges, Majid seems sincere. Viewers have learned, however, that few things in Haneke's film are as they appear to be.[50] Visually, Majid's soft body and miserable home suggest a life in which one dare not express rage. Still, Majid lets Georges know that seeing him on television was "désagréable" ("unpleasant") (Haneke 00:48:30). When Georges recognizes Majid and threatens him, Majid responds with mockery. The aging, impoverished man is unbeaten, and he resists Georges's power by refusing to answer his repeated question, "Qu'est-ce que vous voulez de moi?" ("What do you want from me?") (Haneke 00:46:09). Majid maintains his advantage by letting Georges imagine possible answers—and perhaps realize that he is asking the wrong question. After their meeting, Georges learns that Majid and/or an associate has filmed their confrontation. A video, sent to Anne and to Georges's employer, has recorded Majid's politeness and Georges's threats. It concludes with footage of Majid crying, visually manifesting his suffering to the most important people in Georges's life (Figure 5.1).

At last, Georges is forced to tell Anne and the audience the history of Majid. The French-Algerian boy's parents, who worked for Georges's family, were murdered in the Paris massacre of October 17, 1961. In what may have been the deadliest twentieth-century European "'peacetime' massacre," French police shot fifty to three hundred fifty (the number is still disputed) French-Algerian protesters and threw their bodies into the Seine (Pages 3–4; Penney 77–78). Police Prefect Maurice Papon, who had organized the deportation of Jews from Vichy France, authorized the shooting (Pages 4; Penney 78). Haneke developed the story of Georges and Majid after seeing a documentary on the massacre, which had received no media attention for forty years. "I was totally shocked that I had never heard of this event before," says Haneke, who is Austrian. "[But] I don't want my film to be seen as specifically about a French problem. . . . In every country, there are dark corners—dark stains where questions of collective guilt become important" (Porton 50).[51] Georges can't accept or even fathom the notion of collective guilt. His narrative of the massacre is telegraphic: "Enough said, Papon, the Police Massacre. They drowned 200 Arabs in the Seine, including probably Majid's parents, they never came back" (Haneke 00:51:20–35; qtd. in Pages 11, Pages's translation). This choppy account with sentences stuck end-to-end lacks any analysis of causes (Pages 11).[52] It reveals thinking that admits no reflection on responsibility. Georges tells Anne that his parents adopted Majid because "ils se sentaient responsables" ("they felt responsible") (Haneke 00:58:59). His tone, however, implies that

FIGURE 5.1 Majid (Maurice Bénichou) cries in his kitchen. © Maurice Bénichou in *Hidden* by Michael Haneke. Courtesy of Les Films du Losange. All rights reserved.

such feelings exceeded anything they owed the boy. Anne asks Georges what happened to Majid, who never entered her husband's family. Georges replies that Majid was sent to a hospital, but by now, neither Anne nor the audience is likely to trust him. Guided by Haneke, the film's driving question is shifting from "Who sent the tapes?" to "What is Georges hiding?"

One might say that Georges is wrestling with an unknown challenger to control what is visible and what is not. If the tape sent to his employer were shown in public, it could wreck his career (McGill 148). To protect Georges, the Head of Programming destroyed it, but he wants to know who created it and why. "Pourquoi vous hait-il autant?" ("Why does he hate you so much?") he asks Georges (Haneke 01:04:05). His boss's question cuts deeper than "What do you want?" and Georges tries to deflect it from his thoughts. Instead, he focuses on how to stop Majid from "terrorizing" him and his family. When Pierrot fails to come home one night, Georges presumes that Majid is responsible and arrives at Avenue Lenine with the police. He and the viewer learn that Majid, too, has a son—who is arrested for the undocumented kidnapping along with his father. Pierrot returns home the next morning, having neglected to tell his parents that he was staying with a friend. After a humiliating night, Majid and his son are released from jail. Even without knowing most of the facts, the audience may sense why Majid hates Georges.

As a talk show host and television editor, Georges controls the dissemination of images. He asks his production team to cut comments by a guest because they are "too 'theoretical'" (Ogrodnik 58). He deletes footage revealing that Rimbaud's sister destroyed much of his work but keeps a discussion of Rimbaud's sexuality (Penney 90). Significantly, Georges is summoned during this editing by an insistent phone call from Majid. Hoping for a showdown, Georges returns to Avenue Lenine, where Majid thanks him for coming and claims he didn't know about the tapes. "Je voulais que tu viennes, parce-que je voulais que tu sois présent" ("I wanted you to come, because I wanted you to be present,") he says (Haneke 01:25:02). With a sure, determined gesture, Majid pulls a knife from his pocket and slits his own throat. Blood spurts from the wound and sprays his kitchen wall before he falls to the floor. Majid, not Georges, has orchestrated the film's most powerful image. His suicide is "one of the most shocking scenes in the history of cinema" (Seshadri 46).

Haneke calls Majid's cut "the most important shot of the film . . . [a] *terribly realist* shot" (de Baecque 18, qtd. in Celik 60, Celik's trans. and emphasis). As the writer and director, Haneke sees the slash as "a desperate act of self-destruction" but also "an act of aggression directed towards Georges" (Porton 51). If Majid really knew nothing of the tapes, then maybe Georges's re-entry into his life after forty years has simply hurt too much. If Majid did know about them, which is more likely, his cut is an aggressive visual act. By killing himself in front of Georges, he visually proclaims, "You want me to disappear? Well, then you're going to have to watch it happen." Rather than an extreme form of withdrawal, Majid's suicide works as "an explosive accusation" directed not just at Georges but at any viewer who has sympathized with him (Celik 60).

Majid has done to himself what many in his society would like to do to him, but they have to witness the messy process. Majid stages his death as a "performance" that unsuspecting viewers are forced to watch (Pages 18). After years of pain, he externalizes the emotions he has hidden so that the person most responsible for them will have to see them. In his death, Majid comes across not as a "guilty terrorist" but as a "wronged person" (Ogrodnik 59).

Georges's response mirrors the audience's in one key respect, for after stumbling dazedly about, he "goes to the movies" (Pages 15).[53] A distant shot shows him leaving a multiplex cinema, where he has spent two hours trying not to think about Majid. When Georges returns home to Anne, he finally reveals what may have motivated Majid to send the tapes. When Georges was six, he didn't want a new Algerian brother, so he told his parents that Majid was spitting blood. This first plan failed because a doctor found Majid healthy, but Georges lied again, telling Majid that his father wanted a rooster killed (McGill 141). The murder of the cock got Majid evicted because it made the boy look dangerous.[54] In 1961, Majid was taken to an orphanage, and neither Georges nor the viewer knows what he has experienced during the past four decades. Even as a six-year-old, Georges was manipulating visual images to his advantage (Gavarini 196).

Maybe from Georges, Majid has learned how to use imagery to create lasting impressions. Unlike Gregor, he has made the "great cut," and his act influences the minds of the people around him.[55] Georges continues to deny and withdraw, but Majid's son confronts Georges at work. As in the first scene with Georges and Majid, Haneke's shots emphasize the men's differences in height. Whereas Georges stood taller than Majid, his son seems to tower over Georges. The visual impression suggests Georges' emotions: Majid's son scares him, and initially, Georges refuses to speak with him. Instead he withdraws behind barriers (an elevator door, a glass partition) that he hopes the son won't dare cross, but which he repeatedly does. In contrast to Majid, the young man is assertive and demanding. He won't be put off and threatens to go to the press. George finally agrees to speak with him in a bathroom, a space that often conceals sex and violence as well as human waste. With his tense body exuding anger, Majid's son accuses Georges of denying his father a good upbringing. In an orphanage, he says, "on apprend la haine. On n'apprend pas la politesse" ("one learns hate. One doesn't learn politeness") (Haneke 01:40:25). Possibly Majid's son is referring to his own life because viewers know nothing of his mother or his childhood. His hate and Georges's resound off the bathroom walls, whereas Majid is the politest character in the film. The young man denies that he sent the tapes, but Georges doesn't believe him. He warns that there will be consequences if Majid's son keeps terrorizing his family, but the young man mocks, "Menacer, ça vous savez faire" ("Making threats, you know how to do that") (Haneke 01:41:14). From his father, Majid, he seems to have learned how to rattle people who hold power. The young man refuses to name anything he wants. His aim is more to assert himself through his presence. Georges asks him if he wants "que je vous demande pardon" ("for me to apologize to you"). The son responds angrily, "A qui? A moi?" ("To whom? To me?") (Haneke 01:41:21). To Majid's son, Georges's question is absurd. The one who deserves an apology is lying dead with his throat cut.

Emotionally, Majid's son succeeds in his aim. Viewers are likely to suspect that there will be consequences, and that the story of Majid has not ended. Literally and metaphorically, the encounter has given Georges a headache, and the film's final sequence begins with Georges taking a sleeping pill, drawing his drapes, and going to bed. But Majid lives on in Georges's numbed mind as Haneke takes viewers into his dream. Spurred by the encounter with Majid's son, Georges and the viewer witness the crucial turning point in Majid's life. Set in Georges's parents' courtyard, the dream sequence mirrors the earlier one with the rooster (Pages 10). Perhaps from the perspective of six-year-old Georges, the viewer watches from a distance like a remote director. A green car pulls up, and officials seize Majid, who struggles and breaks away. They recapture him, force him into the car, and drive off. Possibly the distance between Georges and Majid in this shot conveys his emotional separation from his "brother" (Gavarini 203–04). Until Georges began to receive the tapes, he never saw Majid again, and Majid's invisibility has made it easy not to think of him. The French-Algerian man and his son have made sure that Georges and the audience will "see" Majid for the rest of their lives.

Viewers of Haneke's film cannot fail to notice the recurrence of the title word, "caché." It arises even in "hidden" forms: for instance, the sleeping pill that Georges takes is known as a "cachet" (Pages 17; Penney 81). In the confrontation with Majid's son, Georges insists, "Je n'ai rien à cacher" ("I have nothing to hide") (Haneke 01:38:44). Here he combines "cacher" with a word fewer critics have noticed, but which riddles Haneke's screenplay like a punctuation mark: "rien" ("nothing"). "Rien" is one of the first words the viewer hears as Georges and Anne try to guess where the surveillance camera lies. Georges tells his mother "rien" when she asks him what's wrong, and Majid answers "rien" when Georges demands to know what the French-Algerian man wants. Pierrot tells his mother "rien" when he returns home, showing how the word is being passed between generations. This word of negation runs through the film, creating glints of affinity among its diverse scenes.

If one could express Majid's goal in a single phrase, it is not to be "rien." He and his son want to be valued as thinking, feeling human beings in a society trying to represent them as nothing. Metaphorically, their desire to be seen conveys their greater demand to be acknowledged. If they created and sent the drawings and tapes, the first step in their strategy is to use visual images to make Georges *see* the consequences of his act.[56] It is arguable whether a six-year-old can be blamed for displacing an unwanted new brother. Probably, at some time, most children of six would be thrilled to see their siblings removed from the house. The question is how to deal with the consequences forty years later, how to seek justice and make amends. As a start, the unknown filmmaker wants to remind Georges and the audience of events that have become invisible. If Majid is the artist, he is using visual images to make his point rather than the verbal language of which Georges is master (Gavarini 195). The videos, drawings, and suicide are visual accusations calling attention to a hidden crime (Seshadri 37).

As a second tactic, the unknown filmmaker wants to assert himself as a force to be reckoned with. Through visual imagery, he sends the message, "I am watching you. I know what you did; I know where you live; and you can't escape me." In the hands of Majid, his son, or an associate, the camera so often used to represent French-Algerians as terrorists reveals the abuses of those more privileged.[57] Through the videos, the filmmaker controls Georges's moves, since he invariably goes to the places they depict (Celik 71).

But the unknown media artist wants to do more than frighten and control Georges. His third and most significant aim is to change the way that Georges and the viewers think about what happened in 1961 and its consequences in 2005. The filmmakers—Haneke and his fictional cameraman—would like to change the question that is being asked. "What do you want?" demands Georges over and over. Majid and his son refuse to answer because no individual act, no payment or apology, can compensate for what they have lost. George's supervisor comes nearer the mark when he asks, "Why does he hate you so much?" Unlike Georges's question, this one demands an inquiry into what happened. It considers not just events but emotions, whose force Georges has underestimated. From the filmmaker's perspective, the best questions to ask might be, "What happened, and what are we going to do about it?" Robbed of his parents and raised in an orphanage, Majid grew up without the senses of memory and history so vital for the formation of self (Gavarini 198–99). If Majid values his emotions and manifests his pain, it is because they are all he has to prove he is alive. Recognition of his suffering would mean recognition of his humanity.[58]

In the film's final shot, a distant view of Pierrot's school, Haneke offers viewers an ambiguous encounter. Majid's son approaches Pierrot as he emerges, greets him, and touches him in an insistent but friendly way. Watching from the perspective of a distant stalker, the viewer realizes that Majid's story has not ended. Nothing has been resolved, and the tension remains unrelieved. The conflict has been passed to a new generation, who will make of it what they will. Some viewers may read the ending as menacing, with Majid's son "going after" Georges's. The shot can also be read optimistically, as a representation of dialogue and cooperation among younger people (Celik 77; Dobrogoszcz 237). Possibly, in the interest of these goals, the two sons collaborated to make the tapes (McGill 149). On literal and metaphorical levels, Haneke leaves his film open. Majid has sprayed out his emotions, and the viewer must decide what to do with them.

Aggressive Visualizations

Notes from the Underground, *The Metamorphosis*, and *Caché* tell tales of necessary and unwanted emergence. Whether this emergence of people and emotions is desirable depends on one's perspective. Dostoevsky and Kafka offer the points of view of two men whose emotions some people don't want to see. Filmmaker Haneke presents the perspective of a privileged, reluctant viewer, so that his audiences are led to think of all the people and emotions they might rather not confront.

To tell these men's stories, Dostoevsky, Kafka, and Haneke rely on metaphors grounded in common bodily experiences. In this way, readers are cued to imagine the characters' sensations and emotions. With his concept of the underground, Dostoevsky develops Dante's association of spite with darkness and dirt. Dostoevsky's *podpol'ya* is a foul, hidden place populated by verminous life. By depicting Gregor as an *ungeheures Ungeziefer* (a monstrous vermin), Kafka conveys the constrictive feeling of long-term anger mixed with fear. If readers can simulate Gregor's sensations as a bug, then they can imagine his emotions. Gregor Samsa dreams of making a "great cut," inviting readers to imagine the bonds holding him like ropes. Haneke's Majid literally makes this slash, although his suicide is more an act of violence than of liberation. Driving each story is a metaphor harder to spot, perhaps because of its familiarity: *Notes from the Underground*, *The Metamorphosis*, and *Caché* all represent the desire to be known emotionally through the desire to be seen.

This metaphor, too, has a bodily grounding, but it reveals the ways that cultural assumptions enter understandings of emotions. The conflicted desires of the Underground Man, Gregor, and Majid to reveal and conceal themselves— and the anger they encounter when they "break loose"—show the social forces ready to slam unhappy people who speak out. In their ironic depictions of ordinary sufferers, Dostoevsky, Kafka, and Haneke seem aware of the metaphorical systems associating chronic anger with darkness, dirt, and bondage, systems that make many marginalized people ashamed to speak. The authors and filmmaker create art by depicting three characters that cultural mandates have failed to silence. Because of these works' narrative structures, the Underground Man and Gregor may arouse sympathy, whereas Majid remains largely unknown. All three characters challenge the rule that miserable people should stay hidden and keep their emotions to themselves.

When asked about Majid's suicide, Haneke tells a disturbing tale. An acquaintance who saw *Caché* told Haneke about "a story that he had heard": "A man who had left his wife was asked by her to meet him at a subway station. They met and, while he was there, she threw herself under a subway car before his eyes" (Porton 51). Haneke continues, "I think that's an interesting comment on my film" (Porton 51). One cannot know whether this third-hand urban legend is true, or how much it may have changed in the retelling. What matters is the shared perception of relevance. Both Haneke and the unnamed viewer saw this staged death as similar to Majid's. Majid's cut is not just a self-destructive but an aggressive act.

In *The Causes of Suicide* (1930), sociologist Maurice Halbwachs wrote that someone planning his or her death may aim "to terrify and torture his survivors, to crush them beneath the weight of remorse, to project on to them clearly the responsibility for his death" (Halbwachs 300; qtd. in Celik 76). Majid and the woman who summoned a witness to her death might describe their situations differently. One knows nothing of Majid's life since 1961, or of this woman's life with her husband. But their determination to act out their emotional pain speaks of its degree and of the witness's involvement. When a system leaves one no other way to prove one is alive, one can publicly manifest one's pain. A violent cut between life and death hurls that pain into the eyes of those who may have caused it.

Notes

1. I thank the anonymous reviewer of this manuscript who pointed out that " 'visibility' seems to increase over time."

2. Roger B. Anderson argues that the philosophy of Part I of *Notes from the Underground* can only be understood in the context of Part II. Only through the relationship between the parts can the work be appreciated as "an artistic whole" (Anderson 413).

3. Anderson points out that ironically, the Underground Man's fantasies about women are not so different from Zverkov's (Anderson 422).

4. Dostoevsky, *Polnoe sobranie sochinenii v tridtsati tomakh*, vol. 28, 9 Oct. 1859, in Dostoevsky, *Notes from the Underground*, trans. Michael R. Katz, 93, Katz's translation.

5. Rene E. Fortin claims that Dostoevsky's "overt intention" in *Notes from the Underground* was "to excoriate a Russian society whoring after the strange gods of modernity" (Fortin 225).

6. Dostoevsky, *Polnoe sobranie sochinenii v tridtsati tomakh*, vol. 28, 15 April, 1864, in Dostoevsky, *Notes from the Underground*, trans. Michael R. Katz, 96, Katz's translation. After Mikhail's death, Dostoevsky wrote to his brother Andrey, "It is as though my life were broken into two. For a long time those two people [Marya and Mikhail] had constituted everything in my life," Dostoevsky, *Complete Letters*, 2: 125, qtd. in Astell, 192.

7. Dostoevsky, *Polnoe sobranie sochinenii v tridtsati tomakh*, vol. 28, 9 April, 1864, in Dostoevsky, *Notes from the Underground*, trans. Michael R. Katz, 95, Katz's translation.

8. Dostoevsky, *Polnoe sobranie sochinenii v tridtsati tomakh*, trans. Michael R. Katz as *Winter Notes on Summer Impressions*, 5: 79–80, in Dostoevsky, *Notes from the Underground*, trans. Michael R. Katz, 98–99.

9. Dostoevsky, *Polnoe sobranie sochinenii v tridtsati tomakh*, vol. 28, Letter of 26 March, 1864, in Dostoevsky, *Notes from the Underground*, trans. Michael R. Katz, 94, Katz's translation.

10. I am grateful to Hilmar Preuss and to the Russian Instructor Frau Heinze at the University of Halle for helping me to understand Dostoevsky's choice of words in Russian.

11. Ann Astell proposes that the underground "symbolizes" not just the main character's past but also Dostoevsky's, "the past that the novelist will bury, along with his wife Marya and his brother Mikhail" (Astell 191). Astell cites René Girard's claim that after 1864, Dostoevsky's writing took on powerful new qualities (Astell 192).

12. Roger B. Anderson writes that the Underground Man "serves as his own warden in the underground prison he himself fashioned at an earlier age" (Anderson 430).

13. Joseph Frank calls the Underground Man's response to determinism "a *total* human reaction" and "the revolt of the personality against a world in which free will . . . has no further reason for being" (Frank 212, 218, original emphasis).

14. Joseph Frank describes the Underground Man's behavior as "the negative revolt of egoism to affirm its existence" and reflects, "the ego thus asserts its independence and autonomy, whatever the price it must pay in indignity . . ." (Frank 235, 228). According to Frank, Dostoevsky regarded this kind of egoism as stunted and wrong-headed, since true self-realization involved a willingness to sacrifice oneself for others (Frank 234–35).

15. Mikhail Bakhtin finds that the Underground Man's "thought is developed and structured as *the thought of someone personally insulted by the world order*" (Bakhtin 155, original emphasis).

16. Mikhail Bakhtin points out how greatly the Underground Man fears that readers will think he is asking forgiveness or offering himself up for judgment (Bakhtin 148). Rene Fortin believes that Dostoevsky is synthesizing Augustine's and Rousseau's approaches to confession, the latter of which the Underground Man deprecatingly mentions (Fortin 225). Whereas Augustine wrote to repent and reveal his former sins, Rousseau wrote to show how the world had corrupted him (Fortin 228–29). Dostoevsky was highly critical of Rousseau's ideas, which he associated with Russian intellectuals of the 1840s (Fortin 234).

17. Roger B. Anderson draws on classic psychoanalytic works to argue that the Underground Man is an emotional adolescent. Anderson points out that teenagers use diaries to establish their autonomy, and that their narratives often include episodes depicting them as heroes or victims (Anderson 418). Like the Underground Man, the adolescent "tries to write himself into being. . . . As long as he writes scripts he retains a hold on his own autonomy" (Anderson 428).

18. J. A. Jackson believes that *Notes from the Underground* continues Dostoevsky's efforts in *The Insulted and the Injured* and *The Idiot* to depict an "egoism of suffering," an emotional pattern in which "one suffers not on behalf of or for another but so that the other person will suffer even more because of one's suffering" (Jackson 181).

19. "Insect" is too specific a word for "Ungeziefer," which can mean any kind of vermin. A closer translation of Kafka's key phrase "ungeheuren Ungeziefer" would be "monstrous vermin."

20. Patrick Colm Hogan points out that literal and metaphorical readings of the story need not necessarily be opposed, since "the narrative representation of a

metaphor may involve some degree of literalization of the metaphor" (Hogan, *How Authors' Minds Make Stories* 136).

21. Leland de la Durantaye reports that Vladimir Nabokov warned "against symbolic (or allegorical) readings of the story" (Durantaye 324). Durantaye later cites Walter Benjamin, who thought that Kafka's parables "are never exhausted by what is explainable," and Theodor Adorno, who found that Kafka's parables resist interpretation (Durantaye 328, 329). Durantaye points out, however, that Nabokov offered just such an allegorical reading of *The Metamorphosis* when he claimed that Gregor represents an ingenious artist surrounded by mediocre, uncomprehending people (Durantaye 325).

22. Rebecca Schuman has observed that "Gregor's literal body is possible for the reader to picture only in bits and pieces" (Schuman 26).

23. The German reads, "Das nicht, bitte das nicht! . . . Das Insekt selbst kann nicht gezeichnet werden. Es kann aber nicht einmal von der Ferne gezeigt werden." Leland de la Durantaye, Robert F. Fleissner, and Simon Ryan all comment on Kafka's prohibition against including a drawing of the vermin (Durantaye 323, Fleissner 225, S. Ryan 16).

24. The German reads, "Die Metaphern sind eines in dem Vielen, was mich am Schreiben verzweifeln lässt."

25. The German reads, "wohnt nicht in sich selbst."

26. Critics try to acknowledge both the literal and metaphorical levels of meaning in Kafka's story. Rebecca Schuman calls the novella a "literal-metaphorical narrative" (Schuman 20). Patrick Colm Hogan finds that "the guiding metaphor in the story is not only explicit, but obtrusive"; but he argues that this central metaphor draws on cognitive models of insect behavior, illness (especially degenerative mental illness), and infancy (Hogan, *How Authors' Minds Make Stories* 135, 131–33).

27. Sheila Dickson reads *The Metamorphosis* as a study of anorexia and comments, "[Gregor] is an *Ungeziefer* when he wakes up that morning because that is how he thinks of himself and particularly of his body" (Dickson 179).

28. According to Patrick Colm Hogan, Gregor suffers from a "sense that other people, even the members of his own family, find him disgusting." In Hogan's cognitive study of how Kafka created *The Metamorphosis*, Hogan argues that the "fundamental sense of other people's disgust is probably what activated the (explicit) model of the insect initially. Kafka then chose to partially literalize the model" (Hogan, *How Authors' Minds Make Stories* 130).

29. I have altered the translation here ("hold myself back") because the Muirs' translation, "hold my hand," does not convey the sense of the original, "mich . . . zurückhielte" (Kafka, *Verwandlung* 8).

30. *The Metamorphosis* is one of three short works that Kafka called *Die Söhne*, since all three depict mistreated, banished sons. The other two in this group are "Der Heizer" and "Das Urteil." Michael P. Ryan points out the relevance of Kafka's own relationships with his parents to the feelings of the sons depicted in these stories (M. P. Ryan 73–74).

31. The German reads, "Ich habe die Eltern immer als Verfolger gefühlt . . . Nichts wollen die Eltern als einen zu sich hinunterziehn, in die alten Zeiten, aus denen man aufatmend aufsteigen möchte."

32. Patrick Colm Hogan defines simulation as "our ordinary cognitive process of following out counterfactual or hypothetical trajectories of actions and events in imagination" (Hogan, *How Authors' Minds Make Stories* xiii). Simulation works by activating relevant sensory memories and other mental patterns while people are reading literature, just as it does when they are negotiating life. Hogan joins critics such as Elaine Scarry in arguing that literature offers "instructions for simulation" and that "we experience some sort of pleasure in simulation as such" (Hogan, *What Literature Teaches Us* 23, 29).

33. Simon Ryan reports that "few writers have agonized as much about the body as Kafka. Few writers have entered so self-consciously into the act of writing as a means of constructing the image of the writer's body" (S. Ryan 5).

34. The German reads, "als hätte ich den Kopf in ein falsches Loch gelegt" and "als wäre ich in einer Nuss eingesperrt gewesen."

35. Simon Ryan concurs with Sander Gilman's argument in *Franz Kafka: The Jewish Patient*, that Kafka "lived as if predestined for the illness to which he finally fell victim" (S. Ryan 10).

36. Sheila Dickson believes that ironically, Gregor seems most human in the moments when anger takes control of him and he hates his family (Dickson 179).

37. Critics disagree sharply about how to read the end of Kafka's tale. Patrick Colm Hogan argues that structurally, *The Metamorphosis* relies on twin "sacrificial narratives," but he mentions nothing uplifting about the ending (Hogan, *How Authors' Minds Make Stories* 132). Lewis Leadbeater finds that Gregor's death revitalizes the Samsa family, allowing them to "emerge into the new life of springtime" (Leadbeater 177). Vladimir Nabokov has the opposite impression. In a marginal note in his personal copy, he wrote, "the parasites have fattened themselves on Gregor" (Nabokov 282). I agree with Nabokov that the ending is chilling, not inspiring.

38. The story fragments show a marked similarity to Dostoevsky's *Notes from the Underground*, since the character addresses someone above ground and refers to his own space as "hier unten" ("down here"). Kafka's character tells the person above ground, "hier unten geht es uns schlecht, ja es geht uns sogar hundsmiserabel" ("we're doing badly down here, we're as miserable as dogs"). My translation.

39. The original German reads, "[der] Kampf des Ungeziefers, welches nicht nur sticht, sondern gleich auch zu seiner Lebenserhaltung das Blut saugt."

40. Michael P. Ryan observes that in the first story of *Die Söhne*, "Der Heizer," a servant chases the protagonist Karl across the room "as though he were hunting a vermin" ("als jage er ein Ungeziefer") (qtd. in M. P. Ryan 80, my trans.).

41. Sokel quotes Kafka, *Briefe 1902–1924*, 336–37, Sokel's translation.

42. Several critics have noted that Haneke's film offers viewers the world from Georges's point of view. James Penney believes Georges serves as a "bourgeois intellectual everyman" and a "personification of liberal middle-class guilt" (Penney 79). Neil Christian Pages writes that Georges "functions as a stand-in for the rest of us," "us" meaning an upper-middle-class art-house audience (Pages 3). Ipek A. Celik observes that in the film's crucial scene, Haneke "situates the spectator and the protagonist side by side" (Celik 60).

43. Jehanne-Marie Gavarini writes that Georges's lies are "almost unbearable to watch" (Gavarini 200).

44. Several critics have noticed the name of Georges's street, "rue des Iris," revealed by a sign that is easy to miss (Dobrogoszcz 230; Penney 81).

45. Except where otherwise indicated, all translations of the dialogue of *Caché* are my own.

46. Interpreters of *Caché* have pointed out the symbolism of Majid's beheading of the Gallic cock. Ipek A. Celik describes the likely emotional effect in France of seeing "the national symbol of the rooster associated with blood . . ." (Celik 68). Tomasz Dobrogoszcz writes that when "Majid cuts off the head of the Gallic rooster," he becomes an "embodiment of the Algerian threat to France" (Dobrogoszcz 236).

47. A number of critics have commented on Georges's collection and display of his taped shows (Gavarini 193; McGill 141). Jehanne-Marie Gavarini notes how Haneke uses the Laurents' television as "a background to their daily activities" (Gavarini 194).

48. Jehanne-Marie Gavarini points out that by addressing Majid as "vous," Georges "signifies that he has completely forgotten Majid" (Gavarini 202).

49. In George Eliot's *Middlemarch*, the shady character Raffles tells the self-righteous banker Bulstrode, who built his fortune on a swindle, that Bulstrode reminds him of "a droll dog of a thief who declined to know the constable" (Eliot 329).

50. Ipek A. Celik writes that Haneke "makes the image a suspect" (Celik 74).

51. Richard Porton's "Collective Guilt and Individual Responsibility: An Interview with Michael Haneke," appeared in the film journal *Cineaste*, https://www.cineaste.com.

52. James Penney observes, "The casually dismissive tone of Georges' remark signals that no further thought in this connection is required" (Penney 80).

53. Neil Christian Pages points out Haneke's self-reflective allusion to film and calls Georges's retreat to a multiplex "psychopharmaceutical solace" (Pages 15–16).

54. Tomasz Dobrogoszcz comments that Georges plays on his parents' "primal fear that the Algerian savage will harm their sweet, innocent child" (Dobrogoszcz 233).

55. Max Silverman analyzes the way that Haneke's self-reflective *Caché* compares cuts made by knives and axes with cuts in relationships and cuts in film editing (Silverman 57).

56. James Penney writes that *Caché* "explores the psychodynamics of postcolonial guilt as they are made manifest in the specific arena of the field of vision" (Penney 79).

57. Benjamin Ogrodnik believes that in *Caché*, the camera is "turned into a weapon of resistance for the formerly colonized" (Ogrodnik 58).

58. Jehanne-Marie Gavarini finds that in *Caché*, Haneke tries to depict the "lack of recognition of another person's suffering." Gavarini believes that "Majid's pain comes from the lack of recognition by another human being, as well as an entire nation, of what took place in his life in 1961" (Gavarini 201).

| Detached and Circling

Metaphors for the Emotions of Women Scorned

> The very systematicity that allows us to comprehend one aspect of a
> concept in terms of another . . . will necessarily hide other aspects of the
> concept.
>
> —GEORGE LAKOFF AND MARK JOHNSON

THE EMOTIONS OF JILTED women have long entertained audiences hungry
for vicarious passion. The combination of rage, humiliation, jealousy, and
loss of self-worth can spark strikingly creative revenge campaigns. Many
people worldwide can understand rejection and have been rejected by a be-
loved person at some time. The sting can be especially keen when the rejecting
person has been inside one's body, and when one has been socialized to build
one's identity through relationships. Psychologist Jean Baker Miller observes
that "for many women the threat of disruption of an affiliation is perceived
not as just a loss of a relationship but as something closer to a total loss of
self" (Miller 83). The sense that one's body and inner essence are no longer
wanted can lead to lacerating violence. Why does the agony of abandoned
women draw readers and film-goers when it can evoke painful memories?[1]
What pleasures emerge when one watches a jilted woman's agony and fury?[2]
Bad behavior makes for good stories, and when a woman refuses to accept
rejection, the audience's pleasure may increase. In representing the emotions
of rule-breaking women, authors and filmmakers not only evoke passion; they
develop cultural metaphors indicating how identity should be constructed and
how relationships should work.

   This chapter analyzes metaphors used by writers and filmmakers to rep-
resent the emotions of seven resistant women: Dido in Virgil's *Aeneid* (29–19
BCE), Miss Havisham in Charles Dickens's *Great Expectations* (1861), Agnes
Wessington in Rudyard Kipling's "The Phantom Rickshaw" (1885), Evelyn
Draper in Clint Eastwood's *Play Misty for Me* (1971), Alex Forrest in Adrian
Lyne's *Fatal Attraction* (1987), Mia Williams in Andrea Arnold's *Fish Tank*
(2009), and Mia Fredricksen in Siri Hustvedt's *The Summer without Men* (2011).

With the exception of the last two works, these stories and films show rejected female characters from a male perspective.

To convey the emotions of abandoned women, these authors and filmmakers draw on some traditional metaphors, such as the avoidance of light. One female character marks a man's home with her scent so that her memory will taunt him for some time. Most of the metaphors that communicate these women's pain involve altered or restricted movement. The rejected female characters move less; they move more; they turn rigid; they fly free; but in the works created by male artists, they move *wrong*. These castoff women drive much of the action, but they move in circles rather than progressive lines. From the perspective of male protagonists, the jilted women become hindrances because they refuse to move forward. To the men eager to shake them off and move on, they remain determinedly, insistently stuck. They follow compulsively, jump on men's backs, and in a sticky, demeaning metaphor, they "cling."

Cultural metaphors that depict unwanted women as offensive increase the agony of abandonment. A recent television advertisement for American Standard VorMax toilets shows a tall, white man trying to run with a dark-haired woman clinging to his back.[3] As he jogs along, she whines, "I love you, I love you, I love you." With a knowing look, the man turns his eyes to the viewer. "No one likes a clinger," he says. He points to a white toilet bowl, where a blue image of him and the clinging woman dissolves and is flushed down the drain. Metaphorically, the ad represents a woman who loves too much as human waste clinging to a toilet bowl. This chapter will seek other ways of representing rejected people and their emotions.

Attachment

Psychological studies of human attachment describe emotional relationships metaphorically, in terms of physical ones. Human languages push scientists toward this choice: it would be hard to describe emotional bonds without using terms like "distant" or "close," which denote spatial positions and may evoke visual and somatosensory images. Characterizing emotional relationships through physical ones may seem like the most natural strategy in the world for humans, whose minds and bodies can't be separated. Still, it is vital to remember that attachment is a metaphor. As Max Black showed, a metaphor makes meaning when it "selects, emphasizes, suppresses, and organizes features of the principal subject by *implying* statements about it that normally apply to the subsidiary subject" (Black, "Metaphor" 291–92, original emphasis). Calling emotional relationships "attachments" invites readers to view them through a cognitive device that makes some of their features visible but occludes others. Attachment has become the most widely used term in psychology for analyzing the ways that humans form emotional bonds. By using spatial experience as a metaphoric source, attachment allows scientists to discuss degrees of closeness but fails to describe situations in which people perceive themselves to have mixed with others to the point that they are occupying the same space.

In his classic study of human attachment, psychologist John Bowlby chose his descriptive terms carefully. Bowlby sought to explain variations in young children's feelings toward their parents, since some children easily tolerated separations, whereas others protested if left even briefly. "Clinging behavior, either literal or figurative, can be seen at every age . . . ," he observed (Bowlby 211). Bowlby rejected terms such as "jealous," "possessive," "greedy," and "over-dependent" because these words carry "an adverse value judgment that is held to be inappropriate and unhelpful" (Bowlby 211). Instead, Bowlby proposed the term "anxious attachment," which "respects the person's natural desire for a close relationship . . . and recognizes that he is apprehensive lest the relationship be ended" (Bowlby 213). Through his own experiments and surveys of other scientists' work, Bowlby showed that anxious attachment was not an inborn character defect. It results from experiences early in life that are carried to later relationships. Children of parents who are physically or emotionally unavailable or who threaten desertion tend to produce anxious children who storm at the first sign of abandonment.

In the past four decades, psychologists have confirmed, revised, and updated Bowlby's claims. Cindy Hazan and Phillip Shaver have proposed that romantic love is an attachment process and can be understood in terms of Bowlby's theory (Hazan and Shaver 511). In an extensive questionnaire study, Hazan and Shaver produced evidence that in adult relationships, people behave in secure (56%), avoidant (24%), or anxious/ambivalent (20%) ways that closely parallel children's stances toward their parents (Hazan and Shaver 521). "Secure" adults, emotionally nurtured by their parents, welcome intimacy, trust their partners, and believe that they are worthy of love. "Avoidant" adults, physically and/or emotionally rejected by their parents, shrink from intimacy and do not trust others. "Anxious/ambivalent" adults, whose parents sent mixed signals, crave intimacy but doubt their worthiness for love and their partners' devotion to them (Hazan and Shaver 512). Childhood experiences never fully determine a person's behavior in adult relationships, which involve sexual and dynamic interactions, but they seem to exert a significant influence (Hazan and Shaver 522).

In the quest to build knowledge about emotional relationships, "attachment" has been the prevailing metaphor, but it needs critical examination. "Attachment" suggests gluing one solid object to another—creating an appendage that the first object did not always have and in the future may not need. This metaphor fails to account for feelings that one has merged with one's partner, and that two formerly independent beings have grown together. As a term, attachment doesn't account for the intermeshing of lives that loving relationships involve.

Attachment also offers a convenient metaphor for anyone who wants to end a relationship. It justifies partners who want to "detach" themselves from unwanted lovers, but it bewilders partners who feel integrated with their mates.

The attachment metaphor validates complaints about "clinging" lovers but offers no language to a partner who feels so entangled with her mate that a breakup would shred her tissues. Bowlby's term, chosen out of respect for people's emotional needs, still excludes much of human experience.

Interweaving, imbricating, blending, growing together, genetically combining—these alternate metaphors for emotional relationships emphasize the fine scale of intimacy and the destruction that can ensue when two people try to live distinct lives after years of interdependence. Humans beings are organic creatures, and associations between organisms are harder to end than those between mechanical parts. "Attachment" and "detachment" carry mechanical connotations. One can separate two Lego pieces more easily than a fungus and a blue-green algae.

The seven fictional works analyzed in this chapter vary in their capacities to provide alternate metaphors. Those created by male authors and directors offer metaphors that largely denigrate the rejected women's emotions, although they sometimes inspire sympathy for the characters. The abandoned female characters hide in darkness, wander in circles, stalk their rejecters, and attack them with knives. All seven of these rejected characters challenge the power men hold over them—and in some cases, they pay for it in their capacities to evoke sympathy. In her analysis of *Great Expectations*, literary critic Adina Ciugureanu observes that "when a woman opposes the patriarchal world . . . she becomes an object of ridicule, a grotesque figure, a monster . . ." (Ciugureanu 354). Readers and viewers may regard these jilted female characters as crazy, selfish, immature, manipulative, destructive, vengeful, and violent. Any one of these labels is likely to halt thought about the content of the women's protests.

Through popular culture, metaphors for fictional characters' emotions can shape real people's inner lives. This is particularly true in the case of Alex Forrest, whose butcher knife and bloodied white dress still haunt millions of minds worldwide. Media scholar Elaine Berland and psychotherapist Marilyn Wechter argue that "films provide a public stock of enabling and constraining images and narratives to image forth what a person can do and be. Such texts function as powerful cultural resources which the individual viewer selectively draws upon to construct, maintain, and transform personal identity" (Berland and Wechter 38). Filmed and literary representations of emotions matter because they can shape people's emotional experiences. When stories push metaphoric models that contradict people's inner lives, they can inculcate fear and shame in their readers.

The Aeneid: *Impeded Motion*

Like Homer's *Odyssey*, Virgil's *Aeneid* tells a story of movement and obstructed motion. In his quest to reach Italy and found Rome, the Trojan warrior Aeneas doesn't progress linearly, but he and his narrative have a defined goal. Virgil composed the epic in 29–19 BCE to solidify Roman culture's founding myth and justify its defeat of Carthage in the Punic Wars (264–146 BCE) ("Third Punic War"). In this narrative context, Aeneas's passionate relationship with the Carthaginian Queen Dido can function only as an obstacle. Much as Circe, the sirens, and the lotus-eaters hindered Odysseus, Dido threatens to hold Aeneas back. The North African (originally Greek) Queen rules a powerful state, whose welfare depends on her physical and mental health. Since the death of her first husband, she has vowed not to remarry—until Aeneas lands on her shores. Virgil's judgmental narrator reproaches her, but with the gods maneuvering in a parallel realm, no human actor in this tragedy is fully responsible for her actions. With vivid descriptions of Dido's feelings, Virgil arouses sympathy for her even as he presents her emotions as a force to be overcome.[4]

Virgil makes Dido's wrath on losing Aeneas believable by showing the intensity of her passion for him. The Roman poet depicts female desire in an evocative, visceral way that few writers in the subsequent two millennia have matched. Throughout his poem, Virgil describes scenes with details that cue readers to form mental images.[5] Like Kafka's depiction of Gregor, Virgil's representation of Dido's desire drives readers to *feel* her urges in their bodies. At first, Virgil conveys her lust through a mixed metaphor: it is "longing that her heart's blood fed, a wound / Or inward fire eating her away" (Virgil 95). This hybrid metaphor gains force when the narrator comments, "The inward fire eats the soft marrow away, / And the internal wound bleeds on in silence" (Virgil 97). Virgil aims to awaken readers' memories, so that they may recreate passionate longing they have felt in the past. When Dido "presse[s] her body on the couch he left," both male and female readers may feel stirrings (Virgil 98). One vivid simile is likely to make readers wonder how responsible Dido is for her pain: she "roamed through all the city, like a doe / Hit by an arrow shot from far away" (Virgil 97–98). Early in Book IV, the reader is urged to feel the burning pain of this arrow.

At the same time, Virgil tries to make his readers see through Dido's eyes. With a few deft descriptions, he makes it clear how attractive the Trojan warrior is. Aeneas "walk[s] / With sunlit grace upon him," and Dido senses "the manhood of the man, his pride of birth" (Virgil 101, 95). The attraction is mutual. When the goddess Juno—who seeks to hinder Aeneas—creates a storm to unite them in a cave, Virgil's poetry arcs with sexual energy: "Torches of lightning blazed, / High Heaven became witness to the marriage, / And nymphs cried out wild hymns from a mountain top" (Virgil 101). Dido's sorrow begins as soon as her desire is fulfilled.

Juno's storm typifies the female forces active in *The Aeneid*, chaotic winds that swirl, circle, and scatter. Even though Juno's storm has a purpose, these forces contrast with Aeneas's fixed desire to found Rome. The Trojan on a mission may sail in curves, but his will is a linear vector. In evocative descriptions, Virgil describes the work of Rumor, whose female mischief serves as a leitmotif:

Through all the African cities Rumor goes—
Nimble as quicksilver among evils. . . .
By night she flies between the earth and heaven
Shrieking through darkness, and she never turns
Her eye-lids down to sleep. . . .
In those days rumor took an evil joy
At filling countrysides with whispers, whispers,
Gossip of what was done, and never done. (Virgil 101–02)

Like wind or water, Rumor exerts powerful effects but lacks an apparent goal or purpose. Throughout Carthage, Rumor reports that Dido and Aeneas "reveled all winter long, / Unmindful of the realm, prisoners of lust" (Virgil 102). While Rumor swirls, forward motion ceases: Aeneas is stuck in Carthage, and Dido's domain deteriorates.

Concerned, Jupiter asks Mercury to send Zephyrs—directed, message-bearing winds. "The man should sail: that is the whole point," says the King of the Gods (Virgil 104). He urges Aeneas to think of his son, Ascanius, even if he is too smitten to think of himself. In depicting Aeneas's reaction to this prod, Virgil takes as much care to evoke bodily responses in the reader as he did with Dido's desire. Aeneas "felt / His hackles rise, his voice choke in his throat" (Virgil 105). The reader is cued to feel his consternation, plus his desire to set things right. The metaphor used to represent lust now depicts Aeneas's will, and he "burn[s] only to be gone" (Virgil 105). Sensing the opposing forces he will face, he decides to leave Carthage quietly.

Unsurprisingly, the female force Rumor alerts Dido that Aeneas is preparing to sail. In lines that mirror Virgil's description of the wounded doe, the Queen "traverse[s] the whole city, all aflame / With rage, like a Bacchantë driven wild" (Virgil 106). In contrast to Aeneas's refocused energy, Dido's will causes only restless wanderings. She berates Aeneas for planning to steal away and demands, "Can our love / Not hold you . . . ?" (Virgil 106). The very terms with which she offers her plea suggest the impeded motion Aeneas fears. As a result of their relationship, Dido tells Aeneas, she has lost her integrity and the respect of her people. If he goes, what will she have left?

In marked contrast to the way Virgil depicts Dido, the Roman poet represents Aeneas as mastering his emotions—with help from Jupiter. Despite Dido's pleas, "The man by Jove's command held fast his eyes / And fought down the emotion in his heart" (Virgil 107). Defensively, Aeneas tells Dido, "I never held the torches of a bridegroom, / Never entered upon the pact of marriage" (Virgil 107). His father, he explains, has appeared to him in dreams and urged him to sail to Italy for his son's sake. According to this defense, Aeneas is not leaving of his own free will. Although he supposedly wants to stay, he has to sacrifice passion for duty. Dido, who has neglected her domain for her passion, comes across as relatively selfish. To Roman readers, this contrast would have made sense: after a long struggle, masculine Roman reason defeated effeminate African sensuality in the costly and painful Punic Wars.

While Aeneas invokes his mission to reach Italy, Dido uses her emotion as a persuasive tactic. She begs Aeneas, "by these tears," to stay, since against his arguments of duty, she can offer only her authentic feelings (Virgil 106). In sexually suggestive terms, she reminds him, "I took the man in, thrown up on this coast / In dire need, and in my madness then / Contrived a place for him in my domain . . ." (Virgil 109). In contrast to Aeneas, Dido makes no apparent effort to quash her emotions. She seems to *be* her humiliation and fury rather than a distinct entity trying to control them. Either she is weak, according to the model that an independent self controls emotion, or the model that excludes emotion from the self is wrong. Dido rages, accuses, insults Aeneas's mother, and vows revenge beyond death. The Trojan is unmoved by her wrath, and in Virgil's metaphoric system, her wild, emotional movement contrasts with the hero's fixed resolve. In a visually evocative simile, Virgil illustrates the difference between Aeneas's and Dido's emotional states:

> And just as when the north winds from the Alps
> This way and that contend among themselves
> To tear away an oak tree hale with age,
> The wind and tree cry, and the buffeted trunk
> Showers high foliage to earth, but holds
> On bedrock, for the roots go down . . . far. . . .
> Just so this captain,
> Buffeted by a gale of pleas . . .
> Felt their moving power in his great heart,
> And yet his will stood fast; tears fell in vain. (Virgil 111–12)

Virgil conveys Dido's feelings through furious, purposeless movement. Although in this metaphor, Aeneas's inner force is "holding on," he seems more capable of motion with purpose.

Aeneas's resolve heightens Dido's desperation, and just as Virgil moved readers to feel her desire, he works to make them sense her rage. The same fire that served as a metaphoric source for her lust now conveys the intensity of her wrath. "Oh, I am swept away burning by furies!" cries the raging Queen (Virgil 109). As Dido watches Aeneas's men prepare their ships, the narrator addresses her directly: "At that sight, what were your emotions, Dido? / Sighing how deeply, looking out and down / From your high tower on the seething shore . . ." (Virgil 110). This question is actually addressed to the reader, who may feel prompted to answer in her place. The response is painful to imagine and harder to articulate. Devastated, Dido "ran / In sickness from his sight and the light of day" (Virgil 109). Knowing that she is going to lose, she behaves like Dante's angry sinners headed for the darkness of hell.

Unable to stand her pain and humiliation, Dido resolves to commit suicide. Her preparations for death parallel Aeneas's outfitting of his fleet, since both are mobilizations. Dido plans her demise as a performance, a dramatic, communicative act. Emotionally, it resembles the suicide of Majid, whose family also comes from North Africa. Summarized as a message, Dido's communication might read, "You've hurt me, and I'm going to show you how much!" Dido asks her sister to prepare a funeral pyre in her "inner court" and to top it with Aeneas's arms, his clothes, and their marriage bed (Virgil 113). Dido doesn't conceive of emotion as something to be controlled, but she does want to control her staging of it. She plans her death as a visible undoing of the passion that unmade her life. Besides allowing her to escape from pain, Dido's suicide functions as a violent accusation, a shrill awakener of guilt. Although she prays for people "bound unequally by love," she is moved mainly by rage (Virgil 114).

Male gods help Aeneas steady his resolve, whereas Juno assists Dido haphazardly. Mercury warns Aeneas that Dido is "whipping herself on / To heights of anger," actively cultivating her emotions, and she may be capable of anything (Virgil 116). Aeneas sails before dawn, and when Dido spots his receding fleet, she wants to tear him to pieces. She vows eternal enmity between her people and his, a legacy that supposedly led to the Punic Wars. Although Aeneas cannot witness her death, she still enacts the gruesome, erotic suicide. On a funeral pyre, she stabs herself with her Trojan lover's sword. In depicting her death, Virgil inspires vivid images just as he did with her desire: "Her chest-wound whistled air. / Three times she struggled up on one elbow / And each time fell back on the bed. Her gaze / Went wavering as she looked for heaven's light / And groaned at finding it" (Virgil 121). Virgil encourages readers not just to see and hear her dying body, but to inhabit it. Dido's death is hideously slow, and even in the end, she seems to harbor swirling impulses rather than a steady will.

With Aeneas gone, only female voices remain behind in the emotional wreckage. "Rumor [goes] rioting" after Dido's death much as it did after her sexual bonding (Virgil 120). Devastated, Dido's sister reproaches Dido for her abandonment. In the sister's voice, readers hear the accusations of her people, whom Dido has left without a Queen. Like Dido's passion, her suicide may come across as selfish when compared to Aeneas's future-oriented gaze. Even after Dido's agonizing death, she remains in suspension. She can enter the Underworld only when Juno takes pity on her and sends Iris to clip her hair. In Dido's final undoing, she scatters in the winds that have represented her emotions throughout Book IV: "Her body's warmth fell into dissolution, / And out into the winds her life withdrew" (Virgil 121). Virgil describes Dido's death so that any reader might feel pity, as most might imagine her intense desire. Pity is not respect, however, of which Virgil's metaphors awaken little. Whether Dido functions as a whirlwind or an obstacle, she is hindering purposeful movement. Readers may cry for her, but their respect may have sailed with the Trojan fleet, cutting the waves in the morning light.

Great Expectations: *Perverse Stasis*

Nearly 2000 years later, Charles Dickens depicted another jilted woman who flees from the light. In *Great Expectations*, his disturbing character Miss

Havisham spends her life commemorating an emotional crime. Grounded in the Christian tradition, Dickens's portrait of Miss Havisham reinforces a metaphorical pattern used to represent many subsequent abandoned women's emotions. Crucially, readers get to know the vengeful heiress not from her point of view but from that of Dickens's male protagonist, Pip. Recounted by an adult Pip, *Great Expectations* tells of his abusive boyhood and emotional growth. Much of his maturing involves his response to financial "expectations," of which he falsely believes Miss Havisham is the source. In Pip's narrative, the vengeful heiress exploits Pip and her ward, Estella, whom she has raised to tantalize men. Although Miss Havisham speaks at length, readers never see through her eyes the cruel act that has left her so embittered. In Dickens's evocative passages depicting the heiress, he invites readers to simulate sensations—but they are more likely to be Pip's than the miserable old woman's. Dickens's choice of perspective affects readers' experiences of the story and their abilities to bond with the characters. Represented by her victim, the angry heiress makes it hard to believe that she was once a victim, too. As Pip suffers and gains compassion, readers may sympathize with her despite the harm she has done him. It is hard to pity Miss Havisham, however, since she demands pity with such force.

According to Pip's youthful companion, Herbert, Miss Havisham was "a spoilt child" (Dickens 178). Her mother died when she was an infant, and her father indulged her. He later married his cook, with whom he had a son, but after this woman's death, Miss Havisham's half-brother grew up "riotous" (Dickens 178). Her father disinherited him, and Miss Havisham's half-brother resented her from then on. In Herbert's account, the half-brother conspired with "a showy-man," who courted her and with whom she fell in love (Dickens 179). Her suitor extracted money from her, and Herbert's father, Matthew Pocket, warned her not to marry the man, but "she was too haughty and too much in love, to be advised by anyone" (Dickens 179). On her wedding morning, she received a letter in which her fiancé "heartlessly broke the marriage off" (Dickens 180). It would be ungentlemanly for Herbert to say so, but his account implies that Miss Havisham deserved her fate. Since Herbert generously supports Pip, readers have little reason to doubt his word.

Like Dido, Miss Havisham finds the life that she wanted laid waste by a man's act of will. And like Virgil's Queen—a character Dickens certainly knew—Miss Havisham tries to regain control by staging symbolic performances. Ideally, she would like the whole world to witness her pain, but she limits her audience to a select few, among them Pip and Estella. She responds to her rejection by trying to freeze time, so that the moment of her agony becomes a lifelong *tableau vivant*.[6] She stops the clocks at twenty minutes to nine, the moment she read her fiancé's crushing letter.[7] She remains in her wedding dress with one shoe off and one shoe on and leaves her wedding feast to rot. In her emotional world, time has stopped, and she uses all her influence to make the outer world conform to her inner life. She makes her life a monument to a long-past emotional crime.

Like Virgil's Queen, Miss Havisham moves in circles. Although she can walk, she prefers her wheelchair, which she directs Pip to push around her rotting feast. "The work I had to do," recalls Pip, "was to walk Miss Havisham round and round the room. . . . Over and over and over again, we would make these journeys. . . . It was like pushing the chair itself back into the past, when we began the old slow circuit round about the ashes of the bridal feast" (Dickens 83, 92–93, 236). Metaphorically, instead of moving forward, Miss Havisham's mind is circling an emotional crime scene. To avenge the outrage committed against her, she has adopted and raised Estella to devastate men and has summoned Pip to suffer as Estella's victim. Driving all of these acts are her beliefs that her suffering matters—that *she* matters—and that the man who has caused her suffering should pay.

Beliefs like these may seem essentially human, but in this female Victorian character, they come across as narcissistic. Adina Ciugureanu has observed how often mirrors appear in Pip's scenes with Miss Havisham, and how her obsession with her image suggests a narcissistic splitting (Ciugureanu 353). Arguing in twenty-first-century terms, Ciugureanu proposes that because Miss Havisham won't "go beyond" the rejection and "leave it behind" her, she "cling[s] to" a happy, ideal past self who believed she was loved (Ciugureanu 353). Ciugureanu draws on the Western metaphorical tradition that represents life as a linear journey and depicts those who reject forward motion as problematic. Miss Havisham's division between victim and aggressor mirrors her narcissistic split, since she wants love as much as she wants revenge (Ciugureanu 356). In the patriarchal, Christian context of *Great Expectations*, Miss Havisham's drive to manifest and perpetuate her suffering will probably be interpreted as vain. Instead of dwelling on her agony, she should forgive the misdeed, dedicate herself to others, and move on.[8]

Dickens's depiction of Miss Havisham's enduring anger depends not just on his narrative structure but on his persistent metaphors. His descriptions of Miss Havisham emphasize contrasting extremes, through which he manifests her emotional state. Among the metaphors that link his creative descriptions, one stands out unmistakably. Like Dido in her final hours, Miss Havisham withdraws from daylight.[9] "You are not afraid," Miss Havisham asks Pip, "of a woman who has never seen the sun since you were born?" (Dickens 57). Like Virgil and Dante, Dickens implies that Miss Havisham's rage consigns her to darkness. She has been nurturing her anger just as she has raised Estella—with malicious purpose rather than love. By the time Pip encounters her, she has reached a stage in which her component substance—and emotional state—can no longer tolerate light. When the mature Pip recalls his first impression of Miss Havisham, he says, "she must have looked as if the admission of the natural light of day would have struck her to dust" (Dickens 59). According to the Western metaphor that represents knowledge as light, she cannot risk being "enlightened" because she might learn that her outlook on life is wrong.

References to spurned daylight initiate the novel's emotional climax, in which Estella defies Miss Havisham, and the old woman realizes the futility of her vengeful life. Pip reflects:

> In shutting out the light of day, she had shut out infinitely more; . . . in seclusion, she had secluded herself from a thousand natural and healing influences; . . . her mind, brooding solitary, had grown diseased, as all minds do and must and will that reverse the appointed order of their Maker; . . . And could I look upon her without compassion, seeing her punishment in the ruin she was, in her pro-found unfitness for this earth on which she was placed, in the vanity of sorrow which had become a master mania . . . ? (Dickens 394)

"Vanity" functions as this passage's key word, indicating both pride and futility. Pip compares Miss Havisham's "vanity of sorrow" to vanities of "penitence," "remorse," and "unworthiness," all emotions likely to corrode personalities (Dickens 394). Dickens' words bring to mind Eric P. Levy's quotation of Samuel Beckett to describe self-pity as "aristocratic vanity": "'Can there be misery . . . loftier than mine?'" (Beckett 2; qtd. in Levy 27). Having turned her life to a monument commemorating her pain, Miss Havisham can't imagine anyone else's. More than love—for which she once so longed—the rejected woman wants revenge. She tells Pip that when she is laid dead on her bridal table, it "will be the finished curse upon him" (Dickens 87). The "vanity" of her actions, in both senses, comes from her lack of a sympathetic audience. For most of the novel, Pip and Estella feel no pity for her, and the readers' feelings are likely to follow Pip's. Her ex-fiancé does not know or care that his wedding feast is rotting; she is performing only for herself. Through these references to rejected sunlight, Dickens creates an Inferno in which an angry, isolated soul is bubbling alone in the mud.

Miss Havisham's unsustainable emotional state builds narrative tension, since Dickens's descriptions indicate that her unstable structure must collapse. On her decaying table, Pip watches "speckled-legged spiders with blotchy bodies running home to [the centerpiece], and running out from it, as if some circumstance of the greatest public importance had just transpired in the spider community" (Dickens 83). The spiders' frantic social movement suggests the natural forces that Miss Havisham can't control despite her efforts to stop time. After a lifetime of effort to maintain rigid structures, the tattered "Witch of the place" ignites (Dickens 83). The conflagration, which comes from sitting too close to a fire, suggests Miss Havisham's stifled desires—not so much sexual ones as her more basic needs for intimacy and love (Hartog 260). Pip recalls her "running at me, shrieking, with a whirl of fire blazing all about her, and soaring at least as many feet above her head as she was high" (Dickens 397).[10] Fire absent from Dante's fifth circle of angry sinners consumes the rage of the self-pitying heiress. Miss Havisham dies more of nervous shock than of burns, still attempting to control those who might pity her. In the last moments that readers spend with her, she is demanding that

Pip write "I forgive her" (Dickens 398–99). There is no evidence that she has forgiven the man who aroused her "dark" passions.

Like Virgil's depiction of the deserted Queen, Dickens's portrait of Miss Havisham offers a model for subsequent representations of jilted women's emotions. Dickens associates the sorrow, humiliation, and rage of abandonment with darkness, decay, stagnation, and compulsive circling—above all, with a refusal to move forward. Miss Havisham differs from Dido in that she is a "Miss": her love was never consummated, and she is probably a virgin. She does not share the agony of having been entered and left, but she has suffered the deadlier shock of learning that her fiancé never loved her at all. In the epic of Aeneas and the humbler story of Pip, these female characters work as forces to be overcome. In some respects, they obstruct motion—unsuccessfully and temporarily. In other senses, they create swirls of activity. Without their emotions, there would be no stories to tell, yet their love and anger seem to hold men back. One might think of them as resistors in a circuit, depicted in terms of darkness but capable of creating narrative light.

"The Phantom Rickshaw": Compulsive Following

Rudyard Kipling's early story, "The Phantom Rickshaw," relies on black and white imagery that works differently than Dickens's darkness and light. Kipling first published this tale of a jilted woman's ghost in the 1885 Christmas volume of the *Civil and Military Gazette*. A revised version appeared in his collection, *Eerie Tales*, in 1888 (Scheick 48). Kipling's protagonist describes himself as "Theobald Jack Pansay, a well-educated Bengal Civilian in the year of grace 1885," but the reader encounters Jack's story within an intriguing frame (Kipling 8). Before meeting Jack, the reader hears two conflicting narratives of what killed him: (1) Dr. Heatherlegh's claim that Jack died of overwork; and (2) the narrator's view that "a little bit of the Dark World came through and pressed him to death" (Kipling 2). In the narrator's opinion, Jack was "hag-ridden," tormented by an unwanted woman (Kipling 2).

"The Phantom Rickshaw" can be read as a fantastic tale, since the frame makes readers "hesitate" between medical and supernatural explanations (Scheick 48–49). In late nineteenth-century India under colonial rule, Dr. Heatherlegh's narrative would have made sense. Simla, the northern town in which the story takes place, was known as a refuge for British administrators exhausted from heat, long hours, and disturbing work (Bandyopadhyay 58). British officials who became mentally ill received treatments such as "prolonged bathing" and "Swedish drills" (Bandyopadhyay 58), much like the "cold-water baths and strong exercise" that Heatherlegh prescribes for Jack (Kipling 12).[11] Simultaneously, the colonial setting makes the "Dark World" narrative plausible in many senses. Jack may have been working too hard, but he also seems to have been haunted by an ex-lover pulled by four native ghosts.

Written for readers familiar with colonial culture, "The Phantom Rickshaw" is extremely funny. Like *The Aeneid* and *Great Expectations*, it comes from a male point of view, and it describes an affair that would have spawned clubroom jokes. Jack meets Agnes on a ship sailing from Gravesend to Bombay, and he recalls that by the journey's end, "both she and I were desperately and unreasoningly in love . . ." (Kipling 3). His ironic tone suggests just how much this love meant to Jack. Agnes is married to a Bombay officer, but her husband's existence seems not to concern the lovers. "In matters of this sort," Jack observes, "there is always one who gives and another who accepts. From the first day of our ill-omened attachment, I was conscious that Agnes's passion was a stronger, a more dominant, and . . . a purer sentiment than mine" (Kipling 3). In describing Jack's relationship with unfortunate Agnes, Kipling ironically employs the classic fire metaphor for passion, evoking laughs at the characters and at his own cliché. Jack's desire lacks the dignity of Dido's, and after one season in Simla, he reports that his "fire of straw burnt itself out to a pitiful end" (Kipling 3). In no uncertain terms, Jack tells Agnes that he is "sick of her presence, tired of her company, and weary of the sound of her voice" (Kipling 3). But Agnes isn't tired of Jack.

When Agnes refuses to accept Jack's rejection, his feelings change from pity to hate. His progression through infatuation, weariness, and frustration to rage makes emotional sense—because he controls the inner, first-person narrative. The reader can know Agnes's emotions only through Jack, and through the narrator who provides the outer frame. Before long, Jack has come to feel "blind hate—the same instinct . . . which prompts a man to savagely stamp on the spider he has but half killed" (Kipling 4). Jack's spider metaphor depicts Agnes as the classic spinning female, but emotionally, it reveals much more. "The Phantom Rickshaw" can be read as a warning about acting without reflecting (Scheick 51). Before starting a relationship that Jack knew would soon end, he "never hesitated to consider how Agnes would feel" (Scheick 51). Jack's confession makes it clear that he suffers attacks of conscience, and that the phantom rickshaw pursuing him after Agnes's death may be a "psychological representation of guilt" (Bandyopadhyay 58). The qualities of this "Dark World" phantom suggest that Jack feels guilty about more than Agnes.

As literary scholar Debashis Bandyopadhyay has noticed, Jack's behavior toward his rejected lover "smacks of British attitude to the colonized Indians" (Bandyopadhyay 63). Although Agnes wanted a relationship with Jack, and the Indians did not want to be colonized, both have been used as disposable objects to fulfill white men's desires; both have been treated as less than human. If the phantom rickshaw represents the return of the repressed, Jack has been repressing more than a frustrating affair. In Jack's narrative, Agnes speaks only a little, but her emotions come through in the descriptions of the rickshaw he still sees even after his cold baths.

When Agnes dies, apparently from despair, Jack becomes engaged to Kitty Mannering, but Agnes's rickshaw reappears. Her spectral vehicle is seen only by Jack; Kitty and her horse pass through it as though it were empty air. Jack tries to convince himself that the rickshaw is an illusion, since "one may see ghosts of men and women, but surely never coolies and carriages" (Kipling 8). In his mind, the four men pulling Agnes can't be ghosts—because *they were never human to begin with*. He learns that the four men who hauled Agnes were brothers, and all four recently died of cholera. For the first time, Jack wonders how much Agnes paid them, what hours they worked, and what they did when unharnessed. Until now, he has never really seen them.

In Kipling's descriptions of the phantom rickshaw, the words "black" and "white" often recur. Both alive and as ghosts, Agnes's men wear black and white uniforms, and Jack recalls Agnes as "a white face flitting by in the rickshaw with the black and white liveries" (Kipling 4). To Jack, the men's uniforms look like magpies' feathers, and he refers to Agnes's "accursed 'magpie' jhampanies" (Kipling 5). The insistent imagery of black against white speaks of the colonial empire Jack is serving.

One other bird figures in Jack's memories of Agnes, who calls to him with an "eternal cuckoo cry" (Kipling 4). "Jack, darling!" she repeats. "I'm sure it's all a mistake—a hideous mistake; and we'll be good friends again someday. Please forgive me, Jack dear" (Kipling 4). By cultural reputation, cuckoos and magpies are parasitic, thieving birds: cuckoos deposit eggs to be raised by others, and magpies steal shiny objects. In one of the story's many reversals, the terms that Jack imposes on Agnes and her men suggest his own theft and parasitism as a colonial official.

Jack calls Agnes a cuckoo because to his ears, she repeats the same notes each time he hears her. Close examination reveals that this is not true; Agnes repeats some key phrases, and her utterances are similar, but they never match exactly.[12] Jack's reference to "the irksome monotony of her appeal" (Kipling 4) typifies the complaints of those who hold power. Unhappy women and natives often *do* repeat accusations—because no one is listening and taking them seriously. Central to Agnes's appeals is a plea to be forgiven, perhaps because she thinks she has been rejected for being bad. This tactic, too, suggests the moves of oppressed people. One can disrupt a system, Sianne Ngai has observed, by following its rules too well (Ngai 67). When direct confrontation is not an option, one can demoralize rulers through exaggerated humility. In Agnes's endless requests to be forgiven, she communicates that Jack should be asking forgiveness of her. "Why can't I be left alone—left alone and happy?" he demands (Kipling 15). On many levels, he is sick of hearing about the situation he has created.

In Kipling's hands, Jack feels these circumstances all the more keenly because little by little, he slips into Agnes's role.[13] Once he is engaged to self-confident Kitty, he finds himself following her. When Jack and Kitty ride, she gallops off, "fully expecting . . . that I should follow her" (Kipling 7). Kipling's language creates striking parallels between the reversed relationships. Jack's final words to Agnes "might have made even a man wince" and "cut the dying woman . . . like the blow of a whip" (Kipling 5). When Kitty learns of Jack's relationship with Agnes, she breaks off their engagement with a literal blow: "My answer was the cut of her riding-whip across my face from mouth to eye, and a word or two of farewell that even now I cannot write down" (Kipling 14). As a rejected man, Jack finds himself harboring the emotions that Agnes once felt for him (Scheick 51). He ends his story by asking readers, "Pity me," as he has begun to pity Agnes (Kipling 19).

As a rejected lover, Jack learns what it means to be as invisible as the natives he has ruled. Kitty and her new suitor ride past him, and "for any sign she gave I might have been a dog in the road" (Kipling 16). To the woman Jack loves, he has ceased to be human, perhaps even to be real. By degrees, he begins to feel as though "the rickshaw and [he] were the only realities in a world of shadows" (Kipling 16). Accompanied by a rickshaw only he can see, he suspects that Kitty and Heatherlegh are ghosts, and only he and Agnes are real. Jack's new state of mind suggests a colonial world of parallel realms, each thriving oblivious of the other. To the British, the dark men doing their labor are ghosts; to the Indians, the white men passing in rickshaws are spectral.

By the end of Kipling's story, Jack has resigned himself to being accompanied by Agnes's rickshaw forever. He ridicules the suggestion that he go home to England, "an application to escape the company of a phantom!" (Kipling 19). His relationship with the supernatural suggests his growing awareness of India, of which he is an integral part (Bandyopadhyay 63). At the story's outset, the medical and supernatural explanations of Jack's illness seemed opposed: either he is hallucinating a phantom rickshaw, or his ghosts are "real." As the story concludes, the narratives begin to merge. Together, the logic of colonial medicine (see to your health, and the rickshaw will disappear) and the persistent rickshaw pulled by men in black and white suggest the quandaries of colonialism. In representing the emotions of a jilted woman, Kipling has captured the feelings of people who occupy the same time and space but whose emotional lives differ so greatly that they experience each other as ghosts.[14] Kipling shows a persistent, vocal ghost, however, who makes her presence known. In his story of a colonial "bitch on wheels," he depicts a woman and a people who will not be ignored.

Play Misty for Me: Constriction

When Clint Eastwood approached Universal Studio executives about directing his first film, they asked, "Why are you so eager to make a picture where the woman has the best part?" (M. H. Wilson 74).[15] Eastwood replied, "The guy is the subject of what's going on, so what difference does it make?" (Thompson and Hunter 25). In Play Misty for Me (1971), a female character drives the narrative, but her feelings and actions are represented from the male protagonist's perspective.[16]

The visual and auditory medium of film depicts emotions in ways that fiction and poetry cannot. In his directorial debut, Eastwood used colorful imagery, visual metaphors, and music to suggest what his characters were feeling.

In some ways, *Play Misty for Me* recreates Virgil's, Dickens's, and Kipling's depictions of abandoned women. For example, Eastwood employs lighting to shape viewers' responses to his female characters. The desired woman (Tobie Williams) appears in bright, natural settings, whereas the unwanted one (Evelyn Draper) is often filmed indoors, at night (Pittman). Viewers know these women only through their interactions with a male character who understands neither of them well. To dismiss *Play Misty* as misogynist would be "procrustean criticism," since the film represents women's emotions in a complex way (Westbrook 38). Eastwood's friend Jo Heims (a woman) wrote the script, although Eastwood later hired writer Dean Riesner to revise it when Eastwood found the protagonist "a little soft" (Kaminsky 89).[7] Ultimately, the film's representation of emotions belongs to Eastwood, who thinks visually. "I compared all of the shots in my mind, laid everything out," he recalls (Thompson and Hunter 24). His vision of an angry, jilted woman has frightened viewers for decades.

Play Misty takes place in Carmel, California, and the film's opening shot shows waves crashing against a rocky cliff. Throughout the film, images of waves breaking on rocks recur as a visual metaphor, suggesting the power of natural forces. The protagonist, disc jockey Dave Garver, broadcasts soft jazz at a local radio station, where a female caller has been requesting Errol Garner's tune, "Misty." One night after his show, Dave meets Evelyn Draper, to whom he makes advances despite his emotional attachment to artist Tobie Williams. In the bar scene in which Dave and Evelyn meet, Eastwood alternates shots offering Dave's view of Evelyn—whose bright yellow dress draws the eye—with shots showing Evelyn's view of Dave. Several of these images are indirect and involve reflections in mirrors (Knee 92–93). Dave and the bartender (played by Eastwood's directorial mentor, Don Siegel) attract Evelyn with a nonsensical game, and Dave leaves thinking that he has "picked up" Evelyn. Really, Evelyn has gone to the bar to initiate a relationship with him. It is she who has been requesting "Misty."

Dave tells Evelyn about his feelings for Tobie and indicates that he doesn't want to "complicate his life," a phrase offered by Evelyn (Eastwood 00:12:40). "Well, neither do I," she says, "but that's no reason we shouldn't sleep together tonight if we feel like it" (Eastwood 00:12:45). Dave agrees, and they spend the night together. When Dave leaves at sunrise, Eastwood's camera reveals Evelyn watching at the window. Later that day, she startles Dave by appearing at his house with groceries to cook him dinner. He communicates conditions that she seems not to have grasped: if and when he wants to see her again, he will call her. Evelyn responds, "Well, there are no strings, but I never said anything about not coming back for seconds" (Eastwood 00:17:13). She and Dave enjoy sex again, but she shocks him on the way out by screaming at a neighbor. Like Dave, the viewer may begin to realize how volatile Evelyn is.

Tobie's return from Sausalito makes Dave even more eager to get rid of Evelyn. Although Tobie seems to love Dave, she left him because his promiscuity was turning her into a "jealous female," a person she did not want to be (Eastwood 00:23:13). Many of Evelyn's scenes occur in semidarkness, and her very name ("Draper") implies obfuscation and concealment. Dave's and Tobie's scenes take place outdoors (Pittman), and the open landscape and sunlight suggest the natural flow of their relationship, which is progressing without deceit or planned maneuvers. In contrast, Evelyn's efforts to maintain contact with Dave grow more aggressive and dramatic. She waits for him at his favorite bar, pops up in the back of his convertible, and fights with him for his car keys. She appears at his house with a large, stuffed dog and drops her coat, under which she is naked. Dave confronts Evelyn, saying, "I never told you that I loved you" (Eastwood 00:38:21), but she, who can't imagine they are *not* in love, replies, "not in words, maybe, but there are lots of ways of saying things that have nothing to do with words" (Eastwood 00:38:33). Evelyn has read—or imagined—love in Dave's movements, his voice, and his desire for her body. As Dave continues to deny there is a bond between them, Evelyn's anger escalates. "What am I supposed to do," she demands, "sit here all dressed up in my little whore suit waiting for my Lord and Master to call?" (Eastwood 00:39:03). Dave replies that he has never wanted her to wait. "Get off my back, Evelyn!" he seethes (Eastwood 00:39:07). His words recall a metaphor for heroin, a "monkey on the back" that first brings pleasure but then clings with a life-controlling grip. This same metaphor may have inspired the American Standard VorMax toilet ad.

From Dave's perspective, Evelyn's grasp on his life feels like that of a life-destroying drug. Like Agnes, she continually reappears, apologizing and invoking their nonexistent relationship. Evelyn attempts suicide by slitting her wrists, so that Dave is obliged to care for her. She disrupts his lunch with a female media executive, who is offering him an opportunity to run a San Francisco show. "Is this your idea of a dish? . . . She couldn't get laid in a lumber camp!" screams Evelyn, who is anything but a feminist (Eastwood 00:51:11–29). Dave physically forces her into a taxi, and as it pulls away, her bright yellow arms reaching out the window look like a sea-monster's tentacles. With a long, shining knife, Evelyn slashes up Dave's apartment and wounds his cleaning lady, Birdie. Eastwood's camera reveals Evelyn swinging the knife like a scythe rather than stabbing. Increasingly, she comes across as a mythological destroyer rather than a human woman.

Dave enjoys a brief respite when Evelyn is hospitalized, and he and Tobie make love in a series of idyllic outdoor scenes. Eastwood's choice of music for these scenes is ironic, since Roberta Flack's "The First Time Ever I Saw Your Face" fits Evelyn's idealized notion of love better than Dave's or Tobie's.[18] The romantic lyrics describe love that begins at first sight and lasts forever, whereas Dave and Tobie are working to repair a relationship. Dave warns Tobie about Evelyn, who reappears and threatens him with a knife, but like Victor Frankenstein, he presumes that the rejected creature is after him.

Perhaps a little ahead of Dave, viewers may guess the identity of Tobie's new roommate, Annabel. Evelyn's final burst of violence is "an attack on his gaze" (Knee 99): she slashes the eyes of Tobie's portrait of Dave, binds and gags

Tobie, and cuts off her hair. "God, you're dumb," she taunts, as she stands over the terrified artist (Eastwood 01:26:23). Evelyn murders the police sergeant who comes to investigate, so that Dave has to finish her himself. In Tobie's dark house, he and Evelyn hunt each other, and she slashes, screams, and flees (Figure 6.1). Their maneuvers parallel their initial games in the bar, except that now the aim is death, not sex. Wounded and bleeding, Dave hits Evelyn in the face with a closed fist, just as if she were a man. She crashes through a window, falls screaming from a cliff, and lands in the surf below. The film's final shot mirrors the opening one, except that in the waves foaming against on the rocks, Evelyn now floats, her arms outstretched.

When Eastwood discusses film direction, a few key metaphors emerge. Even more than the visual images of his first film, these metaphors resonate with literary depictions of rejected women's emotions. As an actor, Eastwood admired Don Siegel's direction because Siegel maintained his "forward momentum" and didn't get "bogged down" (Kaminsky 83). Eastwood imitated Siegel by maintaining his vision and staying on budget, but he made sure to leave himself room to improvise. "I hate to be the prisoner of a diagram," he says (M. H. Wilson 75). Eastwood welcomes input from actors and sometimes

"PLAY MISTY FOR ME"
Dave Garland (**CLINT EASTWOOD**) the most popular disc jockey in the Monterey-Carmel area of California, tries to stop crazed psychotic Evelyn Draper (**JESSICA WALTER**) from killing his girlfriend Tobie Williams (**DONNA MILLS**), in UNIVERSAL PICTURES, LIST OF A LIFETIME II's electrifying, "PLAY MISTY FOR ME."

MCATV

FIGURE 6.1 Evelyn Draper (Jessica Walter) and Dave Garver (Clint Eastwood) struggle in *Play Misty for Me*. © 1971 Universal City Studios, Inc. and the Malpaso Company. Courtesy of Universal Studios Licensing LLC. All rights reserved.

incorporates his own new ideas. Overall, his choice of words suggests a commitment to linear, progressive motion with freedom to maneuver.

In *Play Misty for Me*, these are exactly the qualities that Dave feels that Evelyn has taken from him. In two interviews, Eastwood described *Play Misty's* central theme as "misinterpretation of commitment" (Kaminsky 93; Thompson and Hunter 25). Eastwood specified that he wanted to convey a feeling of "constriction, the blanket thrown over one . . . the bound-in feeling" (Kaminsky 94). He expected that many viewers would have experienced "somebody [who] has just tried to move in too fast, or has just held on too hard" (Kaminsky 93). In the film, Dave asks his fellow DJ, "You ever find yourself being completely smothered by somebody?" (Eastwood 00:33:39). As a first-time director, Eastwood wanted to convey a sense of "suffocation" so that viewers could feel it in their bodies (Thompson and Hunter 25). Together, his metaphors imply a desire for progress driven by one's own will and a horror of having one's motion restricted by someone else.

Eastwood seems sincere in his belief that both men and women can experience suffocating relationships. *Play Misty* was never designed as a myth to portray unwanted women as deadly, clinging octopi. Written by a woman, it represented the actions of a real stalker—a woman known to Eastwood and to script-writer Jo Heims. In separate interviews, Eastwood described this stalker's actions, which included attempting suicide, cutting up a man's clothes, threatening his life in the night, disguising herself with wigs, and appearing in bars he frequented to see whether he was dating other women (Kaminsky 92–93; Thompson and Hunter 25). Eastwood has also indicated that he experienced an oppressive, one-sided relationship, although it was "less dramatic" (Thompson and Hunter 25; M. H. Wilson 73–74). In *Play Misty*, he believed he was telling a well-known story, one to which male and female viewers could relate. "It is a type of behavior that you can observe in either sex," Eastwood insisted (M. H. Wilson 74). If *Play Misty* is a horror movie, it creates emotional horror because of the familiarity of its subject. Eastwood believed that on a visceral level, most viewers would understand unwanted love. In their bodies, they would shudder at the prospect of having their motion impeded and their freedom denied. But one wonders how decades of female viewers have related to a character whose lover has left him due to his promiscuity, and who sleeps with a stranger just as he is trying to win her back.

Play Misty denies viewers any possibility of understanding Evelyn because she does nothing but pursue Dave. She has no job, no friends, no family, and almost no history. Eastwood says he denied Evelyn background for a reason, despite pressure from his advisers. He wanted to reinforce the audience's identification with Dave, so that "we see her unfold as he does" (Kaminsky 91). Eastwood thought that scenes relating Evelyn's psychological history would contribute nothing to the story. On the contrary, "explaining" Evelyn could hurt the work artistically by giving readers less to imagine. Rather than advancing the tale, adding background for Evelyn would bog it down. Within the narrative frame Eastwood has constructed, he is right. Dave doesn't care about Evelyn's background; he didn't when he was trying to sleep with her, and he doesn't when he is trying to get rid of her. As an erotic and murderous force undamped by human inhibitions, she lies open to any narratives that viewers want to project upon her. To film critic Duncan Pittman, Evelyn is a "clingy, needy mess" (Pittman).[19]

Like "The Phantom Rickshaw," Eastwood's film about a jilted woman addresses much more than one unhappy person's emotions. Idyllic Carmel lies close to Berkeley and San Francisco, which in 1971 were dynamic centers of social change (Knee 89–90; Pittman). Duncan Pittman reads *Play Misty* as a warning from members of older generations about the selfish excesses of the Baby Boomers (Pittman). Interpreted from Garver's perspective, Evelyn certainly suggests a situation that has run out of control.

More significantly, Eastwood's film raises questions about how human relationships need to evolve to accommodate the social changes underway. Eastwood wanted to explore a challenging problem: "To what extent are we responsible for the relationship we establish?" (M. H. Wilson 74). Taken as a whole, *Play Misty* offers a complex response to the director's question. Like "The Phantom Rickshaw," the film indicates that sexual relationships without consequences simply do not exist. Supposedly, Dave has enjoyed a number of these, but he now wants an emotionally richer life with Tobie. The film's narrative construction makes it hard to identify with Evelyn, who wants intimacy but seems not to know what love involves. It is Tobie who voices the issue that women articulated in the 1970s, a question equally relevant to men: How can one maintain a relationship while retaining one's autonomy and sense of self? (Westbrook 47). In this broader, social sense, the metaphor of constriction applies equally to women and men.

Fatal Attraction: *Boiling the Rabbit*

In 1971, *Play Misty for Me* had little cultural impact. Financially, the film did well, but during struggles to attain equal rights and end a war, the tale of one rejected woman's rage left few ripples. In 1987, in contrast, Adrian Lyne's film depicting an unwanted woman's fury struck the media with hurricane force.

Fatal Attraction resembles Eastwood's film on many levels.[20] Both are shot from the viewpoint of a male protagonist rewritten to win sympathy. The characters' names, Dave Garver and Dan Gallagher, suggest unconscious borrowing. Both films involve undeveloped "villainesses" who initiate sexual relationships, knowing that the men they desire are committed to other women. Both movies use color and lighting to make these antagonists appear inhuman and frightening. In both films, a woman attempts suicide by slitting her wrists, and both refer to *Madame Butterfly*. Both involve a large, gleaming knife, and both have been compared to Alfred Hitchcock's *Psycho*.[21] At screenings of both films, male audience members yelled "Hit her!" and "Kill the bitch!"[22] *Fatal Attraction* follows Eastwood's film so closely, it might be viewed as an East-Coast remake. Why, sixteen years after *Play Misty*, did the representation of a jilted woman's emotions arouse so many viewers?

Unlike *Play Misty*, *Fatal Attraction* has a didactic feel. Whereas the married protagonist, Dan, and his wife, Beth, emerge as flawed, well-meaning characters, the seducer Alex Forrest lacks a complete personality. When Dan refuses to continue their relationship after a passionate weekend, Alex expresses anger with increasing violence. She articulates her rage in lines that viewers still quote, but Lyne's visual images of her emotion register more strongly. In the steam and hiss as her acid dissolves Dan's Volvo, audience members can feel her fury. Viewers may experience Alex's rage most strongly in the film's most horrifying image, that of Dan's daughter's rabbit boiling in a pot. Lyne offers this image from Beth's perspective, and it involves the eerie sound of the lid tapping as well as scum, bubbles, and white fur. More than any other sequence in the film, these images establish Alex's lack of humanity. She has attacked Dan's family in its softest spot, and if she could have, this modern-day witch might have boiled Dan's six-year-old daughter, Ellen. In Lyne's representation, viewers may find it hard to sympathize with Alex. Her rage seems unjustified by the circumstances—because of the way Lyne and screenwriter James Dearden have constructed them.

Dearden created *Fatal Attraction* from his 45-minute film, *Diversion*, about a married man who spends a weekend with a single woman and then apparently gets caught (Faludi 28–29). Producer Sherry Lansing, at the time one of the most influential women in Hollywood, wanted to develop *Diversion* into a feature film because she "always wanted to do a movie that says you are responsible for your actions, that there is no such thing as a one-night stand" (Faludi 29). The theme of the "obsessive lover" interested Lansing, who had often noticed "the lack of self-esteem when someone is left" (Mass 31). As Dearden developed his script, director Lyne and studio executives "pressured" him to make the married man more sympathetic; the single woman, less so (Faludi 30). Just as Eastwood brought in Riesner to solidify his "soft" character (Kaminsky 89), producers asked Dearden to make Dan "more lovable" (Faludi 30). In the original story, Dearden's protagonist had contacted the woman; in his new version, she becomes the sexual aggressor. Dearden was also encouraged to develop Dan's wife, who evolved from a "teacher . . . preparing to return to work" to a dedicated, full-time homemaker (Faludi 30). Most important, Dearden changed the ending—twice. His original film ended when the "other" woman called the protagonist's house, his wife answered, and the screen went black (Faludi 29). In contrast, *Fatal Attraction* focuses on Alex's actions following her rejection, even after Dan's revelation of their intense weekend to Beth. In the film's first ending, Alex commits suicide while listening to *Madame Butterfly*, and Dan is incarcerated for her murder until Beth proves him innocent. In previews, audiences found this ending emotionally unsatisfying, and they made their unhappiness known. At Lyne's and the producers' request, Dearden then wrote a more "cathartic" ending in which Beth and Dan jointly kill Alex, who dies dramatically in a bathtub (Faludi 49). As Paramount

Marketing President Sidney Ganis told Susan Faludi, "We set out first and foremost to make a movie that would sell" (Faludi 49–50). Achieving this goal did not involve representing Alex's emotions in a realistic way.

As executives sensed with *Play Misty for Me*, the woman in *Fatal Attraction* has the best part.[23] Alex dominates the action and drives the story because she refuses to accept Dan's rules. "You knew the rules," he says as he prepares to return home—rules he has not articulated but presumes she accepts (Lyne 00:32:25). "What rules?" she challenges (Lyne 00:32:27). Alex refuses to follow the patriarchal script for adultery, which requires her to withdraw quietly (Babener 31). If Alex had done so, there would have been no story to tell; there rarely is when characters conform. Probably, she would have escaped unharmed, at least in a physical sense (Berland and Wechter 42).[24] Instead, Alex calls Dan, confronts him at work, enters his home, kills his pet, kidnaps his child, and tries to murder his wife. Alex's actions invite viewers to dismiss her as mad, but if she is, what is the nature of her illness? Probably Alex's craziness lies in "her refusal to play the culturally accepted role of the jilted heroine" (Conlon 152). Unlike Dido and Madame Butterfly, Alex doesn't want to die, although she attempts suicide to show Dan how much she is suffering. "I'm not going to be *ignored*, Dan," she warns, when he berates her for entering his home as a prospective buyer (Lyne 01:01:13). Dan's erasure of Alex feeds her growing anger. Even after hearing that she is pregnant with his child, he refuses to acknowledge any moral bond. More than Alex wants Dan, she craves "non-invisibility" (Sherwin 176), and her insistence on acknowledgment drives the narrative. In the face of all cultural opposition, she believes that she has a right to be "in" Dan's life. In an uncritical way, the film represents a culture in which the "owners" of lives view them as bounded, with full power to determine who is "in" and who is "out."

Alex's demand to be acknowledged resonated with some female viewers, whose responses to the film defied executives' expectations. *Fatal Attraction* sparked conversations about how to murder disrespectful ex-husbands and ex-boyfriends (J. Thompson 14). Alex's fearless violation of Dan's boundaries pleased some viewers because "she enacts a revenge fantasy that anyone who has ever been rejected can enjoy" (Sherwin 182). Above all, Alex wants to show that she won't disappear; she cannot simply be thrown away (Larson 82). Having been treated like a thing, she takes out her anger on Dan's things, and her outrage registered with women who felt that a society had tossed them aside and "trivialized their rage" (Larson 77, 83). It can be fun to watch Alex disrupt the "overwhelming niceness" of Dan's family with its strangely androgynous child (Jermyn 256).[25] When Alex views the Gallaghers and vomits, some audience members may share her nausea.

Dearden's revisions largely dehumanized Alex, but he left her some wonderful lines. When Dan tells her he's happily married, she asks, "So what are you doing here?" (Lyne 00:29:48). Recalling their first conversation, she chides, "You thought you'd have a good time. You didn't stop for a second to think about me" (Lyne 00:32:24). Dan tells Alex that she's sick, and she asks if that's because "I won't let you treat me like some slut you can just bang a few times and then throw in the garbage" (Lyne 01:07:59). Alex tells Dan, "I'm going to be the mother of your child. I want a little respect" (Lyne 01:08:04). In female viewers, these statements sparked powerful responses. In *Vogue*, Molly Haskell wrote that "women everywhere can applaud Close's diatribe against the one-night stand as a convenience for men" (qtd. in Mass 32). Alex's claims also resonated with producer Sherry Lansing, who approved of Alex's responses to a point. "What I like about the Glenn Close character," she said, "is that she is a woman who fights back; she's equal. She says, 'You can't fuck me and then throw me in the trash can.' She is a strong feminist, and she is saying, 'I will not be ignored'" (Mass 32). Unlike Riesner, who revised Heims's script for Eastwood, Dearden included some background for Alex: the fact that her father had died when she was seven. Dearden may have planted this fact to explain her behavior, or—less likely—to win her sympathy. In a game with Dan, however, Alex uses this information deceitfully, first hurling it to upset him, then withdrawing it as a lie. Her ability to lie about her father's death suggests an underlying coldness.

Viewers who experienced Alex as empty responded not just to what the film shows but what it does not. As a character, she is only slightly more developed than Evelyn Draper. Alex has no family, no friends, and as an associate editor, she wouldn't last a week. Like Evelyn, she never works and seems to live only to pursue Dan. Film critic Pauline Kael noted that when Alex shifts from a confident to an unstable woman, "the violence that breaks loose doesn't have a thing to do with the character who has been set up" (qtd. in Mass 32). It would be an understatement to describe this character as "soft." As a human person, Alex barely exists.

Visually, Lyne and his designers conveyed Alex's emotional emptiness through her white, minimalist apartment and its setting in Manhattan's meat district. Her home can be approached only through a hellish alley lined with bloody slabs of beef and fires burning in cans (Babener 29; Bromley and Hewitt 20; Mass 33). This environment suggests an isolated emotional life like those of Dante's angry souls in hell. Alex's family name, "Forrest," implies wildness (Conlon 152), and her tendency to appear in black or white, "spookily" lit and framed, encourages viewers to see her as a "mythic destroyer" (Davis 52). If Alex represents chaotic natural forces, she may be a goddess of turbulent flow, since so many scenes associate her with water (Davis 52; Berland and Wechter 38). Dan and Alex bond during a rainstorm in which he "cannot get his umbrella up" (Hala 77). They make love and later fight viciously beside Alex's sink. It is raining when Alex slits her wrists, and her showdown with Dan alternates shots of a boiling kettle with those of an overflowing tub. Together, the stark imagery and flowing water present Alex more as an emotional force than as a human being. The multisensory images of fluids convey emotion through the liquid-in-a-container pattern Zoltán Kövecses has noticed (Kövecses, *Emotion Concepts* 144–48)—especially with the whistling kettle at the film's climax.

Even for viewers who experience Alex as a person, Lyne's film implies that her rage can't be justified. She knows that Dan is married, but with her line, "we're two adults" (Lyne 00:16:02), she implies that she'll accept sex without long-term involvement. She lies to Dan repeatedly, although she may be deceiving herself. Viewers may sympathize when she defaces his car, but probably not when she kidnaps his child. Alex merely takes Ellen to an amusement park and buys her ice cream, but child abduction is abhorrent.

In discussing Lyne's and Dearden's representation of Alex, cultural critics repeat three terms: "invalidate," "trivialize," and "dismiss." These verbs describe what Lyne's film does to Alex's grievances. *Fatal Attraction* offers Alex subversive lines—only to void their legitimacy through her actions (Berland and Wechter 40). In this film of the 1980s, "the authentic rage of woman scorned is robbed of its legitimacy . . ." (J. Thompson 12). As Sianne Ngai describes in *Ugly Feelings*, narratives such as this one represent emotions as illnesses or character defects rather than valid responses to injustice (Ngai 128–30). Alex demands that a man who has entered her body acknowledge her existence, and that he take responsibility for the child he has fathered—but the film deflects attention from what Alex says to what she does. Within the context of *Fatal Attraction*, her criticisms lack credibility, as do her boiling emotions.

Clint Eastwood made *Play Misty* partly to ask, "To what extent are we responsible for the relationship we establish?" (M. H. Wilson 74). *Fatal Attraction* tends not to ask but to tell, and it warns against relationships outside of marriage. The film approaches a powerful emotional issue: how to strike a balance between domesticity and passion, "how to manage marriage and yearning" (Berland and Wechter 41).[26] Rather than conceiving of this issue in social terms, it reduces the problem to an individual one and presents an unmarried woman's longing as the unhappiness of someone who has made poor choices, is too selfish to maintain a relationship, or is simply crazy.[27] Unlike *Play Misty*, *Fatal Attraction* turns away from the greatest quandary of relationships, one vital to both sexes: how to maintain a robust sense of self while living as a partner and parent.[28] In 1987, *Fatal Attraction* may have pleased audiences because of a cultural reluctance to face this question. Certainly awareness that AIDS could infect white heterosexuals created a climate welcoming the fears the film visualized. But *Fatal Attraction* also resonates with fears that extend beyond sexuality. The outraged, jilted woman it creates and destroys is angry about more than one man's rejection.

Fish Tank: *Learning to Move*

Whereas Dave orders Evelyn off his back, Connor invites fifteen-year-old Mia to climb on. Andrea Arnold's film *Fish Tank* follows their complex interactions as Mia comes of age in a British housing project. Arnold's film, which won the 2009 Cannes Jury Prize, differs from Eastwood's and Lyne's by presenting rejection from a female perspective. It also varies in the way it represents Mia's

emotions, which are depicted through movement.[29] Visually and metaphorically, Arnold presents a young woman who takes control of her own motion.[30]
Mia, whose name suggests a "stubborn sense of self," acts out her feelings
in deft, sometimes violent moves (Cuming 336). Drawn to hip-hop dancing,
she practices in an empty apartment that offers a bird's-eye view of her terrain. Arnold's film is all about movement, and at key emotional points, the director depicts flocks of swirling birds or wind-blown grass. Arnold's hand-held
camera follows Mia around, since she is the center of the action (Cuming 336).
Consigned to a space for England's poorest families, Mia will let no one dictate
how she moves through it.

Mia is not a good hip-hop dancer, but viewers may see that her dancing is
art. It involves her whole body and differs radically from the sexual belly-rolling
of the girls she fights. Arnold rejects the cliché of "salvation through show
business" offered by some films of underclass girls (Mullen 17). Mia practices
conscientiously and imitates African American dancers because improvising
on their movements develops her sense of self (Cuming 337). Mia's kinesthetic
intelligence makes her even better at fighting, which matches her dancing in
its daring. Twice she takes on entire groups, and in a shocking early scene, she
bloodies a girl's nose with a lightning-fast head-butt. From her family, Mia has
learned to use her body as a weapon, since she, her mother, and her younger
sister Tyler are shown hitting, pinching, and pushing each other. "Cunt! Bitch!
Fuck-face!" they scream (Arnold 00:16:35). In one horrifying move, Mia's
mother digs her hand into Tyler's hair, grabs hold, and hurls her daughter
from the room. Because Mia values movement so greatly, she tries to enable it
in others. In an early scene, she attempts to free a Traveler's horse—with which
she may identify—by breaking its chain with a hammer. Attacked by three
Traveler boys and their dog, she circles like a martial artist. "Get off of me!"
she screams, a line that runs through the film like a refrain (Arnold 00:12:43).
Arnold communicates the psychological forces operating on Mia through the
sense of being bodily restrained.

A "fish tank" suggests an environment where one is confined and observed
to give pleasure to someone more powerful. As a metaphorical source, it
first seems like an odd choice for Mia's housing project because no one is
watching.[31] Mia's "estate" is filled with people listening to music and hanging
laundry, but more privileged Londoners don't want to see them. If anything,
Mia's tower—like Majid's—was built to keep her and her family out of sight.
Arnold's camera hesitates over a guinea pig in a glass cage, but the image
doesn't function as a visual metaphor. It forms part of the camera's playful
dwelling on the feminine objects in Mia's flat: underwear dangling on a line;
a scallop-shell mobile that catches the light. By selectively aligning qualities of
fish tanks and projects in ways that Max Black described, Arnold's metaphor
avoids emphasizing entrapment. Her film focuses on movements within the
tank and the gaze of one predatory observer.

Arnold shot *Fish Tank* on the Mardyke Estate in the distant suburbs of
London. Created in the 1960s for Ford Dagenham workers, the housing

complex has since been torn down (Cuming 335–36). Emily Cuming, who has studied female coming-of-age stories set in public housing, notes that some narratives represent towers as enforcing "class apartheid" (Cuming 334). When one is "housed" and has no money for decorations, one's home does not express one's individuality (Cuming 329). As Cuming points out, however, Arnold's *Fish Tank* doesn't represent public housing as a crushing environment. "I actually think estates are great places," says Arnold. "They're full of people, they're full of life. I mean, that's how most people live. It's probably a better way to live than a lot of middle-class lives which are more isolated and more lonely and have less community" (Mullen 17). Arnold's images of the objects in Mia's flat suggest that its inhabitants do have individual lives. Arnold's sound-scape conveys the vibrancy of Mia's environment, which is full of shouts and pounding music (Cuming 336). In intimate scenes, the soundtrack offers only breathing, hinting that private selfhood is possible. Visually, Arnold reveals grassy expanses broken by roads that suggest possibilities rather than oppres-siveness. The active, open world below Mia's practice room seems to inspire her as she dances. Although impoverished, she has found "a room of her own" and "a room with a view" (Cuming 337). Unlike many social realist films, *Fish Tank* doesn't focus on an environment that shapes individuals (Roddick 19). Every person represented in Mia's world is distinct, and the characters may surprise the viewer. Rather than depicting an entrapping space, Arnold shows one in which movement is possible.

Arnold, who wrote the script herself, follows two relationships that offer motion to Mia. The possibilities are provided by two men, who hold more power in her society. Increasingly, these relationships create paths that lead in different directions. One morning, while dancing to a hip-hop video in her kitchen, Mia realizes she is being watched by an attractive, bare-chested man. "You dance like a black," he tells her, and she takes it as a compliment (Arnold 00:14:40). The man is her mother's boyfriend, Connor, who has a job and a car and offers her family new opportunities. With pinches, punches, and verbal threats, Mia's mother tries to keep her girls away from Connor, whom she wants all to herself. The sexy young mother seems to have had Mia and Tyler in her teens, and there is no mention of their father(s). Her mother appears to wish intensely that Mia and Tyler weren't there. In the film, Mia will be rejected in many ways, but her keenest pains come from her rejection as a daughter.

Connor offers attentiveness and tenderness unknown to Mia, and he seems to like her and Tyler, who is about ten. Over their mother's objections, he includes them on a drive to a lake. Arnold's footage of this sequence, rich in movement and color, suggests how much the trip means to the women, who rarely leave their housing project. Connor's car offers motion and space on a new scale and shows Mia what the world has to offer (Cuming 338). When Mia cuts her foot, Connor invites her to ride piggyback, using his body to keep her mobile. Most important, Connor praises Mia's dancing and encourages her to audition for a professional job. He even lends her his camera so that she can prepare an audition video. Mia doesn't trust Connor and searches his wallet, pocketing his cash. But when he moves in with her family, claiming that his mother has thrown him out, she grudgingly accepts him. She confides to him that if she could be any animal, she would like to be a white tiger, like the one in the poster on her bedroom door. Connor tells her she's limiting her possibilities by choosing a creature on the ground. He would like to be an eagle—another predator—and he asks her, "Don't you want to fly?" (Arnold 00:31:30). As the eagle fixes his eye on the tigress, both animals seem headed for trouble.

Simultaneously, Mia bonds with the Traveler boy Billy, the youngest of the three with whom she fought. He returns her portable CD player and invites her along on a junkyard raid to find a part for his Volvo. Like Mia, Billy wants to be mobile, which for him means repairing his car (Cuming 338). Mia leads Billy to the store where Connor works, jumps on Connor's back, and asks him for money. Effectively, Connor has become her father, and she rides off on Billy's back with the jump and grip she has learned from Connor. As a substitute father, Connor acts concerned about Mia's relationship with nineteen-year-old Billy. He warns Mia that Billy is too old for her, whereas Mia's mother appears unconcerned. "She's never had a boyfriend," she says, and Mia replies, "I just fucked him upstairs, actually" (Arnold 01:02:53–56). Connor tells Mia that she needs "sorting out," but she challenges, "You're nothing to me. So why should I listen?" (Arnold 01:03:55–01:04:00). A few nights later, Connor and Mia's mother come home drunk, and after helping her mother upstairs, Connor asks Mia to dance for him and mentions her coming audition. Connor is the only person who has ever supported Mia's dancing, and she hesitatingly agrees. As Arnold's camera alternates Mia's movements with Connor's gaze, the viewer may begin to feel dread. His touches grow increasingly sexual, and Mia doesn't resist. She seems to have been attracted to him from the first, and she is competing sexually with her mother, who wants to send her away to a "special" school. Connor is competing with Billy, and while inside of Mia, he seethes, "Is his cock this big?" (Arnold 01:16:22). Viewers may fear that some night when Mia has passed out, Connor will move on to Tyler. Mia awakens to the sound of her mother's sobs. "Connor's gone," announces Tyler (Arnold 01:19:05).

Every image Arnold has offered of Mia's movements indicates how she will take Connor's flight. In rejecting her, he has denied her as a lover and a daughter, plus he has abandoned her family. As the white tiger, Mia acts as the protector in a family where no man can fill the role. Her mother seems not to think of confronting Connor, and only Mia has bothered to learn where he works and lives. When Connor doesn't respond to her calls at work, Mia seeks him at home. Connor lives in a small stand-alone house a short train ride from Mia's project. Apparently, it hasn't occurred to him that his project women would pursue him there. Maybe, like Dave Garver and Dan Gallagher, he has thought that they wouldn't dare. "Jesus Christ!" exclaims Connor when Mia appears at his door (Arnold 01:23:53). He drags her down the street, drives her to the station, and gives her money for train fare home. A shot of Mia against a scratched, dirty glass wall shows her hesitating—should she retire to her project, or fight? Her previous actions point toward her response. With the sure, bold movements of her dancing, she climbs Connor's fence, opens a back window, and breaks into his house, which is momentarily empty. Mia dances the way that she lives, and her motions convey her anger and pain.

Arnold reveals Connor's secret to viewers in the same instant that Mia discovers it. She seizes Connor's camera, which comes alive with the sounds and images of his wife and daughter Keira, a girl of about six. In quick flashes, Mia spots Keira's toys. In this awful moment, Arnold restricts the soundtrack to Keira's singing, Mia's breathing, and the patter of her urine on the carpet as she squats and pees. Emily Cuming reads this act as "childlike" and "anti-social" (Cuming 338), but Mia's behavior is more that of a tiger marking its territory—or challenging the boundaries of another's.[32] Mia wants to send Connor an unmistakable message: "I was here. I exist. What are you going to do about it?" Like Alex Forrest, she feels that she has been used as a thing, and her family has been treated the same way. Mia responds by wrecking Connor's rug and unleashing her anger on his family.

Mia's rival isn't Connor's wife, who barely appears on screen. The rage of the unwanted daughter focuses on the wanted one. Arnold uses sound to mark Mia's growing emotion as Keira rattles by on a silver scooter. The little blonde girl in the sparkly pink dress takes no notice of her larger, darker "sister." In a terrifying sequence that echoes *Fatal Attraction*, Mia grabs Keira's hand and tells her they are going to get ice cream. Arnold conveys the girls' confused fear and rage with images of swaying grass in the fields they cross. As Mia drags Keira farther from home, the little girl fights, and Mia turns brutal. She tears the pink dress, which catches on a fence. Mia seems to have no plan, but viewers' fear may mount as the girls approach a desolate waterfront. Given what Mia has suffered, given her rage and physicality, will she be capable of murder?[33] Keira kicks and screams as Mia shakes her and finally hurls her into the water. For a few sickening seconds, she disappears. At last her tiny, white face re-emerges, and when Mia helps her out of the water, viewers know that the unwanted daughter can't kill the wanted one. It isn't Keira who is keeping Mia from moving.

As in the popular film Arnold cites, the male rejecter responds violently. The soundtrack conveys Mia's growing fear as she trudges home alone in the dark. On the black road, a car approaches, then passes, and viewers' dread may rise. A second motor roars, and tires screech. As Mia sprints across a black field, Arnold offers only the sound of her breath. Soon it is mixed with the rush of Connor's, since he is in hot pursuit. Connor catches Mia easily and hits her with the back of his hand. Like Dave Garver's knockout blow, this rejection is absolute and final. With his body, Connor tells Mia who holds the power: only he has the right to move freely, watching, choosing, entering, and abandoning women. Undefeated, Mia refuses to accept that only men can control motion.

In its ending, Arnold's film grants Mia the power of choice—in an exotic dance club, the location of her audition. In a dark room filled with judging eyes, she is asked to dance one more time. After seeing the gyrations of a fat, older woman, Mia leaves the platform without performing. The managers seem genuinely interested in her, but given the looks of the other applicants, it is probably her youthful body they want. There is nothing remotely artistic about this dancing, and Mia refuses to dance badly to give men pleasure. Instead, she chooses to leave with Billy, who has repaired his car and is driving to Wales. With few good options for mobility, Mia joins forces with the young man with whom she has the most in common (Cuming 338). Mia takes time to say goodbye to her mother, whom she discovers dancing to her hip-hop CDs. Through an image of concerted motion, Arnold conveys the bonds among the mother and daughters, which involve love as well as hate. The film's final shot offers upward movement: the rise of a silver balloon soaring over Mia's project.

Arnold's balloon suggests that Mia is moving on—she may be moving up, flying free. "Move on" can work as a humiliating command when one is ordered to march after a forced detachment. The metaphor of resuming motion assumes a different meaning, however, when one chooses the time, rate, means, and direction of motion. In *Fish Tank*, Mia comes to control the way she will move her body, who will see it, and with whom she will share it. As depicted by Arnold, Mia's motion differs from that of Dido, Miss Havisham, Agnes, Evelyn, and Alex, who were created mainly by male artists. In their rejection of linear motion, these characters serve as negative examples. One gets the feeling they are balking to show that they exist because life offers them no better ways to realize themselves. Despite enormous social disadvantages, Mia Williams manages to move on her own terms. She may ride briefly on men's backs, but she will dance through life as she chooses.

The Summer without Men: *Brain Shards*

Probably not by coincidence, Siri Hustvedt also called her jilted protagonist Mia, a name that draws attention to her wounded sense of self. The sharp, witty heroine of *The Summer without Men* plays with her name, musing, "Mia. . . . I am. I am Mia" (Hustvedt 31). Mia Fredricksen suffers a psychotic breakdown when her husband of thirty years asks for a "pause" so that he can live with a younger woman (Hustvedt 1). It infuriates Mia that her life has been smashed by a cultural cliché: the flight of men who realize that "what IS does not HAVE TO BE and then act to free themselves from the aging women who have taken care of them and their children for years" (Hustvedt 3). The fact that Mia's abandonment sends her to a hospital suggests that in defining herself, she has overemphasized her relationship with Boris.[34] But this fifty-five-year-old poet and scholar has plenty of creative brilliance left. Rather than destroying her, Mia's illness and recovery shatter a confining case and free her identity to assume more complex forms.

As a poet, Mia lives her metaphors, imagining them in literal, amusing ways. Mentally, she hears a guitar chord when her therapist tells her that she has "struck a chord" (Hustvedt 50). Initially, Hustvedt depicts Mia's emotions through metaphors of explosive shattering. Mia, from whose point of view the novel comes, opens by describing thoughts that "burst, ricocheted, and careened into one another like popcorn kernels in a microwave bag" (Hustvedt 1). In the hospital, Mia records her thoughts in a notebook that she ironically labels "Brain Shards" (Hustvedt 2). References to fragments recur early in the novel, but in this story of recovered identity, shattering constitutes only one metaphoric system.

Hustvedt's line drawings offer a visual metaphor for Mia's changing emotional state. In the first, a woman is confined in a square, and the viewer sees only her desperate face and reaching arms. The second shows her with her head and shoulders above the box, gripping it and looking aside with ironic amusement. In the third, the woman—who is always naked—lies atop the square, narrating to a larger woman who is looking down sympathetically. In the final image, the woman flies happily across the page, ignoring the box below. If one flips through these drawings fast, one experiences Mia's summer without men as an animated sequence. What has shattered isn't herself but a familiar structure encasing her identity, which has long been needing room to grow.

As in the story of Mia Williams, Mia Fredricksen's relationship with space works metaphorically. Whereas fifteen-year-old Mia finds a room of her own, the fifty-five-year-old poet recalls writing at her kitchen table while her daughter Daisy was napping. Mia realizes that she hasn't "fought for [her]self" and reflects, "Some people just take the room they need, elbowing out intruders to take possession of a space" (Hustvedt 6). The narrative relies on Mia's decision to leave New York and teach for a summer in her native Minnesota town, Bonden. In her determination to heal, she returns to old space, but her move is not regressive. She starts by cleaning the dusty house she has rented and takes pleasure in the sharp edges and clear surfaces she creates. In the past, Mia has not taken command of her space. Now that she does, Hustvedt's description of her hard-edged house suggests the changing state of Mia's mind.

Although Mia was diagnosed with Brief Reactive Psychosis, her delusions were metaphorically, if not literally, accurate. As a poet, she recalls, "for years I had been toiling away at work few wanted or understood. . . . Rejection accumulates; lodges itself like black bile in the belly. . . . Paranoia chases rejection" (Hustvedt 55–56). When Mia was delusional, she thought that Boris would move into their apartment with "the Pause" and force Mia out onto the street (Hustvedt 42). Convinced that Boris was in league with "them," Mia heard voices saying, "Of course he hates you. Everyone hates you" (Hustvedt 43). Although Mia seems to have imagined a conspiracy, her perception of one rejection too many rings true, and her fear of homelessness is socially realistic. How many women, interned and medicated for mental illness, have merely been reporting their internalizations of the contempt they perceive all around them?

Whatever the nature of Mia's madness, her illness doesn't recede suddenly. Her pathology mirrors her health, and the two fold into each other like yin and yang.[35] During the summer, Mia exchanges e-mails with a mysterious "Mr. Nobody" (Hustvedt 54). Mia suspects that her correspondent may be Leonard, a learned patient whom she met at the hospital, but several hints indicate that Mr. Nobody is a lingering voice.[36] Nobody torments Mia with messages saying that she is worthless, until she realizes how much the cruel words on her screen sound like the "accusing voices" in her mind (Hustvedt 56). As Mia reflects on these messages, she realizes that Boris has treated her as a "Ms. Nobody," interrupting her "as if [she] were an airy nothing" (Hustvedt 74). Also, no one in the novel but Mia can match Nobody intellectually, since the two toss word-bombs full of arguments from Sigmund Freud, Jacques Derrida, and Lev Vygotsky. Mia's narrative substantiates her early claim that she can "out-think just about anybody" (Hustvedt 18). Probably, Nobody's messages are coming from Mia's mind.

While Mia is an intellectual contender, she has more trouble dealing with her emotions. References to her family make it clear that she is ashamed to cry because she was raised to suppress her feelings. Mia's mother "roared" at her for "crying jags and . . . eruptions," and her father stammered, "I can't. I can't," unable to express any emotion at all (Hustvedt 69, 44). "I always thought you felt too much," her mother tells her, an opinion her father and sister shared (Hustvedt 13). As a teenager, Mia hid in toilet stalls to cry when other girls tormented her. Her therapist, Dr. S., hypothesizes that the women in Mia's family "stepp[ed] around" her father's feelings (which included unfulfilled love for another woman), and that Mia recreated this scenario in her marriage (Hustvedt 51). Considering her circumstances, Mia cries relatively little during the summer, although she refers ashamedly to her weeping in the months before. Her references to crying, both her own and that of other characters, tend to be dismissive and sarcastic. When she learns that Boris has moved in with "the Pause," Mia reports that she "took it like a woman. [She] wept," and she "leaked a small bucket of tears" to Dr. S. (Hustvedt 73, 81). Mia's older sister calls her a crybaby, and she doesn't fight the charge. She can see nothing positive in tears; crying is a phase to move beyond, to transcend.

More than crying, Mia despises self-pity, as most twenty-first-century Americans have been taught to do. In a metaphor that recalls Bunyan's Slough of Despond, Mia realizes, "I had fallen into the ugly depths of self-pity, a terrain just above the even more hideous lowlands of despair" (Hustvedt 59). In a narrative whose images convey upward motion, crying and self-pity represent sludgy depths. Mia dislikes her mother-in-law, "self-pitying Dora," whose adoration of Boris strikes her as selfish (Hustvedt 44). Having lived with a partner for thirty years and raised a child, Mia feels contempt for people who are self-absorbed, and she worries that she is becoming one. On the ward, which is never far from her mind, "crying jags" revealed the patients' pathological self-enclosure, and health meant letting the world in (Hustvedt 10). Mia feels exhilarated when a June storm reminds her how vast and wondrous the world is.

When Dr. S. tells Mia that she seems to be enjoying life, Mia initially feels shocked. Always harsh with herself, she is emotionally honest and asks, "Had I been clinging to an idea of wretchedness while I was secretly enjoying myself?" (Hustvedt 51). In this question, cultural contempt for self-pity meets the rawest of female emotions. Enjoying oneself would mean "moving on." Despite one's rejection, the world has continued its motion, so why not enjoy it? For others who have been hurt, the observation that one is enjoying oneself may come as a knowing jeer. It reminds one that life will continue, injustice will be forgotten, and no one has cared about one's pain. Mia's use of the pejorative word "clinging" shows that she takes the former perspective. In this story of recovered motion, "clinging" has no positive connotations.

Unlike the sorrow and self-pity Mia shuns, her anger manifests itself through movement. Her rage inspires dramatic, creative, and extremely funny revenge fantasies. At first, Mia imagines herself as a woman who "blasts into space and bursts into bits that scatter and settle over the little town of Bonden" (Hustvedt 15). This first metaphor of rage resembles that of shattering, which conveys her initial feeling of disintegration. But as Mia rises from her confining box over the summer, her rage-fantasies increasingly involve others. Just as fifteen-year-old Mia tried to free Billy's horse, Mia dreams of liberating Boris's lab rats. She imagines freeing "all the tormented rats from their prisons" and watching "as their milk-white bodies shoot across the floor" (Hustvedt 47). Drawing on Victorian models, she pictures herself returning from the dead to haunt Boris and his Pause in their Manhattan apartment. In her fantasies, she flies out to others, even if it is to make them suffer for the pain they have caused her.

As Hustvedt's title suggests, relationships with other women help Mia heal. During her summer in Bonden, learning from women at the beginnings and ends of their lives gives Mia a broader perspective on her situation. She responds most strongly to her mother, who may be looking down in Hustvedt's third sketch. Like Mia, her mother has prioritized other people's needs over her own and now has mixed feelings about it. Mia's mother never recovered from her brother's death from polio and always suspected that her parents wished she had died instead. Having spent her life serving Mia, Mia's sister, and their father, Mia's mother has no interest in remarrying because she doesn't want to spend her remaining years tending a man. Instead, she dedicates herself to her friends, women aged 84 to 102 whom Mia calls the "Five Swans" (Hustvedt 8). Among these aging women, Abigail stands out as the most ferociously alive. A former art teacher bent ninety degrees from osteoporosis, Abigail reveals her "private amusements" to Mia (Hustvedt 35). Throughout her life, she has stitched out her frustration in subversive, hidden embroidery. Under a flap in a blanket, she has sewn a woman sucking up a town with her vacuum cleaner; inside a Christmas table runner, she has embroidered five women masturbating. In a tragically ironic statement, Abigail tells her fellow book club members that "stepping on one's desires is deforming" (Hustvedt 149). In Mia, Abigail senses a kindred spirit and entrusts her with the "amusements," plus a secret she has concealed all her life. Abigail's greatest love was for a woman, seventy years ago. Watching the swans slip away and taking responsibility for Abigail's art inspire Mia to live differently in her remaining years.

Mia also develops respect for her neighbor, Lola, who is verbally battered by her husband, Pete. Without his help, Lola is raising their infant son Simon and four-year-old daughter Flora, who deals with her painful home life by building an imaginary world. Despite Lola's exhaustion, the young woman creates art: metal earrings in the shape of well-known buildings. Mia's empathy for abused Lola may stir a visceral response in readers. As Pete bellows obscenities at Lola, Mia reports that "with every verbal assault my body stiffened as if from a blow" (Hustvedt 132). Overnight, Mia shelters the children and Lola, who is just two years older than her own daughter, Daisy.

Emotionally, Mia develops most intensely by teaching poetry to thirteen-year-old girls.[37] Led by a sociopathic teenager, her students viciously torment Alice, a student who is "kinda different" (Hustvedt 90). In their abuse of Alice, the students spark painful memories of Mia's own bullying. Recalling taunts like the voices she once heard, Mia reflects, "I, wimp and crybaby, allowed them to taint me" (Hustvedt 130). Rather than blaming her abusers, Mia blames herself for letting her tormentors hurt her. Her assignments to her poetry students suggest her evolving emotional state. Mia asks them to write "secret me" poems, nonsense poems, and poems that emerge from close observation (Hustvedt 49). She intervenes in their abuse of Alice by making them tell the story from each other's points of view.

In narrating her own story, Mia rarely accuses, attributing injustice less to individuals than to systems. Looking at the Swans, she thinks that they "may all have been born in the Land of Opportunity, but that opportunity had been heavily dependent on the character of their private parts" (Hustvedt 150). Despite her fantasies of tormenting Boris, Mia depicts her neuroscientist husband as a round character whom the reader may start to like. Mia points out that Boris is "scrupulously honest" (Hustvedt 140). It hasn't occurred to him to have an affair, stay married, and not tell Mia about it. The reader learns that Boris's penis, named Sidney, once almost popped out at a Berkeley lecture. He cried copiously at *A Tree Grows in Brooklyn* but cannot cry in real life—but then Mia corrects herself: Boris cried when their daughter Daisy was born. The renowned scientist who studies "the neural correlates of consciousness" cannot follow philosophy, through which Mia has led him stepwise (Hustvedt 24). Boris has also failed to master the washing machine, with which she has tried the same approach. He leaves his dirty clothes on the floor, and after several weeks of cohabitation, the Pause throws him out. Mia feels no glee in learning of his eviction and does not seem to want revenge. As Boris makes clumsy, earnest overtures, Mia realizes that she cannot continue their relationship on their old terms. She can accept only a partnership that permits autonomy and growth, a bond that lets husband and wife "make meaning" together (Bein 18). When Boris asks Mia what he can do, she commands him to woo her. As he arrives at her house in Bonden, she says that Boris must come in to her. The novel's ending indicates that if Boris wants Mia back, he will have to accept her as an equal. Thanks to Mia's shattered container, her emotions and identity have changed shape and will continue to assume dynamic forms.

Representing the Emotions of Rejected People

In representing female characters' fights to be acknowledged, these films and stories draw on some of the same metaphoric families. Their three main metaphoric groups have roots in biology as well as culture. First and foremost, these stories' emotion metaphors represent the agony of rejection through motion or arrested movement. Depending on one's perspective, an abandoned woman's feelings may be conveyed through impeded motion, compulsive circling, or an effort to move freely. Dido's emotions hinder Aeneas's progress, and Miss Havisham tries to stop time's flow. Agnes, Evelyn, and Alex circle men who don't want them rather than "moving on" with their lives. The young and middle-aged Mias seek ways to escape confining structures and fly. The association of emotion with movement makes sense biologically, since the word "emotion" conjoins mental and bodily motion ("Emotion"). Bodily experiences invite artists to convey emotion through movement, but culture enters these metaphors by implying what kinds of motion are desirable. Dido's aimless roaming and Miss Havisham's compulsive circling suggest sick minds that need "straightening out."

A second metaphoric source works in concert with movement to make these fictional women's emotions feel real. This second family of emotion metaphors involves the embrace of darkness and the avoidance of daylight. Dido and Miss Havisham flee from the sun, although Miss Havisham ignites in a roaring blaze. Evelyn and Alex are often filmed indoors, or at night. The darkness metaphorically associated with them suggests mental darkness, in terms of emotion as well as knowledge. The protagonists of Arnold's and Hustvedt's stories differ, since nothing about the Mias conveys rejection of the natural world. Their fights to find a place in it never direct themselves against nature's cycles. In the cases where metaphors characterize rejected women as emotionally "dark," negative cultural connotations emerge. Like Dante, artists who stress this metaphor often imply that angry, rejected people are *choosing* darkness rather than admitting their faults and seeking better ways to live. Metaphors of emotional darkness imply a perverse, petulant refusal of wisdom and happiness.

A third family of emotion metaphors employed here depicts women's emotions in equally daunting terms: those of bondage and freedom; constriction and expansion; encasement and shattering. These metaphors align with the "folk model" characterized by Zoltán Kövecses, which represents emotions as liquids in vulnerable containers (Kövecses, *Emotion Concepts* 144–48). Depending on who is telling the story, the emotions of an unwanted woman may be represented as a suffocating blanket or as an explosive burst from a confining case. *Play Misty for Me* implies that Evelyn's emotions aren't just stifling Dave; they are restricting her from leading a meaningful life. Mia Fredricksen's shattering, on the other hand, leads not to a loss of identity but to the liberation of someone trapped in a brittle shell. These metaphors of bondage and liberation reveal how differently male and female characters—and artists—can imagine the same emotions. Feelings that restrict a male protagonist from moving may allow a female character to move freely.

It would be facile to attribute the differences among these works merely to the genders of their creators. In representing emotions, these stories rely on a common cultural heritage, and by showing jilted women breaking social rules, they expose codes of conduct that benefit some people more than others. As the lovers of disenchanted men, these female characters are supposed to retire quietly (Babener 31). Instead, they wreak havoc. Dido and Miss Havisham stage performances that physically re-enact their pain. Dido commits suicide, and Evelyn and Alex attempt it, although their wrist-cutting seems more like a ploy to make their pain horrifyingly visible. Mia Williams urinates on a rug, and when Boris e-mails Mia Fredricksen to ask her how she is, she wants to send him a gob of spit. To the eyes, ears, skin, and noses of their rejecters, these female characters try to make themselves perceptible. If there is anything common in their fictional offenses, it is their desire to make themselves known.

Men's violent responses to these unruly women indicate that these works concern more than jilted individuals' emotions. Kipling's "The Phantom Rickshaw" and Arnold's *Fish Tank*, especially, suggest that anger, humiliation, and determination to make one's presence known characterize the emotions of many marginalized people. In the mind of a colonial official, the insistent reappearance of a rickshaw pulled by "magpie jhampanies" recalls the exploited natives he rules (Kipling 5). *Fish Tank* depicts the insistent humanity of people housed in places where more privileged people won't detect them. Only individuals like Connor, who seek them out for pleasure, need perceive them at all—with the condition that he can leave at any time and can't be followed.

In a prescient reading of *Fatal Attraction*, literary scholar John Rohrkemper proposed that Lyne's film aroused audiences because it brings to mind "global terrorism" (Rohrkemper 86). By using a familiar, domestic setting, the film frightens viewers by showing the chaos one unhappy person can cause. *Fatal Attraction* draws dramatic force from fears of seemingly irrational acts by angry, disadvantaged individuals with grievances (Rohrkemper 86). In 1992, Rohrkemper reflected that:

> Terrorism is almost always an attempt by the disenfranchised to reclaim control
> from the empowered. . . . As we would have to admit in the case of most political
> terrorism, Alex's anger stems from a genuine cause. . . . It is often the intransi-
> gence of the powerful . . . that leads to such egregious attempts at counter control.
> (Rohrkemper 88–89)

The creators of *Fatal Attraction* may have feared more than one unwanted woman's rage and projected their broader fears onto Alex. The violence of many of the characters discussed here indicates that they are avenging more than one offence and acting on more than their own behalf.

Some of these rejected characters' actions are hard to justify, but even their most outrageous behavior sends the message: "I exist! I am human! I am here!" In their refusal to take rejection quietly, these female characters convey a wish to have their humanity acknowledged. To prove that they are sentient, feeling creatures, they externalize their emotions, since people have treated them as though they had no inner lives. Sensually evocative emotion metaphors dominate their stories because these characters make their emotions perceptible to the senses in order to show that they exist.

In the twenty-first century, narratives depicting jilted women as selfish, crazy, and violent still sell. Hustvedt's story of Mia Fredricksen, however, promises that in the representation of rejected people's emotions, what *is* does not *have to be*. With creativity and intelligence, artists can craft emotion metaphors that will convey the humanity of unwanted people.

Notes

1. In What *Literature Teaches Us about Emotion*, Patrick Colm Hogan asks, "Why is it that we engage in simulation of emotionally aversive situations?" Hogan hypothesizes that "we experience some sort of pleasure in simulation as such" and "our emotion systems may require something like calibration" (Hogan, *What Literature Teaches Us* 29, 31).

2. Adina Ciugureanu asks this question in a study of Charles Dickens's *Great Expectations* and hypothesizes that readers experience both "the misogynic pleasure of seeing a woman put in her place" and "the sadistic pleasure of holding a woman prisoner of her own faults and misfortunes" (Ciugureanu 360).

3. This advertisement can be viewed at: www.ispot.tv/ad/7xDJ/american-standard-vormax-toilet-clinger.

4. I am indebted to Marjorie Curry Woods, whose presentation, "Classical Emotions in the Medieval Classroom," inspired me to include *The Aeneid* in this project.

5. In *Dreaming by the Book*, Elaine Scarry analyses the techniques that poets and novelists use to help readers form mental images (Scarry 3–5). Scarry focuses on visual mental imagery, but Virgil encourages auditory and somatosensory imagery as well.

6. Eiichi Hara compares Miss Havisham to sleeping beauty, "forever living in that moment when her heart was broken . . ." (Hara 603).

7. Adina Ciugureanu points out that although Miss Havisham has stopped her clocks, she seems aware of time's flow. She knows what day of the week it is and when her birthday falls (Ciugureanu 355).

8. Curt Hartog argues that because Dickens "equates motherhood with feminine identity," Miss Havisham appears monstrous because she rejects motherhood

(Hartog 248). In Victorian culture, Miss Havisham is villainous not just because she refuses to forgive but because she exploits children.

9. Dido's death reveals that she is ambivalent in her withdrawal from daylight, since "her gaze / Went wavering as she looked for heaven's light / And groaned at finding it" (Virgil 121). By metaphoric logic, she still wants to live and love.

10. Curt Hartog reads Pip's rescue of Miss Havisham as a rape, since the two are "struggling like desperate enemies" (Dickens 397) on the ground as Pip tries to put out the fire. Miss Havisham's mistreatment of Pip, Hartog argues, leads to resentment and vindictiveness in Pip that mirror her own (Hartog 259).

11. Debashis Bandyopadhyay points out how problematic mentally ill Europeans were in a culture determined to show white supremacy. After European asylum patients in Calcutta were seen "driving scavenger carts," officials moved asylums from major cities to smaller towns, where the patients would be less visible. According to Bandyopadhyay, Heatherlegh's improvised hospital "is modelled on these asylums," and Kipling "was acquainted with these treatments" (Bandyopadhyay 58).

12. Compare Agnes's first "cuckoo cry" with some of her subsequent ones: "Please forgive me, Jack; I didn't mean to make you angry; but it's true, it's true!" (Kipling 5) and "Jack! Jack, darling! . . . It's some hideous mistake, I'm sure. Please forgive me, Jack, and let's be friends again" (Kipling 7).

13. William Scheick observes the finely crafted symmetry of Kipling's story. Just as Jack failed to hesitate before starting a relationship, his fiancée Kitty fails to reflect before leaving Jack. In Scheick's reading, "The Phantom Rickshaw" encourages readers to reflect before acting and to feel compassion for those who have acted too hastily (Scheick 51).

14. Kipling, who advocated British colonialism, was aware of its complexities. Tabish Khair urges readers to avoid facile comparisons of Rudyard Kipling to E. M. Forster as "patriarchal colonialist" and "liberal and humane" writers, respectively. Even though Kipling supported the British Empire, he was "not only under the influence of one set of discourses" (Khair 9–10).

15. Eastwood worded the question differently in a 1976–77 interview with Richard Thompson and Tim Hunter: "Why would you want to do a part in a picture where the woman has the best part?" (Thompson and Hunter 25).

16. Adam Knee observes that Evelyn controls most of the action and moves the narrative forward (Knee 92).

17. In interviews with Richard Thompson, Tim Hunter, and Michael Henry Wilson, Eastwood describes how he "optioned" Heims's script, which he had always admired but was unable to sell. Universal later bought the script directly from Heims, and Eastwood, who had a three-picture contract with Universal, arranged to direct the film (Thompson and Hunter 24; M. H. Wilson 73).

18. Evelyn seems to have fallen in love with Dave at first sound rather than first sight, since her feelings for him developed long before she met him face to face in Murphy's Bar.

19. Richard Thompson and Tim Hunter, on the other hand, find the film satisfying because Jessica Walter, who plays Evelyn, "is such a wonderful villainess" (Thompson and Hunter 23).

20. Surprisingly, only a few critics have pointed out the similarities between *Play Misty for Me* and *Fatal Attraction*: Jim Hala, who wrote that *Play Misty* "is in so many ways the same story as *Fatal Attraction* . . ." (Hala 77); Adam Knee, who calls Evelyn Draper "a clear model for the Glenn Close character in *Fatal Attraction*" (Knee 91–92); and Gale Jardine, who refers to *Play Misty* as "the grandmother of all *Fatal Attraction* films" (qtd. in Pittman).

21. John Rohrkemper analyzes in detail the ways that Lyne's shots in *Fatal Attraction* reproduce Hitchcock's in *Psycho* (Rohrkemper 85). In a 1971 interview, Stuart Kaminsky told Eastwood that *Play Misty* would be compared to *Psycho*, but Eastwood replied that he was not attempting to duplicate Hitchcock's film (Kaminsky 94).

22. In an interview, Eastwood reported that at a preview, men in the audience were calling, "Hit her, hit her" (Kaminsky 92). According to a concession stand worker quoted by Susan Faludi, male viewers of *Fatal Attraction* regularly screamed, "Beat that bitch! Kill her off now!" (Faludi 27).

23. Glenn Close wanted to play Alex Forrest so badly, she offered to do a screen test, which was "unheard of" for an actress of her calibre. Even after director Lyne saw Close's performance, he opposed casting her in the role. Casting agent Billy Hopkins and his associates pointed out Close's intelligence and talent, but Lyne said, "Look at her. She's not pretty enough" (Faludi 30).

24. Kathe Davis proposes that if Alex had ignored Dan and raised his child "in cheerful independence of its father," the film might have been subversive, and Alex would also have avoided harm (Davis 55).

25. Jim Hala and Bonnie Dow have both noticed how much Dan's six-year-old daughter Ellen looks and acts like a boy. Hala finds that this depiction fits the film's gender reversals, which convey a plea for a return to traditional roles (Hala 78). Dow reads the tomboyish daughter as a sign of postfeminist culture, since neither Dan nor Beth tells Ellen to act more like a girl. Dow proposes that the film offers a postfeminist scenario in which women's lives depend on their choices, and two women have chosen—and are fighting for—the same postfeminist man (Dow 124–25).

26. James Conlon argues that *Fatal Attraction* posits passion and domesticity as separate. In Conlon's reading, Dan Gallagher embraces Alex Forrest out of a natural need for passion that his marriage is not fulfilling. Dan violently ejects Alex from his world because in his ideology, domesticity and passion cannot coexist. Conlon points out the instability and danger of trying to exclude passion from one's life (Conlon 151–54).

27. Janet Karsten Larson interprets *Fatal Attraction* in spiritual and economic terms and finds the film "as anti-male as it is anti-female" (Larson 85). She expresses concern about women "whose failures we more readily dismiss in personalist terms than understand in social and demographic ones . . ." (Larson 84).

28. Sandra R. Joshel observes that "the film effectively inhibits the more difficult consideration of how women's autonomy might coexist with their affective relationships" (Joshel 66).

29. Emily Cuming notes that "body language and movement are [Mia's] dominant means of expression" and that "mobility" is crucial in Arnold's film narrative (Cuming 337–38).

30. Lisa Mullen calls *Fish Tank* "the story of a troubled girl trying to relate to her own physicality" (Mullen 17).

31. Arnold's title makes excellent sense if one reads Connor as the viewer who derives pleasure from watching women trapped by poverty.

32. Emily Cuming argues that Mia becomes "an interloper within [an] environment of private domesticity" (Cuming 338). She interprets the break-in and Mia's raid on Connor's wallet as signs of her lack of respect for boundaries (Cuming 337). When Mia urinates on Connor's rug, she may simply be overcome by stress, but she is also leaving a trace of herself that Connor can't easily remove. By marking his home with her scent, she is challenging a man who has been exploiting her family.

33. In an interview, Arnold commented, "I'm really interested in characters who behave in quite difficult ways. I like to see whether it's possible to have empathy with somebody who does that" (Mullen 18).

34. Britta Bein proposes that before Mia's illness, "Boris seems to be the one who has been providing meaning for her" (Bein 2). It takes considerable talent and self-confidence, however, to earn a PhD in Comparative Literature and teach poetry at Columbia University. Even before Boris's "pause," Mia found meaning in life through her work and her Minnesota background, and she will use these alternate sources to reconfigure her identity.

35. Britta Bein argues that for Mia, giving meaning to her illness is inseparable from giving meaning to her life: "The question of Mia's story is not how to get rid of her illness, but rather, how to deal with it in order to bring about a more positive self-definition" (Bein 7).

36. I agree with Britta Bein that "Mr. Nobody" is a part of Mia "rather than an independent being" (Bein 13).

37. Britta Bein observes that as Mia teaches the girls to create meaning through writing, she learns along with her students. As Mia tells her story, she "finds increasing pleasure in her narrative agency" (Bein 15).

CHAPTER 7 | ## Conclusion
Metaphors Matter in Emotion Regulation

Regulatory strategies may accomplish one person's goals at the expense of another's.

—JAMES J. GROSS

ALTHOUGH HUMAN EMOTIONS ARE bodily grounded, anyone studying the regulation of emotions needs to consider their social as well as their biological aspects. Psychologist James J. Gross points out that worldwide, most cultures teach that emotions "can and should be regulated in certain situations" (Gross, "Emotion Regulation" 3). In the years that human beings have lived in complex cultures, emotion regulation has probably done more good than harm. There remains the problem of which emotions to regulate, when, and how. Who has the right to decide what people should feel, and which emotions they should express? Each society answers these questions in its own way, but social rules of emotion regulation rarely benefit all members equally.

Western cultures, especially the United States, currently discourage the expression of "negative" emotions such as unhappiness and fear. On an individual level, people may have reasons for "up-regulating" these emotions, such as "promoting a focused, analytic mindset; fostering an empathic stance; and influencing others' actions" (Gross, "Emotion Regulation" 9). The best strategy for emotion regulation depends on context, and neuroscientists and psychologists who study emotion regulation tend to avoid universal, prescriptive rules. They also steer clear of models in which a human self separate from emotions battles them like dragons. Gross, a leader in the emotion regulation field, refers to "emotion regulation *in self*" rather than the regulation of emotions distinct from a self (Gross, "Emotion Regulation" 6, original emphasis).[1]

Instead, Gross offers a "process model" in which multiple factors enable the emergence of emotions: "situation selection," "situation modification," "attentional deployment," "cognitive change," and "response modulation" (Gross, "Emotion Regulation in Adulthood" 215). Emotions can be regulated at any of these five levels, but the behavioral and neuroimaging studies of Gross's group have shown that interventions early in the process benefit a person more than those enacted later, when an emotion is already being experienced.

Gross and his colleagues have found diverse evidence that cognitive reappraisal (reinterpreting a situation) modulates emotion more effectively than suppression (stifling an emotional response). In a 1998 study, Gross's team showed participants a film of a "disgusting arm amputation" and asked them either to think about the film in a way unlikely to arouse emotion (for example, as if it were a medical class teaching tool) or to conceal their emotional responses to the film (Gross, "Emotion Regulation in Adulthood" 216). Control subjects watched the film without any instructions. As a group, the participants who suppressed their responses showed less disgust but also suffered increases in blood pressure. Participants who reappraised their responses not only exhibited but *experienced* less disgust, and they did not respond physiologically (Gross, "Emotion Regulation in Adulthood" 216). In a related study, participants looked at images of injured men under similar reappraisal, suppression, or "just watch" conditions, and those who suppressed their responses remembered the images less well, based on test performances, than participants who reappraised or responded spontaneously (Gross, "Emotion Regulation in Adulthood" 217). In a subsequent study, Gross's group asked pairs of women who did not know each other to watch a disturbing film and then discuss their responses. One woman in each pair was asked to reappraise, suppress, or respond spontaneously. In the pairs where one woman had suppressed her emotions, *both partners* experienced increases in blood pressure. Gross believes the reason is that when people suppress negative emotions, they also suppress the positive ones that ease social interactions and reduce stress (Gross, "Emotion Regulation in Adulthood" 217). For two decades, he and his colleagues have been finding evidence that cognitive reappraisal alters emotional experience with few consequences, whereas suppression impairs memory, increases stress for oneself and for others, and leaves the experience of negative emotions intact.

Recent neuroimaging experiments support Gross's finding that suppression is more "cognitively costly" than reappraisal (Gross, "Emotion Regulation in Adulthood" 217). In a review of neuroimaging studies on emotion regulation, psychologist Kevin N. Ochsner and Gross observed an overall trend: participants who reappraised upsetting images or films showed early increases in frontal lobe activity and decreases in amygdala or insula activity with time, but participants who suppressed their responses showed later increases in frontal lobe activity and increased amygdala or insula activity with time (Ochsner and Gross 154–56). These data bear out the behavioral finding that people who suppress negative emotions continue to experience them, sometimes with increased intensity. A 2011 neuroimaging study by neuroscientist Christine D. Wilson-Mendenhall and her colleagues asked participants to imagine themselves in physically dangerous or socially tense situations, and in their responses, either to follow a verbal cue such as "fear" or just to observe what was happening. Participants who merely observed situations from a "third-person perspective" showed more activity in visual cortical areas and less in medial prefrontal cortical areas than those who read them in a "first-person," emotionally relevant way, suggesting that in the "observers," more cognitive resources were being devoted to vision, and fewer to relating the situation to oneself (Barrett et al., "A Psychological Construction Account" 458). This result supports the long-standing belief of some Eastern cultures that through meditation, one can attend more to sensations and less to the emotions they arouse, hence gaining a fuller understanding of what is happening around one. When emotions need to be regulated, cognitive strategies that involve reinterpretation or a change of focus appear to bring greater benefits than those that stifle a response.

In Western cultures, calls to "let go" and "move on" often work as commands to suppress. At first, this claim may seem counterintuitive. Emotionally wounded people need to heal and resume living, and such orders may be given with good intentions. "Let go" and "move on" may sound less humiliating than "suck it up" and "stop whining," but emotionally, they can have the same effects. They shame and bully suffering people into silence rather than encouraging thought. A devastated person needs time to think, above all about the direction in which she wants to "move." By representing emotional life through linear, forward motion, "move on" commits the double violation of prescribing what one should feel by dictating how one should move one's body through space. Metaphorically, the phrase works to stifle questions about the direction one's path should take. Depending on a person's life circumstances, a rest, a circle, or a zigzag pattern might work best for her. "Let go" and "move on" offer no guidance for reappraisal, no information about alternate perspectives.

When Gross and other emotion regulation researchers discuss reappraisal, they do not mean brooding over one's emotions for years. Probably none of them would identify Dostoevsky's Underground Man as an emotionally healthy person. They refer to an instantaneous process in which one quickly imagines a different perspective. Their point is that, however fleetingly, *it is worth thinking about what one feels.* Beating emotions back and refusing to think about them can damage physical and mental health. Calls for suppression do not address the reasons for emotions that have emerged from people's interactions with the world. Ultimately, the best response to emotional devastation is to address the interactions that caused it.

Psychologists Lisa Feldman Barrett, Christine D. Wilson-Mendenhall, and Lawrence W. Barsalou have proposed a model of emotion regulation based on the interplay of current and remembered sensations. These scientists' "psychological construction" model "undergirds [Gross's] process model . . . at a different level of analysis" (Barrett et al., "A Psychological Construction Account" 447, 456). Their approach to emotion regulation stems from Barrett's theory of constructed emotion (discussed in Chapter 2), which regards emotions as emergent, individually variable phenomena rather than fixed entities (Barrett, "Solving the Emotion Paradox" 20). Based on behavioral and neuroimaging evidence, Barrett, Wilson-Mendenhall, and Barsalou argue that both emotions and emotion regulation rely on "situated conceptualizations," recreated patterns of past sensory activity that seem relevant to ongoing sensations (Barrett et al., "A Psychological Construction Account" 448). Situated conceptualizations allow people to understand the meaning of sensations, to predict what will happen next, and to plan a response. They let people form updateable categories and concepts in ways that are fundamental to cognition, not unique to emotions (Barrett et al., "A Psychological Construction Account" 448, 451). According to this model, emotions emerge when incoming sensations confront situated conceptualizations in a continuous, simultaneous process (Barrett et al., "A Psychological Construction Account" 450). Emotion regulation can be understood as "shifting from one situated conceptualization to another," as momentary stimuli are compared to different past experiences and interpreted in new ways (Barrett et al., "A Psychological Construction Account" 448). These shifts need not be conducted consciously and can be learned whether they are made conscious or not. Emotions and their regulation rely on conversations between the present and the past, and these exchanges can shift as easily as face-to-face dialogues.

Gross's model of emotion regulation emphasizes intervention points; and Barrett, Wilson-Mendenhall, and Barsalou's, ongoing shifts, but all of these psychologists agree that emotion and emotion regulation rely on shared neural processes. There is no self that "owns" the emotions and is responsible for herding them, as if they were a flock of sheep threatening to eat a neighbor's grass. Ochsner and Gross's review of neuroimaging studies indicates that reappraisal involves the following brain areas: dorsal regions of the prefrontal cortex (PFC; associated with "working memory and selective attention"), ventral regions of the PFC (associated with "language or response inhibition"), dorsal regions of the anterior cingulate cortex (associated with "monitoring control processes"), and dorsal regions of the medial PFC (associated with "reflecting upon one's own or someone else's affective states") (Ochsner and Gross 154). Reappraisal appears to involve modulations of appraisal, and it uses the systems that conduct appraisal in the first place (Ochsner and Gross 154). "The closer one looks," writes Gross, "the harder it is to draw a bright line between emotion and emotion regulation" (Gross, "Emotion Regulation" 12). Barrett, Wilson-Mendenhall, and Barsalou agree that "the phenomena that we refer to as *emotion* and *emotion regulation* are derived within a common mechanistic framework" (Barrett et al., "A Psychological Construction Account" 456, original emphasis). In human brains, no center exists to regulate emotions that is not somehow involved in generating them.

Despite the differences between their models, Gross, Barrett, and their collaborators also concur that language plays a significant role in emotional life. Based on neuroimaging evidence, Ochsner and Gross hypothesize that the reinterpretation of emotions relies in part on "left-lateralized systems for language and verbal working memory (as one constructs a 'new story' about the meaning of a stimulus)" (Ochsner and Gross 154). Neuroimaging studies have surprised some scientists by revealing that "some forms of emotion regulation can depend upon linguistic and cognitive processes not typically thought of as having emotion-related functions" (Ochsner and Gross 156). Evidence for language's role in emotion regulation supports Barrett's hypothesis that language enables the formation of emotion concepts. She and her colleagues believe that language guides a person who is learning what a particular emotion is: "An emotion concept typically forms when a given emotion word . . . is explicitly uttered . . . during many different instances involving a variety of changes in feelings, physiology, and actions . . ." (Barrett et al., "A Psychological Construction Account" 453). Emotional experience depends on physiology, but the languages that people learn shape their interpretations of their emotions.

Scientists who study emotion regulation pay close attention to their own language. Since their laboratory studies contribute to a young, rapidly growing field, they choose their words with great care. Ochsner and Gross refer to "control," a term already well established in psychology. They write that "reappraisal depends upon interactions between prefrontal and cingulate regions implicated in cognitive control and systems like the amygdala and insula that have been implicated in emotional responding" (Ochsner and Gross 154). Gross claims that "we actually hold considerable sway over our emotions," implying a "we" separate from the emotions to be regulated (Gross, "Emotion Regulation in Adulthood" 214). As studies reveal the complex interplay of systems involved in emotion regulation, however, scientists are increasingly employing terms such as "interactions," as in the previous claim by Ochsner and Gross. Neuroimaging evidence indicates that regulation involves multiple dimensions of feedback, and researchers are seeking language to describe exchanges rather than top-down commands. Gross refers to "engagement of the processes that are responsible for altering the emotion trajectory"; and Ochsner and Gross, to "combinations of interacting subsystems" and "an emerging multilevel model of a functional architecture supporting cognitive emotion regulation" (Gross, "Emotion Regulation" 6; Ochsner and Gross 157, 156). These descriptions imply interactive feedback rather than emotional control by a distinct self.

Some scientists show acute awareness that metaphors can create misunderstandings if misused or outgrown. Barrett, Wilson-Mendenhall, and Barsalou criticize the classic machine metaphor of the human brain, which implies that emotions are generated in one brain region and then "regulated by executive or other cognitive processes located elsewhere in the brain" (Barrett et al., "A Psychological Construction Account" 447). The presumed spatial separation implies a temporal separation, with emotions preceding their regulation. So far, the evidence supports neither kind of disjunction. Barrett and her colleagues point out that with the mechanical metaphor, "regardless of which comes first, the emotion is separate from its regulation. . . . Other working metaphors for the mind and the brain are more apt" (Barrett et al., "A Psychological Construction Account" 448). To replace the machine metaphor, they propose a kitchen metaphor to convey the great variety of emotions and thoughts that a brain can cook from "basic ingredients" (Barrett et al., "A Psychological Construction Account" 456). The gender associations of these contrasting metaphors are obvious, but gender alone can never explain the differences in scientists' thinking. Barrett, Wilson-Mendenhall, and Barsalou favor the kitchen metaphor because based on their experimental findings, the source better meets the target. If the human brain is a kitchen, then everything it produces—not just emotions and their regulation—emerges from the same ingredients. By implying that "each brain state . . . can be understood in terms of more core systems," the kitchen metaphor evokes more accurate mental pictures of the ways that brains work (Barrett et al., "A Psychological Construction Account" 448).

In the 1960s, psychologist Silvan Tomkins used a metaphor to show how politics can enter popular understandings of emotions. He noted that there are "right" and "left" ideologies of emotions. The "right" ideology urges people to "strive toward self-sufficiency and adaptation to existing authorities," as behavioral psychologists once urged (Lutz 147–48). One can see this ideology at work in *G. I. Jane, Bridesmaids,* and *Who Moved My Cheese?* Rather than dwelling on one's pain, whatever the causes, one should invest one's energy in managing what one can control: one's emotions, since only the right combination of feelings will let one progress in the journey of life. This is not the only way to think about emotions' personal value, or about their social role.

As an alternative, Tomkins describes a "left" ideology, which holds that "a person deserves and should expect the help and support of the community" (Lutz 148). The "right" ideology also involves community mindedness because it teaches that dwelling on one's pain can hurt others besides oneself. But the "left" ideology implies that emotions are not merely an individual matter. As psychological studies have been revealing since Tomkins' day, emotions emerge from interactions between single minds and the world, and sometimes they require social responses that match the scale of their external causes.

Philosopher Martha C. Nussbaum has argued that ethical theories need to be informed by human emotions (Nussbaum, *Upheavals of Thought* 2), but she warns that anger has a limited capacity for social good (Nussbaum, *Anger and Forgiveness* 6). Anger can send a signal that a violation has occurred; it can motivate people to act; and it can deter people from committing future abuses, but it is an unreliable motivator and a poor communication device (Nussbaum, *Anger and Forgiveness* 6, 39). Because anger involves the perception of wrongdoing and a desire for retribution, it often focuses on the loss of status a person believes she has suffered and leads to fantasies of revenge (Nussbaum, *Anger and Forgiveness* 15). While inspirational leaders such as Martin Luther King have acknowledged people's anger, King guided them away from thoughts of retribution and toward cooperative social action (Nussbaum, *Anger and Forgiveness* 8, 28–29, 31). Nussbaum encourages angry people to move toward a "Transition" in which they consider the social relevance of the harm they have suffered and work to end this injustice on a broader scale (Nussbaum, *Anger and Forgiveness*

31–33). She believes that "victims are right to demand acknowledgement and accountability . . ." but argues that anger is not necessary for the pursuit of justice and will probably not lead to justice unless a Transition is reached (Nussbaum, *Anger and Forgiveness* 35, 39). Nussbaum rightly admonishes people who think that the poor and uneducated have no avenues for expressing their anger except for "lashing out" (Nussbaum, *Anger and Forgiveness* 40). Her philosophical analysis goes to the heart of the issue because the self-pity and grudges of people denied opportunities are closely related to anger. But the anger that pulses within them is not the kind that leads one to burn down a neighborhood.

At the core of self-pity and other "banned" emotions is the thought, "This is wrong. I don't deserve to be treated like this." In many cases, this is a reasonable response, but metaphors of darkness, filth, paralysis, and foul smells make people feel ashamed of this reaction. Awareness that one has been mistreated and that a wrong-doer (sometimes a whole social system) should be held accountable can be a well-grounded reaction, as likely to lead to action as to paralysis. Thinking "I don't deserve this" can reassure a person that she matters when she has been treated as though she didn't. Every human being has a rich inner life, and cherishing one's emotions can bring comfort and inspiration when life's circumstances are hard to bear. One of the greatest disrespects one human being can pay another is to deny that her emotions have value.

Acknowledging that people's emotions have a basis in the world can mean taking an initial step toward social justice. Psychologist Lisa Feldman Barrett, philosopher Martha C. Nussbaum, and literary scholar Sianne Ngai all agree that emotions are "about something" (Barrett, "Solving the Emotion Paradox" 36; Ngai 179; Nussbaum, *Upheavals of Thought* 27). However socially undesirable, emotions emerge from interactions with an environment and cannot be dismissed as false constructions. Emotions speak not just of the attending mind but of the way that the world works. Along with art historian James Elkins, I challenge the belief that "crying is the fault of the crier" (Elkins 39). Elkins refers to encounters with extraordinary works of art, but in a socioeconomic context, his resistance to blaming the crier for crying also rings true.

A culture that scorns expressions of pain does not work equally well for all its members. Such a culture serves those who are suffering least, and refusals to stifle one's crying can do subversive work. At first, wails of anguish may be dismissed as bouts of weakness and self-indulgence. The crier may be blamed for her unwillingness to help herself and be told to grow up and act like a responsible adult. If she persists, questions about why she is crying may turn toward her social environment. One reason why few people like a "crybaby" is that the question, "Why is she crying?" can send thoughts in unpleasant directions. Maybe she is crying because her job offers no health insurance, and she has learned that she has cancer. Maybe her salary won't cover her rent, and she and her three children are going to be evicted. The tears of those crushed by a socioeconomic system remind its elite that their prosperity may come from more than their hard work. Supposedly, banning self-pity and prolonged crying serves everyone's interest. Whose interest does it serve when crying that calls attention to injustice is dismissed as weakness of character?

Thinking differently about emotions will not stop human life from bringing pain. It won't miraculously bring justice, but it will show greater respect for the humanity of people who are being hurt. In *Illness as Metaphor*, Susan Sontag warns writers against using diseases as metaphoric sources (Sontag 3). She cites a host of metaphors in which cancer is aligned with social evils. As a cancer survivor, Sontag argues that using a disease as a metaphor demoralizes its sufferers by reducing their bodies to battlegrounds. But what is the next step? Banning metaphors would mean censorship and would be as pointless as banning emotions one doesn't want to see. Instead, Sontag calls for critical awareness and responsible use of metaphoric language (Sontag 4, 83–87).[2] Like Sontag, I advocate critical analysis of metaphors because it may change people's voluntary use of them. I hope that readers of this book will craft new metaphors to reflect current scientific understandings of emotion.

Studies of emotion regulation such as Gross's and Barrett's speak against a model in which an independent self governs emotions completely separate from it. Neuroscientists and psychologists disagree about whether some basic emotions are universal, or whether individuals learn to create categories of emotions based on their physiological and cultural experiences. But most scientists agree that a human self emerges from every part of interconnected bodies and brains. There is no self uninvolved in emotions that should tailor them to suit social standards.

The model that demands control of emotions by a ruling self does not come from neuroscience or psychology. It predates modern science and has religious roots, which have entwined themselves with economic principles. The notion that one must control one's passions to serve the social good is probably as old as humankind. But the concept of a rational self controlling dark, alien forces imposes oppressive political views on human brains and does not reflect our current knowledge of them. Emotions, even the most unsavory, form integral parts of mental life. Rather than unruly subjects to be controlled, emotions should be viewed as equal citizens worthy of attention and respect. A model stressing cooperation and sharing of mental activity would serve humans better, and it would more accurately reflect what brains do.

Notes

1. Gross contrasts intrinsic emotion regulation, or "emotion regulation *in self*," with extrinsic emotion regulation, or "emotion regulation *in another*," and adds that scientists who study adults usually focus on intrinsic emotion regulation, whereas those who study children analyze extrinsic emotion regulation. As examples of intrinsic and extrinsic regulation, Gross offers, "James regulates his own emotions"

and "James regulates Sarah's emotions" (Gross, "Emotion Regulation" 6). In the first case, his syntax could imply that James's emotions are separate from James, but this reading opposes the gist of Gross's passage.

2. In critically examining cultural uses of cancer metaphors, Sontag works toward "an elucidation of these metaphors, and a liberation from them" (Sontag 4).

BIBLIOGRAPHY

Abbot, Reginald. "What Miss Kilman's Petticoat Means: Virginia Woolf, Shopping, and Spectacle." *Modern Fiction Studies*, vol. 38, no. 1, 1992, pp. 193–216.

Ahmed, Sara. *The Cultural Politics of Emotions*. 2nd ed., Edinburgh UP, 2014.

Alighieri, Dante. *The Divine Comedy of Dante Alighieri: Inferno*. Translated by John D. Sinclair, Oxford UP, 1979.

Alighieri, Dante. *Purgatorio*. Edited and translated by W. S. Merwin, Alfred A. Knopf, 2008.

Anderson, Roger B. "*Notes from the Underground*: The Arrest of Personal Development." *Canadian American Slavic Studies*, vol. 24, no. 4, 1990, pp. 413–30.

Arnold, Andrea, director and screenwriter. *Fish Tank*. Curzon Artificial Eye, 2009.

Arnold, Magda B. *Emotion and Personality: Vol. 2, Neurological and Physiological Aspects*. Columbia UP, 1960.

Astell, Ann W. "The Writer as Redeemed Prostitute: Girard's Reading of Dostoevsky's *Notes from the Underground*." *Religion and Literature*, vol. 43, no. 3, 2011, pp. 186–94.

Babener, Liahna. "Patriarchal Politics in *Fatal Attraction*." *Journal of Popular Culture*, vol. 26, no. 3, 1992, pp. 25–34.

de Baecque, Antoine. Interview with Michael Haneke. *Libération*, October 5, 2005.

Bahri, Deepika. *Postcolonial Biology: Psyche and Flesh after Empire*. U of Minnesota P, 2017.

Bakhtin, M. M. *Problems of Dostoevsky's Poetics*. Translated by Carol Emerson, U of Minnesota P, 1984. In *Notes from the Underground*. By Fyodor Dostoevsky. Edited and translated by Michael R. Katz, Norton, 1989, pp. 146–56.

Bandyopadhyay, Debashis. "The Past Unearthed: New Reading of Ruskin Bond's Supernatural Tales." *Children's Literature Association Quarterly*, vol. 30, no. 1, 2005, pp. 53–71.

Barrett, Lisa Feldman. *How Emotions Are Made: The Secret Life of the Brain*. Pan MacMillan, 2017.

Barrett, Lisa Feldman. "Solving the Emotion Paradox: Categorization and the Experience of Emotion." *Personality and Social Psychology Review*, vol. 10, no. 1, 2006, pp. 20–46.

Barrett, Lisa Feldman, et al. "Of Mice and Men: Natural Kinds of Emotions in the Mammalian Brain? A Response to Panksepp and Izard." *Perspectives on Psychological Science*, vol. 2, no. 3, 2007, pp. 297–312.

Barrett, Lisa Feldman, et al. "A Psychological Construction Account of Emotion Regulation and Dysregulation: The Role of Situated Conceptualizations." In *Handbook of Emotion Regulation*. 2nd ed. Edited by James J. Gross, Guilford P, 2014, pp. 447–65.

Barsalou, Lawrence W. "Grounded Cognition." *Annual Review of Psychology*, vol. 59, 2008, pp. 617–45.

Baxter, Charles. *The Art of Subtext: Beyond Plot*. Graywolf P, 2007.

Beckett, Samuel. *Endgame*. Translated by Samuel Beckett. Grove P, 1958.

Bein, Britta. "Present Women/Absent Men in Siri Hustvedt's *The Summer without Men* (2011)." *Current Objectives of Postgraduate American Studies*, vol. 14, no. 1, 2013, pp. 1–19.

Berland, Elaine, and Marilyn Wechter. "Fatal/Fetal Attraction: Psychological Aspects of Imagining Female Identity in Contemporary Film." *Journal of Popular Culture*, vol. 26, no. 3, 1992, pp. 35–45.

Berlant, Lauren. "Cruel Optimism." In *The Affect Theory Reader*. Edited by Melissa Gregg and Gregory J. Seigworth, Duke UP, 2010, pp. 93–116.

Black, Max. "Metaphor." *Proceedings of the Aristotelian Society*, vol. 55, 1954–55, pp. 273–94.

Black, Max. "More about Metaphor." *Dialectica*, vol. 31, no. 3–4, 1977, pp. 431–57.

Bowlby, John. *Attachment and Loss: Vol. 2, Separation: Anxiety and Anger*. Basic Books, 1973.

Bradberry, Travis, and Jean Greaves. *Emotional Intelligence 2.0*. TalentSmart, 2009.

Bromley, Susan, and Pamela Hewitt. "*Fatal Attraction*: The Sinister Side of Women's Conflict about Career and Family." *Journal of Popular Culture*, vol. 26, no. 3, 1992, pp. 17–23.

Brown, Tony. "Edward Carpenter, Forster and the Evolution of *A Room with a View*." *English Literature in Transition*, vol. 30, no. 3, 1987, pp. 279–301.

Bunyan, John. *The Pilgrim's Progress*. Edited by Roger Sharrock, Penguin, 1987.

Celik, Ipek A. "'I Wanted You to Be Present': Guilt and the History of Violence in Michael Haneke's *Caché*." *Cinema Journal*, vol. 50, no.1, 2010, pp. 59–80.

Chasar, Mike. "G. I. Jane and D. H. Lawrence." *Poetry and Popular Culture*. 12 Feb. 2011. mikechasar.blogspot.com/2011/02/gi-jane-dh-lawrence.html. Accessed 29 May 2017.

Ciugureanu, Adina. "The Victim-Aggressor Duality in *Great Expectations*." *Partial Answers*, vol. 9, no. 2, 2011, pp. 347–61.

"Clinger." American Standard VorMax toilet television advertisement. www.ispot.tv/ad/7xDJ/american-standard-vormax-toilet-clinger. Accessed 16 June, 2017.

Conlon, James. "The Place of Passion: Reflections on *Fatal Attraction*." *Journal of Popular Film and Television*, vol. 16, no. 4, 1989, pp. 148–54.

Cuming, Emily. "Private Lives, Social Housing: Female Coming-of-Age Stories on the British Council Estate." *Contemporary Women's Writing*, vol. 7, no. 3, 2013, pp. 328–45.

Damasio, Antonio. *Descartes' Error: Emotion, Reason, and the Human Brain*. Harper Collins, 1994.

Davis, Kathe. "The Allure of the Predatory Woman in *Fatal Attraction* and Other Current American Movies." *Journal of Popular Culture*, vol. 26, no. 3, 1992, pp. 47–57.

"Despond." *The Compact Oxford English Dictionary*. Oxford UP, 1983, p. 260.

Dickens, Charles. *Great Expectations*. Edited by Margaret Cardwell, Oxford UP, 1998.

Dickson, Sheila. "Two Sides of an Anorexic Coin in *Die Wahlverwandtschaften* and *Die Verwandlung*: Ottilie as *Heilige*, Gregor as *Mistkäfer*." *Orbis Litterarum*, vol. 54, 1999, pp. 174–84.

Dobrogoszcz, Tomasz. "The Hidden Gaze of the Other in Michael Haneke's *Hidden*." *Text Matters*, vol. 1, no. 1, 2011, pp. 226–38.

Dostoevsky, Fyodor. *Complete Letters*. Edited and translated by David A. Lowe, 5 vols. Ardis, 1989.

Dostoevsky, Fyodor. *Notes from the Underground*. Edited and translated by Michael R. Katz, Norton, 1989.

Dostoevsky, Fyodor. *Polnoe sobranie sochinenii v tridtsati tomakh*. Nauka, 1985.

Dow, Bonnie J. "The Traffic in Men and the Fatal Attraction of Postfeminist Masculinity." *Women's Studies in Communication*, vol. 29, no. 1, 2006, pp. 113–31.

Durantaye, Leland de la. "Kafka's Reality and Nabokov's Fantasy: On Dwarves, Saints, Beetles, Symbolism, and Genius." *Comparative Literature*, vol. 59, no. 4, 2007, pp. 315–31.

Eagleton, Terry. *Ideologie: Eine Einführung*. J. B. Metzler Verlag, 1993.

Eastwood, Clint, director. *Play Misty for Me*. Screenplay by Jo Heims and Dean Riesner. Universal Pictures, 1971.

Eliot, George. *Middlemarch*. Edited by Bert G. Hornback, Norton, 2000.

Elkins, James. *Pictures and Tears: A History of People Who Have Cried in Front of Paintings*. Routledge, 2001.

Elson, Miriam. "Self-Pity, Dependence, Manipulation, and Exploitation: A View from Self Psychology." *Annual of Psychoanalysis*, vol. 25, 1997, pp. 5–16.

"Emotion, n." *OED Online*. Oxford UP, March 2017. Accessed 24 May, 2017.

Faludi, Susan. "Fatal Distortion." *Mother Jones*, Feb-March 1988, p. 27+.

Feig, Paul, director. *Bridesmaids*. Screenplay by Annie Mumolo and Kristen Wiig. Universal Pictures, 2011.

Fleissner, Robert F. "Is Gregor Samsa a Bed Bug? Kafka and Dickens Revisited." *Studies in Short Fiction*, vol. 22, no. 2, 1985, pp. 225–28.

Forster, E. M. *A Room with a View*. Penguin Books, 2000.

Fortin, Rene E. "Responsive Form: Dostoevsky's *Notes from the Underground* and the Confessional Tradition." *Essays in Literature*, vol. 7, no. 2, 1980, pp. 225–45.

Frank, Joseph. *Dostoevsky: The Stir of Liberation, 1860–1865*. In *Notes from the Underground*. By Fyodor Dostoevsky. Edited and translated by Michael R. Katz, Norton, 1989, pp. 202–37.

Frazzetto, Giovanni. *How We Feel: What Neuroscience Can and Can't Tell Us about Our Emotions*. Doubleday, 2013.

Frevert, Ute. *Emotions in History—Lost and Found*. Central European UP, 2011.

Gavarini, Jehanne-Marie. "Rewind: The Will to Remember, the Will to Forget in Michael Haneke's *Caché*." In *Millennial Cinema: Memory in Global Film*. Edited by Amresh Sinha and Terence McSweeney. Columbia UP, 2011, pp. 192–208.

Gendron, Maria, and Lisa Feldman Barrett. "Reconstructing the Past: A Century of Ideas about Emotion in Psychology." *Emotion Review*, vol. 1, no. 4, 2009, pp. 316–39.

Gilman, Sander L. *Franz Kafka, the Jewish Patient*. Routledge, 1995.

Goldman, Jane. "Forster and Women." In *The Cambridge Companion to E. M. Forster*. Edited by David Bradshaw, Cambridge UP, 2007, pp. 120–37.

Goleman, Daniel. *Emotional Intelligence: Why It Can Matter More Than IQ*. Bantam, 1995.

Gross, James J. "Emotion Regulation in Adulthood: Timing Is Everything." *Current Directions in Psychological Science*, vol. 10, no. 6, 2001, pp. 214–19.

Gross, James J. "Emotion Regulation: Conceptual and Empirical Foundations." In *Handbook of Emotion Regulation*. 2nd ed. Edited by James J. Gross, Guilford P, 2014, pp. 3–20.

Hagelin, Sarah. *Reel Vulnerability: Power, Pain, and Gender in Contemporary American Film and Television*. Rutgers UP, 2013.

Hala, Jim. "*Fatal Attraction* and the Attraction of Fables: A Morphological Analysis." *Journal of Popular Culture*, vol. 26, no. 3, 1992, pp. 71–82.

Halbwachs, Maurice. *The Causes of Suicide*. Routledge and Kegan Paul, 1978.

Hall, J. R. "Abstraction in Dostoevsky's *Notes from the Underground*." *Modern Language Review*, vol. 76, no. 1, 1981, pp. 129–37.

Haneke, Michael, director and screenwriter. *Caché*. Les Films du Losange, 2005.

Hara, Eiichi. "Stories Present and Absent in *Great Expectations*." *English Literary History*, vol. 53, no. 3, 1986, pp. 593–614.

Hartog, Curt. "The Rape of Miss Havisham." *Studies in the Novel*, vol. 14, no. 3, 1982, pp. 248–65.

Hazan, Cindy, and Phillip Shaver. "Romantic Love Conceptualized as an Attachment Process." *Journal of Personality and Social Psychology*, vol. 52, no. 3, 1987, pp. 511–24.

Heath, Jeffrey. "Kissing and Telling: Turning Round in *A Room with a View*." *Twentieth-Century Literature*, vol. 40, no. 4, 1994, pp. 393–433.

"Heinz Kohut." en.wikipedia.org/wiki/Heinz_Kohut. Accessed 29 May, 2017.

Herz, Judith Scherer. "A Room with a View." In *The Cambridge Companion to E. M. Forster*. Edited by David Bradshaw, Cambridge UP, 2007, pp. 138–50.

Hinojosa, Lynne Walhout. "Religion and Puritan Typology in E. M. Forster's *A Room with a View*." *Journal of Modern Literature*, vol. 33, no. 4, 2010, pp. 72–94.

Hoff, Molly. "Woolf's *Mrs. Dalloway*." *Explicator*, vol. 58 no. 3, 2000, pp. 148–50.

Hogan, Patrick Colm. *How Authors' Minds Make Stories*. Cambridge UP, 2013.

Hogan, Patrick Colm. *The Mind and Its Stories: Narrative Universals and Human Emotion*. Cambridge UP, 2003.

Hogan, Patrick Colm. *What Literature Teaches Us about Emotion*. Cambridge UP, 2011.

Hustvedt, Siri. *The Summer without Men*. Picador, 2011.

Jackson, J. A. "Freedom and Otherness: The Religious Dimension of Dostoevsky's *Notes from the Underground*." *Religion and Literature*, vol. 43, no. 3, 2011, pp. 179–86.

James, William. *The Principles of Psychology*. 2 vols. Henry Holt, 1904.

Jermyn, Deborah. "Rereading the Bitches from Hell: A Feminist Appropriation of the Female Psychopath." *Screen*, vol. 37, no. 3, 1996, pp. 251–67.

Johnson, Spencer. *Who Moved My Cheese? An A-Mazing Way to Deal with Change in Your Work and in Your Life*. Vermilion, 1999.

Joshel, Sandra R. "Fatal Liaisons and Dangerous Attraction: The Destruction of Feminist Voices." *Journal of Popular Culture*, vol. 26, no. 3, 1992, pp. 59–70.

Kafka, Franz. *Brief an den Vater*. Fischer, 2013.

Kafka, Franz. *Briefe*, 4 vols. Edited by Hans-Gerd Koch, Fischer, 1999–2013.

Kafka, Franz. *Briefe 1902–1924*. Edited by Max Brod, Schocken Books, 1958.

Kafka, Franz. *The Metamorphosis*. In *The Metamorphosis and Other Stories*. Translated by Willa and Edwin Muir, Schocken Books, 1995.

Kafka, Franz. *The Metamorphosis/Die Verwandlung*. Translated by Willa and Edwin Muir, Schocken Books, 1978.

Kafka, Franz. *Tagebücher 1910–1923*. 3 vols. Fischer, 2008.

Kafka, Franz. *Tagebücher 1910–1923*. Books on Demand, 2018. Accessed 11 May, 2018.

Kaminsky, Stuart M. "Eastwood on Eastwood." In *Clint Eastwood*. Signet, 1974.

Kandel, Eric R., et al. *Principles of Neural Science*. 5th ed. McGraw Hill, 2013.

Katz, Michael R. Notes. In *Notes from the Underground*. By Fyodor Dostoevsky. Edited and translated by Michael R. Katz, Norton, 1989.

Keltner, Dacher, and Paul Ekman. "Introduction: Expression of Emotion." In *Handbook of Affective Sciences*. Edited by R. J. Davidson, et al. Oxford UP, 2003, pp. 411–14.

Khair, Tabish. "Kipling on the Phantom Rickshaw: Between Words and a Hard Place." *Poetry Nation Review*, vol. 1, no. 135, 2000, pp. 9–10.

Kipling, Rudyard. "The Phantom Rickshaw." In *The Man Who Would Be King and Other Stories*. Dover, 1994.

Knee, Adam. "The Dialectic of Female Power and Male Hysteria in *Play Misty for Me*." In *Screening the Male: Exploring Masculinities in Hollywood Cinema*. Edited by Steven McCohan and Ina Rae Hark, Routledge, 1993, pp. 87–102.

Knight, Holly, and Mike Chapman, songwriters. "Love Is a Battlefield." Sung by Pat Benatar. *Live from Earth*. Chrysalis Records, 1983.

Kövecses, Zoltán. *Emotion Concepts*. Springer, 1990.

Kövecses, Zoltán. *Metaphor and Emotion: Language, Culture, and Body in Human Feeling*. Cambridge UP, 2000.

Kring, Ann M. "Gender and Anger." In *Gender and Emotion*. Edited by Agneta H. Fischer, Cambridge UP, 2000, pp. 211–31.

Lakoff, George, and Mark Johnson. *Metaphors We Live By*. 2nd ed. U of Chicago P, 2003.

Lakoff, George, and Zoltán Kövecses. "The Cognitive Model of Anger Inherent in American English." In *Cultural Models of Language and Thought*. Cambridge UP, 1987, pp. 195–221.

Larson, Janet Karston. "Filming the Poor in Spirit." *Cross Currents*, vol. 38, no. 1, 1988, pp. 76–86.

Lawrence, D. H. *Pansies: Poems by D. H. Lawrence*. Martin Secker, 1929.

Leadbeater, Lewis W. "Aristophanes and Kafka: The Dung Beetle Connection." *Studies in Short Fiction*, vol. 23, no. 2, 1986, pp. 169–78.

LeDoux, Joseph. *Anxious: Using the Brain to Understand and Treat Fear and Anxiety*. Penguin Books, 2015.

Levenback, Karen L. "Clarissa Dalloway, Doris Kilman and the Great War." *Virginia Woolf Miscellany*, vol. 37, 1991, pp. 3–4.

Levy, Eric P. "Self-Pity Neurosis." *San José Studies*, vol. 20, no. 1, 1994, pp. 18–29.

Leys, Ruth. "The Turn to Affect: A Critique." *Critical Inquiry*, vol. 37, no. 3, 2011, pp. 434–72.

Lunt, Dennis. "World Spirit as Baal: Marx, Adorno, and Dostoevsky on Alienation." *Journal of Speculative Philosophy*, vol. 26, no. 2, 2012, pp. 485–95.

Lutz, Tom. *Crying: The Natural and Cultural History of Tears*. Norton, 2001.

Lyne, Adrian, director. *Fatal Attraction*. Screenplay by James Dearden. Paramount Pictures, 1987.

Markley, A. A. "E. M. Forster's Reconfigured Gaze and the Creation of a Homoerotic Subjectivity." *Twentieth-Century Literature*, vol. 47, no. 2, 2001, pp. 268–92.

Mascolo, Michael F. "Wittgenstein and the Discursive Analysis of Emotion." *New Ideas in Psychology*, vol. 27, 2009, pp. 258–74.

Mass, Roslyn. "The Mirror Cracked: The Career Woman in a Trio of Lansing Films." *Film Criticism*, vol. 12, no. 2, 1987, pp. 28–36.

McConkey, James. *The Novels of E. M. Forster*. Cornell UP, 1957.

McElrath, Joseph R. "Plumbing the Swamp: The Modern Mode of Self-Pity." *Southern Humanities Review*, vol. 7, 1973, 53–65.

McGill, Justine. "Bad Memories: Haneke with Locke on Personal Identity and Post-Colonial Guilt." *Film and Philosophy*, vol. 17, no. 1, 2013, pp. 134–53.

Messner, Elizabeth M. "Emotionale Tränen." *Der Ophthalmologe*, vol. 106, no. 7, 2009, pp. 593–602.

Miller, Jean Baker. *Toward a New Psychology of Women*. Beacon P, 1986.

"Miriam Elson, Leader in Social Work Education." *UChicagoNews*. 12 May 2009. news. uchicago.edu/article/2009/05/12/miriam-elson-leader-social-work-education-1909-2009. Accessed 9 May 2018.

Molek-Kozakowska, Katarzyna. "Coercive Metaphors in News Headlines: A Cognitive-Pragmatic Approach." *Brno Studies in English*, vol. 40, no. 1, 2014, pp. 149–73.

Moon, Kenneth. "Where is Clarissa? Doris Kilman and Recoil from the Flesh in Virginia Woolf's *Mrs. Dalloway*." *College Language Association Journal*, vol. 23, no. 3, 1980, pp. 273–86.

Moretti, Franco. "Kindergarten." In *Signs Taken for Wonders: Essays in the Sociology of Literary Forms*. Verso, 1983, pp. 157–81.

Mullen, Lisa. "Estate of Mind." *Sight and Sound*, Oct. 2009, pp. 16–19.

Nabokov, Vladimir. *Lectures on Literature*. Edited by Fredson Bowers. Weidenfeld and Nicolson, 1980.

Negra, Diane. "Gendering the Recession." Keynote Address. International Society for the Study of Narrative Conference. 27 June, 2013. Manchester, UK.

Ngai, Sianne. *Ugly Feelings*. Harvard UP, 2005.

Nussbaum, Martha C. *Anger and Forgiveness: Resentment, Generosity, Justice*. Oxford UP, 2016.

Nussbaum, Martha C. *Upheavals of Thought: The Intelligence of Emotions*. Cambridge UP, 2001.

Ochsner, Kevin N., and James J. Gross. "Cognitive Emotion Regulation: Insights from Social Cognitive and Affective Neuroscience." *Current Directions in Psychological Science*, vol. 17, no. 2, 2008, pp. 153–58.

Ogrodnik, Benjamin. "Deep Cuts." *Film International*, vol. 7, no. 1, 2009, pp. 56–59.

Pages, Neil Christian. "What's Hidden in *Caché*." *Modern Austrian Literature*, vol. 43, no. 2, 2010, pp. 1–24.

Paz, Octavio. *El laberinto de la soledad*. Fondo de Cultura Económica, 1989.

Penney, James. "'You Never Look at Me from Where I See You': Postcolonial Guilt in *Caché*." *New Formations*, vol. 70, 2010, pp. 77–93.

Peters, Robert. "The Self-Pity Poem." *Paintbrush*, vol. 14, 1987, pp. 39–42.

Pittman, Duncan. "West of Eden: Eastwood's Silent Generation Warning to California in *Play Misty for Me* (1971)." *Cine-Files*, vol. 3, Dec. 2012. www.thecine-files.com/past-issues/2012-savannah-film-festival/featured-scholarship/featured-scholarship-three/. Accessed 12 May, 2018.

Plato. *Phaedrus and Letters VII and VIII*. Edited and translated by Walter Hamilton. Penguin Books, 1973.

Porton, Richard. "Collective Guilt and Individual Responsibility: An Interview with Michael Haneke." *Cineaste*, vol. 31, no. 1, 2005, pp. 50–51. www.cineaste.com.

Primamore, Elizabeth. "A Don, Virginia Woolf, the Masses, and the Case of Miss Kilman." *Literature, Interpretation, Theory*, vol. 9, no. 2, 1998, pp. 121–37.

Rahman, Tarir. "The Double-Plot in E. M. Forster's *A Room with a View*." *Cahiers Victoriens et Edouardiens*, vol. 33, 1991, pp. 43–62.

Reitano, Natalie. "American Squander: *Sideways* and the Extravagance of Self-Pity." *Senses of Cinema*, vol. 34, 2005. sensesofcinema.com/2005/on-recent-films-34/sideways/. Accessed 9 May, 2018.

Richards, I. A. *The Philosophy of Rhetoric*. Oxford UP, 1936.

Roddick, Nick. "Do We Know Where We're Going?" *Sight and Sound*, Oct. 2009, pp. 19–20.

Rohrkemper, John. "*Fatal Attraction*: The Politics of Terror." *Journal of Popular Culture*, vol. 26, no. 3, 1992, pp. 83–89.

Royde-Smith, John Graham, and Dennis E Showalter. "World War I." *Encyclopedia Britannica Online*. 20 February 2018. wwwbritannicacom.proxy.library.emory.edu/event/World-War-I/Killed-wounded-and-missing. Accessed 26 May, 2018.

Ryan, Michael P. "Kafka's *Die Söhne*: The Range and Scope of Metaphor." *Monatshefte*, vol. 93, no. 1, 2001, pp. 73–86.

Ryan, Simon. "Franz Kafka's *Die Verwandlung*: Transformation, Metaphor, and the Perils of Assimilation." *Seminar*, vol. 43, no. 1, 2007, pp. 1–18.

Sampaio, Sofia. "'I Wish Something Would Happen to You, My Friend!' Tourism and Liberalism in E. M. Forster's Italian Novels." *Textual Practice*, vol. 26, no. 5, 2012, pp. 895–920.

Sanborn, Pat. "Nasty Pleasures in *Notes from the Underground*." *North Dakota Quarterly*, vol. 54, no. 2, 1986, pp. 200–211.

Saunders, Max. "Forster's Life and Life-Writing." In *The Cambridge Companion to E. M. Forster*. Edited by David Bradshaw, Cambridge UP, 2007, pp. 8–31.

Scarry, Elaine. *Dreaming by the Book.* Farrar, Strauss, Giroux, 1999.

Schachter, Stanley, and Jerome E. Singer. "Cognitive, Social, and Physiological Determinants of Emotional State." *Psychological Review,* vol. 69, no. 5, 1962, pp. 379–99.

Scheick, William J. "Hesitation in Kipling's 'The Phantom Rickshaw.'" *English Literature in Translation,* vol. 29, no. 1, 1986, pp. 48–53.

Schuman, Rebecca. "Kafka's *Verwandlung,* Wittgenstein's *Tractatus,* and the Limits of Metaphorical Language." *Modern Austrian Literature,* vol. 44, no. 3-4, 2011, pp. 19–32.

Scott, Ridley, director. *G. I. Jane.* Screenplay by David Twohy and Danielle Alexandra. Buena Vista Pictures, 1997.

Seigworth, Gregory J., and Melissa Gregg. "An Inventory of Shimmers." In *The Affect Theory Reader.* Edited by Melissa Gregg and Gregory J. Seigworth, Duke UP, 2010, pp. 1–25.

"Self Psychology Psychoanalysis." The New York Institute for Psychoanalytic Self Psychology. 2001–2018. www.selfpsychologypsychoanalysis.org/index.shtml. Accessed 9 May, 2018.

Seshadri, Kalpana Rahita. "Spectacle of the Hidden: Michael Haneke's *Caché.*" *Nottingham French Studies,* vol. 46, no. 3, 2007, pp. 32–48.

"Seven Deadly Sins." *Encyclopedia Britannica.* www.britannica.com/topic/seven-deadly-sins. Accessed 8 May, 2018.

Sherwin, Miranda. "Deconstructing the Male: Masochism, Female Spectatorship, and the Femme Fatale in *Fatal Attraction, Body of Evidence,* and *Basic Instinct.*" *Journal of Popular Film and Television,* vol. 35, no. 4, 2008, pp. 174–82.

Shouse, Eric. "Feeling, Emotion, Affect." *M/C Journal,* vol. 8, no. 6, 2005. journal. media-culture.org.au/0512/03-shouse.php. Accessed 22 July, 2015.

Silverman, Max. "The Violence of the Cut: Michael Haneke's *Caché* and Cultural Memory." *French Cultural Studies,* vol. 21, no. 1, 2010, pp. 57–65.

Simon, Richard Keller. "E. M. Forster's Critique of Laughter and the Comic: The First Three Novels as Dialectic." *Twentieth-Century Literature,* vol. 31, no. 2, 1985, pp. 199–220.

Sinclair, John D. Introduction. In *The Divine Comedy of Dante Alighieri: Vol. 1, Inferno.* Edited and translated by John D. Sinclair, Oxford UP, 1979.

Sinclair, John D. Note. In *The Divine Comedy of Dante Alighieri: Vol. 1, Inferno.* Edited and translated by John D. Sinclair, Oxford UP, 1979.

"Sins, Virtues, and Tales." www.deadlysins.com/. Accessed 8 May, 2018.

Sokel, Walter H. "Kafka as a Jew." *New Literary History,* vol. 30, no. 4, 1999, pp. 837–52.

Sontag, Susan. *Illness as Metaphor and AIDS and Its Metaphors.* Picador, 1996.

Stone, Oliver, director. *Wall Street: Money Never Sleeps.* Screenplay by Allan Loeb and Stephen Schiff. 20th Century Fox, 2010.

"Third Punic War." *Encyclopedia Britannica.* www.britannica.com.proxy.library.emory. edu/event/Third-Punic-War. Accessed 12 May, 2018.

Thompson, Joyce. "From *Diversion* to *Fatal Attraction*: The Transformation of a Morality Play into a Hollywood Hit." *Journal of Popular Culture,* vol. 26, no. 3, 1992, pp. 5–15.

Thompson, Richard, and Tim Hunter. "Eastwood Direction." In *Clint Eastwood: Interviews Revised and Updated*. UP of Mississippi, 2013, pp. 20–39.

Tomkins, Silvan. *Affect, Imagery, Consciousness*. 4 vols. Springer, 1962–92.

Tomkins, Silvan. *Shame and Its Sisters: A Silvan Tomkins Reader*. Edited by Eve Kosofsky Sedgwick and Adam Frank, Duke UP, 1995.

"The Twelve Steps of Alcoholics Anonymous." Alcoholics Anonymous Publishing. www.aa.org/assets/en_US/smf-121_en.pdf. Accessed 9 May, 2018.

Toubiana, Serge. Interview with Michael Haneke. *Caché* DVD. SONY, 2006.

Urzidil, John. "Recollections." In *The Kafka Problem*. Edited by Angel Flores, Octagon Books, 1963, pp. 20–24.

Virgil. *The Aeneid*. Translated by Robert Fitzgerald, Random House, 1983.

Warhol, Robyn R. *Having a Good Cry: Effeminate Feelings and Pop-Culture Forms*. Ohio State UP, 2003.

Westbrook, Brett. "Thoroughly Modern Eastwood: Male/Female Power Relations in *The Beguiled* and *Play Misty for Me*." In *New Essays on Clint Eastwood*. Edited by Leonard Engel, U of Utah P, 2012, 36–52.

Williams, Linda Ruth. "Ready for Action: *G. I. Jane*, Demi Moore's Body and the Female Combat Movie." In *Action and Adventure Cinema*. Edited by Yvonne Tasker, Routledge, 2004, pp. 169–85.

Wilson, Carnie, Chynna Phillips, and Glen Ballard. "Hold On." ©1990 EMI Blackwood Music Inc., Smooshie Music, Universal Music Corp. and Aerostation Corporation.

Wilson, Michael Henry. "'Whether I Succeed or Fail, I don't Want to Owe It to Anyone but Myself': From *Play Misty for Me* to *Honkytonk Man*." In *Clint Eastwood: Interviews Revised and Updated*. UP of Mississippi, 2013, 72–92.

Wilson-Mendenhall, Christine, et al. "Grounding Emotion in Situated Conceptualization." *Neuropsychologica*, vol. 49, 2011, pp. 1105–27.

"Woman Suffrage." *Encyclopedia Britannica Online*. 8 Feb., 2018. www-britannica-com.proxy.library.emory.edu/topic/woman-suffrage. Accessed 26 May, 2018.

Woods, Marjorie Curry. "Classical Emotions in the Medieval Classroom." History of Emotions Colloquium. 18 Nov., 2014. Max Planck Institute for Human Development, Berlin, Germany.

Woolf, Virginia. *The Diary of Virginia Woolf*. 5 vols. Edited by Anne Olivier Bell, Hogarth P, 1977–84.

Woolf, Virginia. *The Letters of Virginia Woolf*. 6 vols. Edited by Nigel Nicolson and Joanne Trautmann, Hogarth P, 1978.

Woolf, Virginia. *Mrs. Dalloway*. Edited by Bonnie Kime Scott, Harcourt, 2005.

appraisal, emotion as, 17–18

Arnold, Andrea, *Fish Tank*, 7–8, 134–39
  articulation of rage in, 138
  choice of movement in, 139
  dwellings in, 135–36
  gender and power in, 138
  movement in, 134–36
  relationships and movement in, 136–37
  response to abandonment in, 137–39
  sexualizing of relationships in, 137

Arnold, Magda, emotion as appraisal, 17

attachment
  anxious attachment, 81
  as metaphor for relationships, 80–83
  patterns of behavior, 81

autonomy, growth of in *The Summer without Men*, 143–44

Bandyopadhyay, Debashis, on "The Phantom Rickshaw," 97, 147n11

banned emotions
  cultural perspectives on regulating, 151
  diversity of metaphors representing, 36
  and metaphors of movement, 36
  resemblance to seven deadly sins, 25
  roots of, 9n5

Barrett, Lisa Feldman
  basis of emotions, 157
  brain, machine metaphor for, 155–56
  language in emotional life, 154–55
  psychological construction model, 153–54
  theory of constructed emotion, 18–20
  on William James, 13

Barsalou, Lawrence W.
  brain, machine metaphor for, 155–56
  memory of sensory experiences, 58
  psychological construction model, 153–54

basic emotions, theory of, 16, 18–19

Baxter, Charles, emotions and visibility to others, 5

Beckett, Samuel, self-pity as aristocratic vanity, 95

Bein, Britta, on *The Summer without Men*, 149n37

Berland, Elaine, 82–83

Berlant, Lauren, 9n8

biology
  and conveying emotion, 1
  emotions and interaction with culture, 20

birds, in "The Phantom Rickshaw," 98–99

Black, Max
  aligning source and target in metaphors, 80, 82
  creating resonant metaphors, 31–32
  interaction theory of metaphor, 20–21
  on metaphors, 20

bodily sensations, in *The Metamorphosis*, 91–93, 94

Bowlby, John, 81

Bradberry, Travis, *Emotional Intelligence 2.0*, 32, 33

brain
  cortex and amygdala, role in emotions, 15–16
  metaphors for, 155–56
  neuroimaging and studies of emotion, 17, 18–19, 154–55

breathlessness, and bodily sensation in *The Metamorphosis*, 92–93

Bridesmaids (Feig), 6–7
  change in, 50
  emotional freedom in, 51
  envy in, 49–50
  self-pity in, 47–51

bullying, response in *The Summer without Men*, 143

Bunyan, John, *The Pilgrim's Progress*
  metaphorical transgression and bodily suffering in, 25
  metaphors of swamping and flooding in, 32

cultural hegemony, and stifling
    language of emotion, 4
cultural values
    and contempt for self-pity, 39–40
    crying, assumptions regarding,
        52–55, 157–58
    crying, prohibitions against, 41–42
    emotions and interaction with
        biology, 20
    emotions and interaction with
        physiology, 24–25
    and expressing emotion, 1, 30
    and facial expressions, 17
    and regulation of emotion,
        151–52, 153
    and shaping of emotion, 2
    and visibility of emotion, 5, 6
Cuming, Emily, 135–36

Damasio, Antonio
    corporeal nature of emotions,
        15, 37n1
    emotions and decision-making, 55n3
    on William James, 13
dance, in *Fish Tank*, 135–36, 138–39
Dante. *See* Alighieri, Dante
darkness
    and character development in *Play
        Misty for Me*, 103
    metaphoric use of in *A Room with a
        View*, 61
    metaphoric use of in *Great
        Expectations*, 94–95
    and representing emotions of rejected
        people, 144
Dearden, James, 131–32
death, in *The Metamorphosis*, 94
deception, and character development
    in *Fatal Attraction*, 134
delusions, metaphorical accuracy of, 140
Descartes' Error (Damasio), 55n3
despondence, in narratives of spiritual
    journey, 25

destruction
    and character development in *Fatal
        Attraction*, 133
    and character development in *Play
        Misty for Me*, 103
detachment, as metaphor for broken
    relationships, 81–82
Dickens, Charles, *Great Expectations*,
        93–96
    abandonment, metaphors of, 96
    attachment, metaphors of, 82
    choice of perspective in, 93
    female forces in, 96
    gender and experiencing emotion, 2–3
    movement of characters, 94
    narcissism, representations of, 94
    narrative tension in, 95
    plot development in, 93
    time, representations of, 93
    vanity, representations of, 95
disease, and metaphors of emotion, 33
Diversion, 131–32
Dostoevsky, Fyodor, *Notes from the
        Underground*, 7, 80–88
    aggressive visualizations in, 105–6
    assertions of humanity in, 87
    biographical context of, 80–81
    character of Underground Man, 80,
        81–82, 84–86, 88, 107n17
    "egoism of suffering" in, 107n18
    feelings of Underground Man, 85
    metaphor of underground in, 82–84,
        85, 87–88, 107n11
    pain and pleasure in, 86
    self-injury of the Underground
        Man, 85–86
    social relationships in, 87
    visual manifestations of suffering
        in, 79–80
Dostoevsky, Fyodor, *The Insulted and the
        Injured*, 84
Dostoevsky, Fyodor, *Winter Notes on
        Summer Impressions*, 81–82

gender
  and expressing emotion, 2–3
  in *Play Misty for Me*, 105–6
  and power in *Fish Tank*, 138
  reversal of roles in *Fatal
    Attraction*, 148n25
Gendron, Maria, 13
Goleman, Daniel, *Emotional
    Intelligence*, 30–32
Gramsci, Antonio, 9n7
Great Expectations (Dickens), 93–96
  abandonment, metaphors of, 96
  attachment, metaphors of, 82
  choice of perspective in, 93
  daylight and darkness in, 94–95
  female forces in, 96
  movement of characters in, 94
  narcissism in, 94
  narrative tension in, 95
  plot development in, 93
  time in, 93
  vanity in, 95
Greaves, Jean, *Emotional Intelligence 2.0*,
    32, 33
Gross, James J., 151–52
guilt, in "The Phantom Rickshaw,"
    97

Hagelin, Sarah, 45–46
Halbwachs, Maurice, *The Causes of
    Suicide*, 106
hand movements, and metaphors of
    emotion, 32–33, 71
Haneke, Michael, *Caché*, 7, 96–104
  aggressive visualizations in,
    105–6, 110n46
  background of, 100–1
  confrontation in, 99–100
  imagery, manipulation of, 102–4
  male characters and cultural rules of
    emotion, 7
  metaphor of underground in, 99
  nothingness, references to, 103–4

secrecy in, 98–99, 100–1
suffering, visual manifestations of,
    79–80, 101–2
suicide in, 101–2
surveillance in, 98, 104
visual appearance and
    contrasts in, 99
Haskell, Molly, 132–33
Having a Good Cry (Warhol), 52–53
Hazan, Cindy, 81
hegemony, and stifling language of
    emotion, 4, 9n7
hesitation, self-pity and, 54–55
hijacking metaphor, and theory of
    emotional intelligence, 31–32
Hogan, Patrick Colm
  depictions of emotion, societal
    reaction to, 3
  engagement with fictional
    characters, 58
  literalization of metaphor,
    107–8n20, 108n28
  simulation, defining, 109n32
  simulation, of emotionally aversive
    situations, 146n1
homoeroticism
  in *G.I. Jane*, 56n8
  in *Mrs. Dalloway*, 73
  in *A Room with a View*, 67
hopelessness, in narratives of spiritual
    journey, 25
housing project, in *Fish Tank*, 135–36
hunger
  and embodied metaphors in *Mrs.
    Dalloway*, 70–71
  as represented in *The
    Metamorphosis*, 93
Hustvedt, Siri, *The Summer without
    Men*, 7–8, 139–44
  abandonment, response to, 139
  anger, articulation of, 142
  bullying, response to, 143
  crying, perspectives on, 141

narrative frame of, 96–97
plot development in, 97–98
knowledge, represented as light, 94–95
Kohut, Heinz, 51
Kövecses, Zoltán
  aligning source and target in
    metaphors, 82
  conceptualization of emotions, 22–23
  patterns and prototypes of emotion
    metaphors, 23–25, 38n6
  rejected people, representing
    emotions of, 144–45

Lakoff, George
  aligning source and target in
    metaphors, 82
  conceptualization of emotions, 22–23
  metaphors as cognitive tools, 21–22
  patterns and prototypes of emotion
    metaphors, 23–25
language
  role in emotional experience,
    11–12, 154–55
  and shaping emotional
    experience, 19, 20
  and social interaction, 13
language of emotion
  hierarchy of, 4
  societal stifling of, 4
Lansing, Sherry, 131–32
LeDoux, Joseph
  corporeal nature of emotions, 15
  defining feelings, 12
  neural mechanisms of emotion,
    31, 37n1
  on William James, 13
Levy, Eric P.
  on self-pity, 42–44
  self-pity and self psychology
    psychoanalysis, 51
  self-pity as aristocratic vanity, 95
light
  and character development in *Play
    Misty for Me*, 103

metaphoric use of in *A Room with a
  View*, 60–61
metaphoric use of in *Great
  Expectations*, 94–95
and representing emotions of rejected
  people, 144
lighting, and depicting emotions in
  film, 101–2
literary scholarship, on the "tenor" and
  "vehicle" of metaphor, 20–21
losing, and expression of banned
  emotions, 5
Lutz, Tom, 40–41
Lyne, Adrian, *Fatal Attraction*, 106–34
  audience reaction to, 130–31, 132–33
  backstory of, 132–33
  character development in, 131–33
  comparisons to *Play Misty for Me*, 130–31
  craving for visibility in, 132
  deception, role of, 134
  demands for respect, 132–33
  dialogue in, 132–33
  gender roles, reversal of, 148n25
  multiple endings of, 131–32
  passion *vs.* domesticity in, 148
  and personal responsibility for
    relationships, 134
  rage, articulation of, 131, 132
  rejected people, representing
    emotions of, 145
  set design, 133
  treatment of emotions in, 134
Lyne, Adrian, gender and experiencing
  emotion, 2–3

magpies, in "The Phantom
  Rickshaw," 98–99
Mascolo, Michael F., 13
McElrath, Joseph, self-pity and poetry, 43–44
McKuen, Rod, 43
memory
  as emergent phenomenon, 19
  and engagement with fictional
    characters, 58

Metaphors We Live By (Lakoff & Johnson), 21–22

Miller, Jean Baker, 79

mirrors

and imagery in *Play Misty for Me*, 102

and narcissism in *Great Expectations*, 94

modulation of emotion, analysis of, 8

Molek-Kozakowska, Katarzyna, 5

Moretti, Franco, 41

movement

of characters in *Great Expectations*, 94

choice of in *Fish Tank*, 139

crying as break from forward motion, 41–42

depicted in *G. I. Jane*, 47

effect of rage and anger on, 35

fear as immobilizing, 34, 35

in *Fish Tank*, 134–36

of images in literature, 61

and life as linear journey, 94

and metaphors of abandonment, 96

and metaphors of banned emotion, 36

and metaphors of emotion, 33, 34–35

and metaphors of female emotion, 88–91

and metaphors of self-pity, 54–55

and plot development in *Play Misty for Me*, 104

and relationships in *Fish Tank*, 136–37

and representing emotions of rejected people, 144

Mrs. Dalloway (Woolf), 69–75

characterization in, 73–76

clothing as metaphor in, 72

diary entries regarding, 72–73

embodied metaphors in, 70–71

female characters and cultural rules of emotion, 7

grievances of characters in, 72

hand movements, references to, 71

homoeroticism in, 73

metaphoric patterns in, 69–70

narration in, 70

odor, as embodied metaphor in, 71–72

self-pity, implications of, 74

socioeconomic restrictions and womanhood in, 76, 77n17

suffering, depictions of, 75–76

suffering, manifestation of, 57–59

music, in *Play Misty for Me*, 103–4

narcissism, as represented in *Great Expectations*, 94

narration, in *Mrs. Dalloway*, 70

narrative frame, of "The Phantom Rickshaw," 96–97

narrative tension, in *Great Expectations*, 95

neural activity patterns

and characterizing emotions, 15

and emotion regulation, 154

and emotion suppression, 152–53

and reappraisal, 154–55

and theory of constructed emotion, 18–19

and theory of emotional intelligence, 31–32

neuroimaging

and studies of emotion, 17

and theory of constructed emotion, 18–19

neuroscience

and "base" and "target" of metaphor, 20–21

and emotion research, 12

Ngai, Sianne

basis of emotions, 157

oppression, reactions to, 99

social stigma of undesirable emotions, 3–4, 134

Notes from the Underground (Dostoevsky), 80–88

aggressive visualizations in, 105–6

assertions of humanity in, 87

biographical context of, 80–81

violence, escalation of, 104
  wave imagery in, 102
pleasure, and self-pity, 44
plot development
  in *Great Expectations,* 93
  in "The Phantom Rickshaw," 97–98
poetry
  as response to bullying, 143
  and self-pity, 43
Principles of Neural Science
    (Kandel), 37n1
Principles of Psychology (James), 13, 15
privilege, displays of anger and, 2
Protestantism, narratives of spiritual
    journey in, 25, 30
prototypes, of emotion
    metaphors, 23–25
psychological construction model, of
    emotion regulation, 153–54
psychology, and "base" and "target" of
    metaphor, 20–21
Purgatorio (Dante Alighieri)
  metaphorical transgression and
    bodily suffering, 25
  rage, bodily suffering and, 26–28
  and religious roots of metaphor, 6, 11–12, 30
Puritanism, narratives of spiritual
    journey in, 28–30

rage
  bodily suffering and, 26–28
  conceptualization of, 22–23
  in *Fatal Attraction,* 131, 132
  in *Fish Tank,* 138
  prototypes for, 23–25
  as response to change, 35
  in *The Summer without Men,* 142
reappraisal, and emotion regulation,
    153, 154
Reitano, Natalie, review of *Sideways,* 43–44
rejection
  metaphors associated with, 79–80
  rejected people, representing
    emotions of, 144–46

relationships
  and accommodating social change, 105–6
  and movement in *Fish Tank,* 136–37
  personal responsibility for, 134
  and sense of suffocation, 104
  sexualizing of in *Fish Tank,* 137
religion
  and metaphors of emotion, 6
  narratives of spiritual journey, 25
  seven deadly sins, 25
  See also metaphors of emotion,
    religious roots of
repair, metaphors of in therapy, 52
repetition, in "The Phantom
    Rickshaw," 99
research, fields of emotional
  communication, scholarly field of, 12
  neuroscience, 12
restoration, metaphors of in therapy, 52
restraint, confronting in *Fish Tank,* 135
Rohrkemper, John, 145
Room with a View, A (Forster), 59–69
  biographical background of, 68–69
  character development in, 59, 62,
    64, 67–68
  electric trams in, 61–62
  female characters and cultural rules
    of emotion, 7
  and Forster's study of Dante, 76n4
  homoeroticism in, 67
  light in, 60–61
  metaphoric patterns in, 59, 62, 69–70
  suffering, depictions of, 63–64
  suffering, manifestations of, 57–59
  water in, 59–60
  womanhood and social forces in,
    64–66, 67–69
  womanhood and socioeconomic
    restrictions in, 66–67
  writing of, 77n14

Scarry, Elaine
  fiction and depicting emotion, 3
  movement of images in literature, 61

Schachter, Stanley, 17–18
Scott, Ridley, *G. I. Jane*, 6–7, 45–47
    cultural context of, 45–46
    homoeroticism in, 56n8
    movement depicted in, 47
    representation of self-pity in, 45–47
secrecy, theme of in *Caché*,
    98–99, 100–1
self-help books, and metaphors of
    emotion, 6
self-injury
    and suicide in *Caché*, 101–2
    and the Underground Man, 85–86
self-pity
    and admonitions to move forward, 54
    in *Bridesmaids* (Feig), 47–51
    core thoughts in, 157
    cultural attitudes toward crying,
        40–42, 54–55
    cultural contempt for, 39–40, 55
    defining, 42
    developmental roots of, 51
    as empathy with self, 52
    and empowering tears, 51–54
    in *G. I. Jane* (Scott), 45–47
    and hesitation, 54–55
    as least-loved emotion, 42–47
    metaphors for, 6–7, 44–45
    and metaphors of restoration and
        repair in therapy, 52
    in *Mrs. Dalloway* and *A Room with a
        View*, 57–59
    in *Mrs. Dalloway* (Woolf), 74
    and physiology of crying, 52–53
    and preserving pain, 44
    psychological narrative of, 42–43
    and reflection of social issues, 54,
        55, 58–59
    sin and representations of, 54
    in *The Summer without Men*, 141
"Self-Pity," D. H. Lawrence, 45, 47
Self Psychology in Clinical Social Work
    (Elson), 51
self psychology psychoanalysis, 51

sensory detail, in *The
    Metamorphosis*, 91–92
serfdom, and *Notes from the
    Underground*, 81
set design, in *Fatal Attraction*, 133
seven deadly sins, resemblance to
    banned emotions, 25
Shaver, Phillip, 81
Shouse, Eric, 12
Sideways (Payne), 43–44
Siegel, Don, 104
simulation
    definition of, 8n1, 109n32
    of emotionally aversive situations, 146n1
sin, and representations of self-pity, 54
Sinclair, John D., 26
Singer, Jerome, 17–18
skin, and metaphors for self-pity, 44–45
smoke, and anger in Dante's
    Purgatorio, 27–28
social change, and *Play Misty for Me*, 105–6
social class
    and authentic *vs.* inauthentic
        emotion, 52–53
    changes in post-World War I Europe, 39
social forces, and womanhood in *A
    Room with a View*, 64–66, 67–69
social inequities
    alerting others to, 5–6, 35–36, 55
    crying and powerlessness, 41, 157–58
    emotion language and protest of, 4,
        35–36, 55
    and representing emotions of rejected
        people, 145–46
social interaction, and language, 13
social issues, and expressions of
    self-pity, 54, 55
social relationships, in *Notes from the
    Underground*, 87
societies
    depictions of emotion, societal
        reaction to, 3
    social elites and stifling language of
        emotion, 4